EDMUND SPENSER: THE CRITICAL HERITAGE

THE CRITICAL HERITAGE SERIES

GENERAL EDITOR: B. C. SOUTHAM, M.A., B.LITT.(OXON.)

Formerly department of English, Westfield College, University of London

---

Volumes in the series include

JANE AUSTEN	B. C. Southam
BROWNING	Boyd Litzinger and Donald Smalley
BYRON	Andrew Rutherford
COLERIDGE	J. R. de J. Jackson
DICKENS	Philip Collins
DRYDEN	James and Helen Kinsley
HENRY FIELDING	Ronald Paulson and Thomas Lockwood
THOMAS HARDY	R. G. Cox
HAWTHORNE	J. Donald Crowley
HENRY JAMES	Roger Gard
JAMES JOYCE (2 vols)	Robert H. Deming
KIPLING	Roger Lancelyn Green
D. H. LAWRENCE	R. P. Draper
MILTON	John T. Shawcross
SCOTT	John O. Hayden
SPENSER	R. N. Cummings
SWIFT	Kathleen Williams
SWINBURNE	Clyde K. Hyder
TENNYSON	J. D. Jump
THACKERAY	Geoffrey Tillotson and Donald Hawes
TROLLOPE	Donald Smalley
OSCAR WILDE	Karl Beckson

SPENSER

THE CRITICAL HERITAGE

Edited by
R. M. CUMMINGS
Department of English, University of Glasgow

LONDON: ROUTLEDGE & KEGAN PAUL

Published in Great Britain, 1971
by Routledge & Kegan Paul Limited
68–74 Carter Lane, London E.C.4
© R. M. Cummings 1971
No part of this book may be reproduced
in any form without permission from
the publisher, except for the quotation
of brief passages in criticism.
ISBN 0 7100 6953 7

Printed in Great Britain by
C. Tinling & Co. Ltd, London and Prescot
and set in 11 on 12 pt 'Monotype' Bembo

TO MY MOTHER AND FATHER

General Editor's Preface

The reception given to a writer by his contemporaries and near-contemporaries is evidence of considerable value to the student of literature. On one side we learn a great deal about the state of criticism at large and in particular about the development of critical attitudes towards a single writer; at the same time, through private comments in letters, journals or marginalia, we gain an insight upon the tastes and literary thought of individual readers of the period. Evidence of this kind helps us to understand the writer's historical situation, the nature of his immediate reading-public, and his response to these pressures.

The separate volumes in the *Critical Heritage Series* present a record of this early criticism. Clearly for many of the highly-productive and lengthily-reviewed nineteenth- and twentieth-century writers, there exists an enormous body of material; and in these cases the volume editors have made a selection of the most important views, significant for their intrinsic critical worth or for their representative quality – perhaps even registering incomprehension!

For earlier writers, notably pre-eighteenth century, the materials are much scarcer and the historical period has been extended, sometimes far beyond the writer's lifetime, in order to show the inception and growth of critical views which were initially slow to appear.

In each volume the documents are headed by an Introduction, discussing the material assembled and relating the early stages of the author's reception to what we have come to identify as the critical tradition. The volumes will make available much material which would otherwise be difficult of access and it is hoped that the modern reader will be thereby helped towards an informed understanding of the ways in which literature has been read and judged.

B.C.S.

Contents

CONTENTS

CONTENTS

CONTENTS

xiii

CONTENTS

xiv

CONTENTS

CONTENTS

xvii

Acknowledgments

To F. I. Carpenter's *A Reference Guide to Edmund Spenser* (Chicago, 1923) and to Dorothy F. Atkinson's *Edmund Spenser: A Bibliographical Supplement* (Baltimore, 1937) I am necessarily indebted. I am fortunate in being able to express a yet larger debt to the generosity of Professor William Wells of the University of North Carolina, who put at my disposal the typescript of the long projected *Spenser Allusion Book*. There is very little indeed that I can add to the labours of its contributors. Professors Heffner, Padelford, and Wells are those who in succession have taken responsibility for the book, but the massive contribution of Miss Dorothy Mason (now of the Folger Library) cannot go unnoticed here. Miss Mason was also kind enough to answer an enquiry for me. For advice, encouragement, and for supplying valuable references, I am grateful to Dr Alastair Fowler of Brasenose College, Oxford, to Professor J. C. Bryce of Glasgow University, and to Mr R. M. Wilding of Sydney University. Dr van Dorsten of the Sir Thomas Browne Institute at Leyden, and the Rector of Lincoln College, Oxford, kindly answered specific enquiries. For other advice I thank Miss Hannah Buchan, and Mr Nigel Alexander, both of Glasgow. The University of Glasgow has been generous in its contributions towards my expenses.

Note on the Text

The original spelling of the passages gathered here has been preserved, though short 's' has in all cases been substituted for long. References to modern editions of works cited have been given only for convenience of consultation: nowhere have I attempted a bibliography of reprintings. All enclosures in square brackets are editorial. Where continuity of sense is not at risk, line references have been substituted for quotations from Spenser and certain other easily accessible authors.

Original footnotes are indicated by a star (*), dagger (†), etc.

Abbreviations

Variorum Spenser *The Works of Edmund Spenser: A Variorum Edition* (Baltimore, 1932–49)
ELH *Journal of English Literary History*
HLB *Huntington Library Bulletin*
HLQ *Huntington Library Quarterly*
MLN *Modern Language Notes*
MP *Modern Philology*
N &Q *Notes and Queries*
PQ *Philological Quarterly*
RES *Review of English Studies*
PMLA *Publications of the Modern Language Association*

Introduction

I

This book ends at a point where it might well begin. 'Before 1715', writes William Mueller, 'we have little more than a series of incidental remarks on Spenser . . . John Hughes, in the critical essays of the 1715 edition, was the first writer to consider the sum of Spenser's work, and not merely fragments of it.'[1] No one could argue with that. Individually the passages printed in this book are unlikely to yield any but an incidental interest. Collectively, they are, I hope, in a variety of ways interesting and useful. In particular, they may draw attention to emphases in Spenserian criticism, from which the modern reader has generally been drawn away. There is almost nothing even in the best of the following pages (excepting the pieces by Hughes), which a modern critic would spontaneously have thought of saying. That is, the seventeenth-century and the twentieth-century impressions of Spenser's work are very different. There is, moreover, very little on the following pages which a modern critic would even think worthwhile saying. The only real argument against the notion that most of the passages printed here are critically useless is to point to the unlikelihood of so many clever and learned men having written nonsense. It will not do to pretend that they were blinkered, that they could never see beyond their own immediate concerns, or beyond Cicero or beyond Bossu. While the modern reader and critic is so isolated from the perceptions (and the ordering of those perceptions) of those closest to Spenser in time and presumably in sympathies, his ground is not the safest. On the other hand, the fragmentary character of most of what is printed here is not something which can be properly apologized for at all. It is merely unfortunate. It can however be said that there is no English poet of the period on whom more extended comment would be available. In Italy or even in France it would have been different. But in England the criticism of vernacular poetry was simply not such an industry then as it was on the Continent. That does not make its errors (when it is certain that they are errors) more those of folly than of carelessness; and it is not in the main an underdeveloped discipline in any but a quantitative sense. In the circumstances it is remarkable that Spenser so early attracted as much critical attention as he did – a good deal more than, say, Shakespeare.

The material offered here, with the exception of chiefly linguistic or chiefly biographical comment, has been arranged chronologically. On the supposition that readers will probably find it more convenient to have all criticisms by any one author set together (for example, those by Harvey, Drayton, or Dryden), even when they must be dated very differently, I have broken the chronological arrangement to accommodate all such pieces under one heading. As well as being more convenient, this sophistication of the arrangement also provides a more coherent perspective on the material: the criticisms of Dryden, for example, are determined more by his own preoccupations than by his reading of other critics. The three larger sections (covering the periods 1579–1600, 1600–1660, 1660–1715) into which all this material falls are fluid (Drayton for example is included in the first, but writes more about Spenser after 1600 than before), but contain material of roughly similar character. The following pages of the Introduction explain what general trends obtain within those periods. The separate grouping of two specialized kinds of comment should not disturb the general reader. There is enough cross-referencing to ensure that he misses nothing. For those specifically interested in the development of Spenser's biography, or in the history of the English language, the gathering together of biographical notices and of linguistic or stylistic comment has such immediate and pressing advantages as to make worth while the disturbance of any straightforward arrangement. Readers who wish to consult the collection of linguistic comment are advised that where material which might properly have been set there forms part of some more general discussion, it has been left in the body of the book. References to such material have been provided at the beginning of the section.

The brief introductory essay which immediately follows is intended only as the most generalized kind of guide. It attempts no extended discussion of any of the passages included in the book, but is meant rather to organize a selection of points into some rough historical pattern. Notions rather different from my own could, I have no doubt, be substantiated from the same evidence.

II

HISTORY OF PUBLICATION

Spenser's first essay in print, the translations for Van der Noot's *Theatre* (1569), went neglected in his time, and except for the brief and often reluctant observations of scholars more recently, have been ever since. His second, *The Shepheardes Calender* (1579), won its author immediate fame – though it was not generally known who the author was[2] – and in Spenser's own lifetime went through five editions. That those editions were printed with successively inferior texts is from a literary critic's point of view unimportant. It shows only that demand for the poems was high, but that expectations of textual accuracy were not. At least up to the mid-eighteenth century, Spenser's reputation rests most securely on that poem. 'Uncouth unkist', but once known, 'beloued of all, embraced of the most, and wondred at of the best'. (No. 1a.) Even before the publication of the *Faerie Queene* (1590), the *Shepheardes Calender* appeared twice more (in 1581 and in 1586), and Harvey had given the publisher Bynneman a correspondence between Spenser and himself which advised the public, though probably only a small public, that they were to expect yet more of the new poet (No. 3c).

Both the *Shepheardes Calender* and the *Faerie Queene* were the products of widely collaborative critical effort. E.K., if he was Edward Kirke, belongs to Spenser's Cambridge circle; if he was Fulke Greville (the most interesting of recent suggestions),[3] then he belongs to the Leicester House circle with which Spenser was associated – how intimately will never be known. The *Faerie Queene* had gone through not only Gabriel Harvey's hands (and changed much in the process, for Harvey by 1590 [see No. 3d] has reversed his earlier judgment of the poem), but through Abraham Fraunce's, and if legend can be believed, through Sidney's as well.[4] In any case both Cambridge and London probably contributed something, and it would be unlikely had Spenser's friends in Dublin not seen and commented on it. There is unfortunately no weight of evidence on which an account of Spenser's composition of any of his poetry can be based. It is generally assumed that the composition of the *Faerie Queene* involved a number of changes in the whole conception of the poem, but precisely what changes of conception can hardly be known. Everyone admires the ingenuity of J. W. Bennet's attempt, in

3

The Evolution of 'The Faerie Queene', to determine Spenser's compositional procedures; but few critics will now accept her conclusions as definitive.[5] There is no way of gauging how Spenser responded to his public, or what shifts he made to satisfy any private audience. Very little he writes is precisely datable, and very little is known of his public.

There is for many people something suspiciously timely about the publications after 1590 of various collections of minor pieces. After the *Faerie Queene* had won 'fauourable passage', Ponsonby published a volume under the title *Complaints* (1591).[6] It is a volume elaborately and variously dedicated, ostensibly, as it is put in the dedication of the *Ruines of Time*, to the Countess of Pembroke, to avoid 'that fowle blot of unthankfulness'. Show and reality in these matters are nicely distinguished in the century, but the instinctive approval that one accords to Professor Danby's brief and suggestive account of Spenser's search for patrons, of his writing poetry 'to maintain him in place in the body of the world', should be qualified by the recognition that Spenser appears most conspicuously on the hunt for patrons only after it quite obviously has to be acknowledged that he is a great poet.[7] There is a cunning ambiguity in the dedication of the *Tears of the Muses* to Lady Strange – 'that by [my] honouring you they might know me, and by knowing me, they might honour you'. Spenser's praise of Leicester is strongest after Leicester is dead.[8] The *Prothalamion* (1596) was presumably commissioned by the Earl of Worcester, and not simply addressed (in as far as it is addressed to anyone) to his daughters. The publication of *Astrophel* (1595) would have been impertinent in a lesser poet. The motions of self-confidence are everywhere. The revision (in the *Complaints* volume) of his contribution to the *Theatre* of Van der Noot could have been motivated only by the mature and famous poet's desire to blot the inferior efforts of the unknown schoolboy. The publication after so long (if the dedication is to be believed) of the *Hymns to Love and Beauty* (1596) is presumably born of the desire to broadcast his better efforts.

Jewel Wurtsbaugh has already comprehensively treated the fortunes of Spenser's text from 1609.[9] A folio edition of the *Faerie Queene* was published just over ten years after Spenser's death by Matthew Lownes (1609), with the enigmatically announced addition of the *Mutabilitie Cantos*. Apart from that addition, Lownes's editorial activity was limited: the Folio is for the most part a reprint of the Second Quarto (1596) – though what changes are made do not suggest to me as they to do Dr Wurtsbaugh that 'the editor emended as he saw fit'.[10] Two

4

years later, in 1611, Lownes published a folio edition of the *Works*. Not only is the editing in this volume distinctly sloppy, but its printing history is complicated. Those complications are dealt with by Dr Wurtsbaugh. They are inherited by the Second Folio of 1617, and that was the text (re-issued in 1628) which served until 1679. The editing of the Third Folio, printed in that year, has been attributed in part to Dryden, but on no good evidence.[11] Its achievement is not in any case, in the usual sense of the word, editorial. What value it must have had lay in its bringing together a lot of material previously neglected or before only published separately – Sir James Ware's edition of *A View of the present State of Ireland* (1633), the Spenser-Harvey correspondence, Bathurst's Latin translation of the *Shepheardes Calender*, together with the glossary attached to it at its first publication (1653), and also the wrongly ascribed *Britain's Ida* first published in 1628. After the Third Folio no edition appeared before Hughes's of 1715. Hughes's editorial procedure did not satisfy Dr Johnson, who saw that he 'perhaps wanted an antiquary's knowledge of the obsolete words', but presumably it was not for that reason that Hughes's edition did not rouse the interest of the public if, as Johnson claims, it did not.[12] It is to Hughes's credit, that first among Spenser's editors, he had thought about the meaning of the text. His emendations are inaccurate and often absurd; but this at least is not wholly the fault of his own limited talents, and he is never, like Bentley with Milton, outrageous.

The availability of texts suggests that Spenser was not neglected. There is however no suggestion of great demand. Indeed, compared with that of the 1750s, when five separate editions of the *Faerie Queene* were published, it may seem rather small.[13] Such matters are difficult to estimate. The early demand for Spenser does not compare with that for, say, Ariosto (of whose *Orlando Furioso* there were more than a hundred editions between 1516 and the end of the century).[14] In respect of the number of editions his work went through, Spenser does not even compare very well with Shakespeare, whose *Works* appeared in four folio editions before Rowe's edition of 1709, while in addition separate plays were published in eighty-five different editions and issues in quarto before that date. On the other hand, J. M. Munro, in his introduction to the *Shakespeare Allusion Book*, is prepared to admit that in the same period allusions to Spenser probably outnumber those to Shakespeare.[15] Whether or not that is so – when the *Spenser Allusion Book* appears, the evidence will speak for itself – Spenser certainly attracted more serious attention. His status is more like that of Jonson.[16]

That is, it is probably safe to say that Shakespeare was more popular than either Spenser or Jonson, but less reputable – in other words, that the level of demand was different.

<h1 style="text-align:center">III</h1>

THE PERIOD 1579–1600

Tacitus relates that once when some lines from the *Aeneid* were recited in the course of a theatrical performance, and Virgil was present, the audience rose to their feet and bowed towards him 'as if he were Augustus'.[17] No such story is related of Spenser, and it is fairly certain that nothing remotely of that order could ever have occurred. It is true that there is a great buoyancy in Elizabethan accounts of Spenser: Spenser was apparently adored by his contemporaries.[18] But the accounts of Spenser in this period come mainly from professional poets. There is no evidence to suggest that he enjoyed a broad fame. What is more, though the criticism does not all come from the *areopagoi* of Cambridge, or Leicester House, or Dublin, there is in most of it a sense of shared assumptions, and most of it does come from closed literary circles. Its tone is intimate as well as buoyant.

The intimacy of tone is a consequence not only of the accidents of Spenser's biography. It may follow partly from a particular and forgotten emphasis on Spenser as a love poet. The aims of most Elizabethan poets were distinctly limited: their strain for the most part was lyrical, and when they spread their wings, it was to attempt the pastoral. Outside scholarly circles there was not, moreover, any emphasis on a generic distinction between the two. Pastoral poetry was for the later Elizabethans primarily erotic, and the *Shepheardes Calender* was seen principally as a love complaint. Spenser, along with Sidney, contributed to the vogue for pastoral trappings in erotic poetry most readily observed in *Englands Helicon* (1600).[19]

This bias appears to contradict that found in those writers who are by various accidents of biography associated personally with Spenser, or in those whose sympathies are most probably in line with Spenser's own. E.K. and, following him, William Webbe take the *Shepheardes Calender* as a warning against love. The contradiction is probably only apparent. Both parties would have admitted the other's points, but each finds a

6

different emphasis useful. And among poets, the erotic emphasis is, naturally enough, the more convenient. In 1582, William Vallans can attempt wholly unerotic pastoral in imitation of Spenser;[20] but later attempts, such as *John of Bordeaux* (1590?) play up whatever specifically concerns love.[21] The apostrophes to Colin which fill the pastoral poetry of the period, even when they acknowledge higher purposes for Spenser's poetry, almost always sentimentalize the man. 'Here *Colin* sits,' writes Barnabe Barnes, 'beneath that oaken tree/*Eliza* singing in his layes.'[22] Mostly the higher purposes are passed over silently. William Smith's dedication of Chloris (1596) to Spenser is addressed to '*Colin* my deere and most entire beloued' and goes on:

> Faine would my muse whom cruell loue hath wronged,
> Shroud her loue labors under thy protection.[23]

'By thee', Barnfield complains to Cupid, 'great Collin lost his liberty,' and when the same poet offers what he calls the 'first imitation of the verse of the *Faerie Queene*', it is a love poem he writes, modelled on Spenser's conceit of Cynthia.[24] No doubt we forget to what extent even the *Faerie Queene* is intended as a love poem, and just how much it might have in common with Ralegh's *Ocean's Love*; but it is no special insight that allows Barnfield to see it. That the *Amoretti* go unmentioned among all this is probably not a circumstance attributable to their late appearance. The first mention of them before Hughes is in Drummond (No. 64), who doubts they are by Spenser they are so bad (a judgment, which, if it includes the *Epithalamion*, is unforgivable). The appeal of Spenser as a love poet is obvious. In the *Shepheardes Calender* he transformed himself into a legend. That the poem is more than an early sort of *Bildungsroman* does not prevent anxious Elizabethan love poets from taking it as such. Spenser is 'chefe of Shepheardes all', and so Thomas Edwards sees the whole poem as 'sweete Affection tun'd in homely layes' (No. 23b).

As the author of the *Faerie Queene*, Spenser is still for Edwards only the 'Heroike Parramore of Faerie Land' (No. 23a). Even Ralegh can hint at a similarity between the Spenser of the *Faerie Queene* and the Petrarch of the *Rime* (No. 10). An anonymous verse preserved in a copy of the 1590 Quarto makes the same point.[25] It would seem that what immediately struck a lot of Elizabethans was that they had a new Ariosto, a poet to 'treat of worthies and of Ladies loue'. But this does not mean that they were ignorant of Spenser's ambitions as a moral or a learned poet, merely that they were not anxious to press the point.

7

The inane jingle by Churchyard (No. 7b) may indicate how much was taken for granted, and Barnfield the sentimentalist also admits the appeal of the deep conceit: Spenser is more than Dowland (No. 27a). But it is those isolated from the preoccupations of the professional poet who first make elaborately explicit a conception of the *Faerie Queene* as primarily ethical or allegorical. The Roman Catholic Anthony Copley in *A Fig for Fortune* (1596) turns the machinery, though not the manner of the *Faerie Queene*, to his own propagandist ends. And the Puritan Francis Rous, on the basis of the same literary assumptions, works out a quite differently aimed adaptation in *Thule, or Vertues Historie* (1598). It is the more intimate perspective which proves more generally congenial, and it is this which allows Spenser's contemporaries so happily to classify him along with so many other modern poets. In evaluating the achievement of Elizabethan poetry, few now would put the names of Spenser and, say, Daniel alongside each other. But Francis Meres for example puts together as lyric poets Daniel, Drayton, Shakespeare (of the 'surged sonnets'), Breton and Spenser, and as pastoral poets Spenser, Gosson, Fraunce, and Barnfield (No. 29).

The nearer to Spenser's immediate circle the critics, the less they are inclined to see him as a model for the fashionable blend of pastoral and erotic. They have at the same time a larger and a more discriminating perception of what his poetry is about. The pretensions evident in E.K.'s prefatory matter direct what they say of the *Shepheardes Calender*, as much as does their reading of the poem. Webbe has already been mentioned in this connexion. 'The occasion of his works,' he says (No. 4), 'is a warning to other young men, who, being intangled in loue and youthful vanities, may learne to looke to themselues in time . . .' More generally, it is a work containing 'many good Morall lessons', by no means specifically on love. And most interesting of all from Webbe's point of view is the poem's excellence as an example of the poet's craft: 'there are in that worke twelue or thirteene sundry sortes of verses . . .' For Webbe, Spenser's achievement consists in having put English poetry on a par with Latin and Greek poetry. Theocritus and Virgil are now matched by Spenser. For Nashe (No. 5a), Spenser has excelled all the moderns. The background of this sometimes oddly chauvinistic emphasis on strictly technical achievement, also evident in the Spenser-Harvey correspondence, has been examined by R. F. Jones in his *The Triumph of the English Language* (1953), to which I refer the interested reader. Spenser's strictly technical pretensions, and the perhaps too sympathetic applause of many of his admirers, also explain the note of dissent in writers as close to the poet as Sidney (No. 133).

The appreciation of the *Faerie Queene* is much slower to catch on. Its rhetorical beauties were noted before publication by Fraunce (No. 134), and perhaps very early imitated by Marlowe.[26] But the *Shepheardes Calender* had a place in the hearts of Spenser's small public which the *Faerie Queene* never had. Campion pretends to be pleased with both – Spenser delights whether writing of rural landscapes or of the horrors of war.[27] But in that little epigram it had perhaps not occurred to Campion to sense the inappropriateness of the facile juxtaposition of the earlier and later poems. When Sir John Davies praises 'Colins fayre heroike style', (*Orchestra*, st. 128) one gets the impression that it is the luxuries of the *Shepheardes Calender* or of Book VI (where Spenser perhaps has deliberate recourse to his own legend) which have appealed most. Only in such a context is it appropriate for Daniel to have made a show of rejecting in *Delia* the trappings of Spenserian chivalry (No. 16a).

'I can imagine no greater birth . . .' Meres (No. 29) echoes Propertius and, even among those best placed to understand the poem, little beyond that is said. The commendatory verses which accompany the first edition of the poem certainly get no further. It seems as if it may have overwhelmed and confused its earliest readers, so that the only accounts of any substance are Spenser's own in the Letter to Ralegh (No. 2c) and that attributed to him by Bryskett (No. 48), whose treatment does presumably reflect Spenser's own conversation about the poem. There is no indication in any published comment of any familiarity with the poem, such as is found among its few (and then learned) admirers in the seventeenth century.

Fortunately there is a corrective to those generalizations made on the basis of published comment. Professor Hough has put before the public an edition of the marginalia on the *Faerie Queene*, written in 1597 by one John Dixon.[28] Nothing to the point is known of Dixon, but it can be assumed that he represents the average serious Elizabethan reader. The interests reflected in his comments are prosaic, but not extraordinarily so; it is clear however that he was not looking to Spenser as a model for his own love poetry. He is apparently confused by the narrative – Sansfoy is mixed up with Archimago, Guyon with Redcrosse, Florimell with Belphoebe, Malecasta with Duessa, and the like. Such confusions are not without interest, for even allowed that Dixon has unawares fallen into error (which is just arguable), they betray not only, as Professor Hough would have it, an indifference to the courtly and romantic aspects of Spenser, but to the literal structure of the whole poem. The other marginalia confirm this. Professor Hough divides them into three categories: the identification of Biblical allusions (in which Dixon anticipates Upton by focusing on the debt to Revelations), the marking of moral characterizations or the moral elucidation of episodes, and the identification of topical allusions. That this last category is especially favoured may serve as a warning to those modern critics who like to think of it as trivial. The marginalia in Cambridge University library Sel. 5.102, and a variety of other early marginalia, indicate a similar preoccupation.[29] It cannot be accidental that Carew in one of the few early comparisons of the author of the *Faerie Queene* with a classical poet chooses to compare him with Lucan (No. 28a).

But it is not, at this period, on such things that the appreciation of Spenser rests. For the poets who wrote most of what is written on Spenser, had little interest in them. Camden relates that at Spenser's funeral a line of poets threw verses, and their pens with them, into his grave (No. 168b). No certain copy of those verses has survived, with the only probable exception of a Latin poem by R.H. (Richard Harvey?).[30] That poem is not printed here since it is so generalized as hardly to be about Spenser at all. There are, however, included in this book a number of obituary and pseudo-obituary pieces, which in spite of varying widely in date, reflect much the same attitudes to Spenser. Almost without exception they represent Spenser as a pastoralist and a love poet – only Fitzgeoffrey's epigrams go further. Pastoral and elegy do adapt well to each other, but the reasons for the predominance of pastoral imagery are, I suspect, more complex, and relate to the sentimentalism already discussed. It is worth pointing out that the presence of poets at Spenser's funeral, and the outburst of obituary versifying more or less immediately on his death, is a singular compliment. Munro was obliged to note that at Shakespeare's death 'the muse shed not one tear', and Jonson did not fare much better.[31]

IV

THE PERIOD 1600–1660

It is too much to say, as H. E. Cory does, that after 1600 there is a reversal in Spenser's critical fortunes.[32] Most of what was written on Spenser in the early part of the seventeenth century, not surprisingly, very much resembles what was written in the 1590s. Very few of those who talk at all about Spenser are prepared to talk ill of him. If only on the principle of *de mortuis nil nisi bonum*, or of the generally observable rise in the reputation (if not the popularity) of recently dead poets of admitted stature, that is what one would expect. Yet there is perhaps (and that may be what Cory meant in speaking of the age of reason following on the age of enthusiasm) some loss of impetus in the appreciation of Spenser. The tone of the criticism fails in spontaneity and intimacy. Also it begins to be more generally discriminating – which means both that it admits more reservations, and that it is more careful than was customary for the Spenser criticism of the last decade of the sixteenth century. There is some change even in the tone of what is unambiguously adulatory. Generally speaking, however, there is a limit to how often the same thing can be said and still persuade us of its genuineness; and there is necessarily a loss of intimacy with Spenser's manner, and of sympathy with the intellectual atmosphere in which he wrote. Moreover, it is commonplace that there was some sort of failure of confidence in the intellectual life of the early seventeenth century.

There are two signs of this loss of impetus. First, those poets, such as William Browne (see No. 60) or Phineas Fletcher (see No. 77), who pretend allegiance to Spenser and Spenser's manner do not write like him. The erotic pastoralists of the late sixteenth century did not write like Spenser either; but then, they made no elaborate claims to, and they had no devious reasons for believing themselves Spenser's heirs. The notions of influence and imitation are notoriously difficult: even decisions about what the terms ought to mean are embarrassing. It should be clear however that the so-called Spenserians of the earlier seventeenth century are engaged on problems quite distinct from Spenser's, and that their debt is only indirect. Historically their position prevented them from being comprehensively interested in Spenser: the new poetry had been forged, and the old problems solved. For the same reason it is in particular doubtful how far Spenser can be said to have contributed to the vogue for mellifluous writing. Nothing that the poets of the earlier part of the century would have wanted to learn from Spenser as practitioners of verse, was not already current. Besides, Daniel is at least as mellifluous as Spenser, and Elizabeth Cooper (of the *Muses Library*) was right to note that it was Spenser and

Fairfax together who 'opened to us a new World of Ornament, Elegance, and Taste'.[33] Fairfax is in fact a good deal more elegant and tasteful than Spenser, and one cannot but feel that seventeenth-century fine writing owes considerably more to him. It is Spenser, however, who in the imagination of his successors remains the type of the elegant and tasteful poet. In one area, Spenser's influence would be obvious were it admitted. But the archaism which is recognized as the distinguishing characteristic of Spenser's style is almost everywhere absent in his supposed imitators. It is present sometimes, but where it is, the suspicion that Spenser's imitators are at some distance from Spenser is only confirmed, for it is used sporadically and mechanically. That is, Spenser's imitators parade debts that are only superficially owed. William Bedell's *A Protestant Memorial* (1605) – a poem which Joseph Hall thinks in Spenser's mould,[34] *Britannia's Pastorall* of William Browne (1613–16), Richard Niccols's *The Cuckow* (1607),[35] the poetry of both the Fletchers,[36] take over features of the movement of Spenser's verse, and features of the diction; but they do so either for incidental convenience, or sentimentally. Often those writers are only in search of the obviously musical. The same mixture of convenience (often one suspects laziness) and sentimentality is manifest in the adaptation of descriptive passages from Spenser. Nathaniel Baxter for example is not, to adapt T. S. Eliot's phrase, mature in his theft of Spenser's description of Belphoebe;[37] Robert Aylett's persistent lifting of whole sections of the *Faerie Queene*, only to vulgarize them, has at least made him useful to a recent critic of Book V.[38] Drayton, whom Douglas Bush may rightly have called 'the chief of Spenser's heirs' exhibits, superficially, little dependence on him.[39]

In general, the attempts to take over structural features of Spenser's work, or to take over his use of allegory, are no more seriously ambitious. Everything, as in Phineas Fletcher's *Purple Island* (1633) is at once exaggerated and on a smaller scale. Indeed the Spenserian allegories of the seventeenth century have this in common, that they are strained beyond the Spenserian manner, and that they are written for an audience more learned or more anxious to learn than that which might safely approach Spenser himself. The allegory is almost exclusively emblematic (Spenser did, it should be remembered, enter the emblem books),[40] and there is rarely supporting narrative. Moreover, perhaps as a consequence of the kind of criticism that Spenser attracted in the period, those allegories have more the quality of fences around philosophy than of pleasant paths to it. Henry More's work is the most

obvious case in point here. The masque also, with its elaborate allegorical apparatus, lent itself easily to the opportunity of plagiarizing
Spenser; and here too the borrowing was mechanical or careless and
the appeal necessarily narrow.[41]

By his imitators, Spenser is made more polite than he is or more
obviously abstruse than he is. That is the first sign of loss of contact
with the spirit of Spenser. The second sign is corollary. Not really
wanting to learn anything from Spenser, or not being able to, some of
his admirers fall into nostalgia. Cory detected this in Joseph Hall;[42]
I do not. But it is evident in some of the obituary material – this sense,
as Boswell puts it in his report of Johnson's death, that a space has been
created which nothing can fill. The less strictly obituary the material,
the more it is free to develop this line in specific directions. It comes out
centrally in some places. The author of *Vindiciae Virgilianae*, for
example, calls up out of the past poets to mend the present state of
poetry: Spenser is among them (No. 76). It comes out incidentally in
other places. Robert Dallyngton wishes that Spenser were alive to
write on the rivers of France for him.[43] Richard Niccols, in lamenting
Elizabeth's death, turns to regret the loss of Spenser.[44] Robert Tofte
heads some verses with apology that Sidney or Spenser would have
done them better.[45] E.G., in his defence of women, acknowledges the
superiority of others' treatment, beginning with Homer's and ending
with Spenser's.[46] Such expressions of inadequacy are common in this
form. In the end, the empty space was either forgotten about or filled.
But before Milton there was hardly any one who could fill it. Sylvester
and Cowley were both possible candidates, but neither was seriously
taken up. The mature Dryden treats his youthful preference for
Sylvester over Spenser as folly (No. 100b). It is difficult perhaps to
distinguish between nostalgia specifically for Spenser and nostalgia for
Spenser's time. The latter strain is never explicit, but the complaint
against more recent poets' inability to write like Spenser, is to that
extent fatuous, that had it been possible it would not have been desirable.

This failure of genuine sympathy allows a special kind of discrimination to develop. But here it is not the dissent which is most obvious or
most interesting. What is remarkable about the mass of comment on
Spenser in this period is the way in which it shows the growth of his
status as a classic author. There is no very good evidence that Spenser
saw himself as an English Virgil, though he contrived his career to
resemble Virgil's and regularly in the *Faerie Queene* courts the compari-

son, and when he planned to overgo Ariosto, presumably he meant in the direction of Virgil. But posthumously, he was regularly honoured with the comparison. Often it is only a lazy tribute, as in the obituary verses of Weever (No. 31) or in Edmund Johnson's trivial piece of Pythagoreanism, '*Virgil's* ghost did wend To *Spenser's* lodge';[47] and it is no very exact characterization of the Water-Poet's to say that Spenser was an exact imitator of Virgil, for he thought that Chaucer was as well.[48] But with Gill (No. 67), who contrives a comparison of Spenser and Homer which sounds like Scaliger's of Virgil and Homer, it takes on meaning. With Digby it flowers. Digby in front of Spenser not only identifies himself with Scaliger in front of Virgil (No. 71a), but it is he who imports into Spenserian scholarship the microscopic criticism (No. 71b) which English readers would associate with the traditions of Virgilian scholarship. Unfortunately, Digby employed his talents in this way only once; and still more unfortunately, he had no worthy successor before Upton.

Other signs of Spenser's classic status are however available. The scholarship of Spenser's seventeenth-century editors is not, as Wursbaugh has shown, of the highest. But that he had editors at all is something. It is a small thing that his first editor Lownes should have troubled to secure missing material, or that in 1628 Walkley should have put out under Spenser's name a poem by Phineas Fletcher in the belief (presumably) that it was missing material. That Ware, a more respectable scholar, should have published a book written thirty-seven years before, no longer (as he admits) wholly relevant to the Irish problem (No. 169) or that a Life should have been attached as early as 1679 to the poet's Works (No. 174): those facts, however trivial in themselves, presuppose what may be called an academic interest in Spenser. With the elaborate apparatus that accompanied the *Shepheardes Calender*, Spenser had announced himself as a poet with academic pretensions. It remained for those pretensions to be taken seriously by a wide public. By Ware they were, and apparently they were by the editors of the Third Folio. It is also worth noting here that the *Shepheardes Calender* appears to have been used as material for Latin translation exercises, though I think it is making a lot of little to suppose that those exercises were either formal or regular.[49]

More singular, Spenser is used from an early date, after the mediaeval fashion, as a sort of *auctor*. To make this plain I have included in the volume a number of passages the critical interest of which is only secondary. The passages from Austin for example (No. 80) are of very little worth; it is merely interesting that he has thought it worth his while to echo Spenser while making a theological point, and to quote him while making a mystical one about the human body. Burton (No. 66) uses Spenser as a supporting authority on human psychology, Selden (No. 18f) on British history, Heylyn on St George (No. 73a). Very early indeed, in 1602, Samuel Rowlands is using Spenser to consolidate commonplaces or as a source of proverbs.[50] Edmund Bolton thinks it worth while citing Spenser 'in his time, the most learned poet of England', if only to contradict him, on the site of Boadicea's defeat.[51] John Speed cites him on the question of whether or not England was once joined to the Continent.[52] And there are many represented on the following pages who are prepared to assure their readers that the Faerie Queene is a compendium of moral law and philosophical lore. When Henry Bold calls him 'our Platonicke Spenser' he only echoes the opinion of Platonist Cambridge.[53]

A third indication, already partly suggested, is the extent to which Spenser was in principle and not in practice imitated. The inadequacy of seventeenth-century imitations of Spenser may be accounted for simply by a loss of familiarity with Spenserian habits of mind, but the reasons for a show of imitation are best seen in terms of the glamour of obvious recourse to classic precedent. More striking yet is the way in which Spenser is adapted or parodied. Both the Pilgrimage to Parnassus and Pasquils Palinodia parody lines from Spenser.[54] The early more extended efforts by Copley and Rous have been mentioned. By mid-century a number are available. The anonymously edited canto from Book V, The Fairy Leveller (1649), is one. Sheppard's Fairy King (see No. 84) is another. Knevett's topically oriented Supplement is yet another (see No. 79). Richard Brathwait, writing under the pseudonym Pamphilus Hesychius, wrote the only deliberately funny parody of the matter of the Faerie Queene of which I know, in the History of Moderation (1669). Such compendious and various tribute is remarkable.

Spenser had aspired to be a classic and his admirers took him as one. It was probably his reception as much as his aspirations which exposed Spenser to attack from those with severer notions of what a classic should be. To judge from the Letter to Ralegh, Spenser regarded the work of Homer, Virgil, Ariosto, and Tasso, as a more or less homogeneous body of heroic poetry, and his immediate successors followed him in this. There are reasons for their view other than lack of discrimination, but since they belong largely to the history of Italian literary criticism they cannot be gone into here.[55] His critics of the mid-seventeenth century were not by and large prepared to accept the earlier view. By no obvious formal criteria is Spenser comparable with Virgil, and Harvey's objection to what is assumed to have been an early draft of the *Faerie Queene* (No. 3c) will hold for later drafts as well.

There is from this particular point of view an interesting reversal in Spenser's critical fortunes. The author of the *Pilgrimage to Parnassus* hints at some early quarrel of the poets in which Spenser is set against Shakespeare.[56] How far the quarrel was particularized it is impossible to know. Most probably it was a quarrel about categories of author rather than authors: about the opposition of learned poetry and native wood notes wild. Fifty years later this quarrel is in some way still alive, for in Samuel Holland's *Don Zara* (No. 93), Spenser is acclaimed by one party of poets – the learned party – and Shakespeare by the other. If so, Holland's conceptions had outlived their proper time. This early quarrel must soon have been forgotten, and another takes its place. It is easier to see Spenser, in the context of the seventeenth-century critical emphasis on design, as a barbarous and gothic poet than as a learned one. The results of his learning are, except incidentally, not immediately apparent; those of his adherence to formally corrupt models and absurd matter on the other hand are. In consequence it is from the neo-classical critics that comes the most stable opposition to Spenser. Spenser becomes at once the object of awe, and a cause for regret. Rymer declared his admiration, but is obliged to put on record a principled disapproval of Spenser's manner (No. 101). That particular combination is commonplace. The sternest censures are generally on his language, but only because it is Spenser's language which is most conspicuously deviant. That will however be discussed later. It is more difficult to know what to make of Drummond's report that as well as disliking Spenser's manner, Jonson objected to his matter (No. 61b). As Drummond states it, it sounds like total condemnation. As such it would make sense. At that date, an objection to the matter of the *Faerie Queene* presumably represents an attack on its 'fabulousness' and reflects an opinion something like Fanshawe's (No. 92). For some, Spenser was not enough of a Lucan. From Jonson, however, the objection sounds like posed overstatement designed to excite Drummond's interest in literary scandal.

There are two classes of reader which Spenser's 'fabulousness' does not discomfit. The first consists of those who read him just for the story, or more generally, for the surface appeal; the second consists of those who do not read him for the story at all. When a child, it was for the story that Cowley read the *Faerie Queene*, and it is of note that he had no understanding at that time of why his mother, who read exclusively in devotional literature, should have had it among her books (No. 87b). Charles I apparently read the *Faerie Queene* 'for alleviating his spirits after serious study'.[57] Sir Aston Cockayne thinks that *Faerie Queene*, along with other romantic and erotic literature, is unsuitable reading for the inexpert (No. 94c). Edmund Gayton classes the *Faerie Queene* as a product of strictly native wit and fancy.[58] The element of fairy tale or romance in the *Faerie Queene* is strong, and it can be enjoyed in isolation. This approach to the poem is however isolated from the main critical currents of the mid-century, though it does come into its own later. In this earlier period articulate readers of the second category well outnumber those of the first. Spenser's poem as well as being enjoyable as romance also invites moral interpretation. That tendency to read almost exclusively as moral allegory, observable from the first, increases throughout the century. Milton (No. 74), and More (No. 82) even as a child, both celebrate Spenser's authority as a moralist, or as a source of arcane knowledge. Put to such uses it hardly matters that the *Faerie Queene* is gothic or the *Shepheardes Calender* quaint. It might not have mattered at all had not Spenser achieved that classic status of which we have spoken. Since he had, it becomes possible for such writers as Lisle (No. 70), or Reynolds (No. 75), or Temple (No. 112) to approve the doctrine, but not the allegory.

That steady disapproval of the neo-classical critics can best be explained in terms of expectations. Earlier in the progress of Spenser's critical fortunes such objections had no ground in which to root themselves. As long as Spenser was classed with his contemporaries (Daniel, Drayton, and the like), or even with Chaucer, then the criteria by which he was estimated were necessarily irregular. Gervase Markham sees Spenser's relation to Chaucer as being like Virgil's to Homer or Ariosto's to Boiardo: that is, more polite and more correct, but not absolutely polite and correct. E.G. does not even trouble with those distinctions: Chaucer and Spenser are comparable because both are learned poets – '*Chaucer's* learned soule in Spencer sung.'[59] Edward Leigh thinks Chaucer, as an English Homer, is superior to Spenser, and in preferring invention to judgment, reveals the very contrary of a neo-classical bias.[60] Jonson is again exceptional. Carpenter believes that the appearance, in *The Golden Age Restored*, of Spenser along with Chaucer, Gower and Lydgate, is high evidence of his poetical canonization.[61] In view of Jonson's remarks elsewhere, the compliment is a little two-edged.

The comparison with Virgil, however, immediately revealed Spenser's formal deficiences. For this reason it is in the end abandoned. It proved in too many respects unsatisfactory, and the passing years diminished its intelligibility. As early as 1631 Robert Henderson substitutes Ariosto for Virgil as the standard by which Spenser is to be measured.[62] It is repeated in the 1650s by R.C. (No. 89a). Thereafter critics sympathetic to Spenser as well as unsympathetic class him with Italian rather than with the ancient poets. The consequences of this procedure are more clearly seen in the period after 1660.

V

THE PERIOD 1660–1715

There are few critics after the Restoration who are prepared to accept Spenser as a poet in the Virgilian mould, and the Ariostan standard was generally adopted. This standard is unfortunately rendered unstable by the beginnings of a more general literary quarrel. For while the battle of the Ancients and the Moderns was not formally open in England before the 1690s, Wotton was not provoked simply by Temple, and the debate was not worked up out of the air. Before that, there were those critics who were satisfied with the literary autonomy of the moderns, and there were those who would quite arbitrarily have preferred their Spenser to be more like Virgil. Rymer, whose reputation suffers a little unjustly on account of his excesses, takes the comparison with Ariosto to be *ipso facto* condemnation (No. 101). Though Rymer concedes a good deal to Spenser, his remains the severest possible neo-classical line. Though hardly anyone can have admired Spenser more, Dryden follows it: 'Spenser wanted only to have read the Rules of *Bossu*; for no Man was Born with a greater Genius, or had more Knowledge to support it.' (No. 100f.) Even earlier, in 1644, when the author of *Vindex Anglicus* is anxious to assert the comparability of English and ancient poetry, he can find it in himself to compare Spenser only with Lucan[63] – he may however, only have been thoughtlessly following Carew. Among the Moderns Spenser might have found readier support had he been more obviously or more consistently a

Christian poet. John Worthington regrets the loss of his *Canticles* (No. 95); Edward Howard (No. 111) and More (No. 82) allow him the advantage of being a Christian poet. But, as Dennis points out (No. 118), even here Spenser damned himself by mixing his Christianity with the vestiges of paganism. For such as Temple, to be a Christian poet was automatically to be disadvantaged (No. 112). Towards the end of the century, Matthew Morgan calls up the image of Spenser.

Depressed when living, slighted now he's dead.[64]

Yet to a poet of Spenser's obvious virtues, concessions had to be made.

Even critics as confident of their own rightness as those of the later seventeenth century, were permitted by the growth of a primitive sort of literary historicism to 'place' Spenser as the product of imperfect time, and his poetry as the product of imperfect principles. A progress from Chaucer to Spenser and beyond is worked out, as in Denham's elegy on Cowley (No. 96) or as in Dryden: 'Even after Chaucer, there was a Spenser, a Harrington, a Fairfax, before Waller and Benham were in being' (No. 100g). *Enfin Malherbe vint*, but Spenser was no Malherbe. He does not in fact come out of this placing process particularly well. Atterbury's astonishment at the recognition that Spenser precedes Waller by only fifty years is a sign of how badly he can come out of it (No. 156). Waller is now underrated, but not so far abused that Atterbury's expression of those notions cannot properly be seen as wrong headed. Once *Paradise Lost* was published, the idea of a literary progress was once more reinforced, but again at Spenser's expense.

Milton was held to be at once ethically and formally superior to Spenser. *Paradise Lost* was not the perfect neo-classical poem, but it was a closer approximation to it than was the *Faerie Queene*. Patrick Hume's notes on *Paradise Lost* for example, where it is a question of a borrowing from Spenser, do not fail to point out the superiority of Milton's version (No. 116). And in an age that rediscovered the sublime, Leonard Welsted in his translation of Longinus can make more use of Milton than of the earlier poet (No. 128).

But except in the imagination of partisans one poet does not supersede another. The failure of the effort to associate Spenser with the ancients, and his betterment in those categories into which his critics had attempted to fit him, led to a revaluation of Spenser's achievement among those not concerned with those *paragoni*, in quite different terms.

Spenser's reputation as a pastoral poet remained throughout the period up to 1715 more or less unimpaired. Congreve in 1695 thinks it not inappropriate to set 'British *Colins* mourning Muse' alongside 'the *Sicilian Bard*, or the *Mantuan* Swain'.[65] Cotton's *Poems* of 1689 show the influence of Spenser still working strongly. Steele in two *Guardian* papers of 1713 – the papers which provoked Pope – considers that both Spenser and Philips have 'copied and improved the beauties of the Ancients'.[66] Pope's reply to those papers, or his adolescent criticism of Spenser in the Preface to his own *Pastorals*, are not at bottom attacks on Spenser but on Philips (Nos. 124, 167). His letter to Hughes better indicates his attitude: 'Spenser has ever been a favourite poet to me; he is like a mistress, whose faults we see, but love her with them all.'[67] Gay's parody of Spenser's pastoral manner in the *Shepherd's Week* (1714) is at least good-humoured. Woodford makes explicit his preference for the minor poems (No. 103). So far is Spenser's reputation as a pastoralist his strength, that by 1717 Thomas Purney attempts a justification of the *Faerie Queene* as a pastoral poem, perhaps on a cue from Hughes.[68]

The *Faerie Queene* required some justification in other than epic terms. Towards the end of the century Spenser hardly counted at all as an heroic poet. A few scattered references are available which suggest that some estimation of him is going on almost in the terms of his contemporaries. Marvell alludes to Spenser as the singer 'In Lofty Notes [of] *Tudor's* blest Race'.[69] And while Evelyn reads Chaucer for his 'facetious Style', he reads Spenser as the celebrator of Elizabeth 'Who aw'd the *French*, and did the *Spaniard* tame'.[70] The *Athenian Mercury* XII (1693) recommends Spenser as a heroic poet, but while the author of the article may have had good taste, he had not strict taste, for he recommends as the best translation of the *Aeneid* that by Gavin Douglas.[71] Then there are signs that a distinction was drawn between heroic and epic poetry, for in *The Journal from Parnassus* of 1688,[72] the 'Examination of Heroics was assigned to Spenser: of Epics and Pindarics to Mr Waller'. One gets the impression that the *Faerie Queene* is being treated as something quite distinct from what it pretends to be, that it was at best being treated as heroic romance.

Unexpectedly two lines of thought on Spenser come together. The approval of the *Faerie Queene* as romance and the rejection of its epic pretensions allow the new revaluation. Spenser's sensuousness and his romance come into their own, and are made respectable. Dryden had said, 'If the design be good and the draught be true, the Colouring is the first beauty that strikes the eye.'[73] After 1700 it hardly seems to matter what the design is like, it is the colouring that strikes the eye. There begins the concentrated emphasis on the specifically pictorial which remains even in this century. Spenser had always, as is clear from the character of early imitations of him, been regarded as a master of descriptive writing. Before the end of the sixteenth century Carew bows to Spenser and Sidney as such (No. 28b), and Richard Haydocke, the English translator of Lomazzo, recommends English painters to the reading of Sidney, Spenser and Daniel.[74] The pictorial emphasis had always been possible. But there is new approval in the tone of Spence's report of the old lady's account of the *Faerie Queene* as a gallery of pictures. Truly, it may as well have been nothing but that.[75]

Addison and Steele combine with an interest in the pictorial, an interest in allegory as such. Now this latter interest (manifested for example in Addison's declaration of a project to write an allegory in the manner of Spenser)[76] does allow Spenser the virtues of seriousness, without tying the critic to any estimation of his poetry in strictly generic terms. The *Faerie Queene* is allowed to be serious, without being epic. Addison approves the allegory of Sin and Death in Milton but thinks it unsuitable for epic (No. 114d). The criteria for seriousness are no longer formal, and this is from one point of view a great step forward. Addison does not deny Spenser's debt to the Italians, but he does make clear that Spenser is not entirely depraved by them: he is free, as he points out, from their use of false wit (No. 114b). These are novel moves in the game of comparisons. They make Spenser, a poet *sui generis*.

All this Hughes develops (No. 131). It is his virtue to have made explicit the tendencies apparent in the criticism of the past fifty years, to have pulled them into order, and to have made sense of them. It would be difficult to overestimate his particular debt to Addison or Steele. All systems of literary classification are for practical purposes abandoned. All attempts to fit the *Faerie Queene* to the pattern of epic or to the pattern of romance are rejected. Spenser is estimated on the basis only of what Hughes finds in him – his fine morality, his noble speeches, his beautiful allegories and most of all his pictorial sense. Hughes is the first modern critic of Spenser. There is no room here to estimate what damage he may have done.

VI

LANGUAGE

Comments on Spenser's language, where not part of more broadly based comment have been excluded from the period division, partly because they can be more conveniently consulted if printed separately, partly because their tenor is independent of the fluctuations that mark general opinion on Spenser.

It is E.K. who determines what course the discussion will take (No. 1a). When he first brings up for discussion Spenser's archaizing procedures, he is aware of possible dissent from his own heartily expressed approval. Valla had objected to archaism in Livy, others to archaism in Sallust. But he considers 'that those ancient solemne wordes are a great ornament, both in the one and in the other.' And so it will be in Spenser. The opinion is defended on a variety of grounds, not all wholly compatible: it suits the decorum of pastoral to use old words, the old word lends gravity to utterance, the common word sets off the uncommon, English is purified by the use of pure Saxon. Subsequent discussion has always the character of a reshuffling of those terms. It is almost always very abstract – no one before this century thought to examine thoroughly the precise quality of Spenser's archaism; and it usually involves generalized praise or blame of Spenser's mode of affectation rather than discussion of how exactly it operates in Spenser's poetry. Francis Beaumont simply follows and quotes E.K. (No. 140), Everard Guilpin states both sides of the case (No. 142), but in E.K.'s terms; Sir Philip Sidney, oddly ungrateful for a dedicatee, states only the case against archaism (No. 133). The viability of both points of view is illustrated by the survival of the same argument into the age of Philips and Pope (No. 167). If Ambrose Philips should be thought too weak-minded an advocate of archaism to matter, then perhaps Oldham (No. 154) or Bentley (No. 161) will not. In practice Oldham or Bentley might have thought it unmannerly to affect archaism, but they understand the principle. Pope, one suspects, only affects astonishment at Spenser's language. It is difficult to believe that he is genuinely as uncomprehending as Edward Howard (No. 151) or Sir Thomas Culpepper (No. 152).

That there was some genuine difficulty even in understanding Spenser is suggested by the publication of a glossary along with Bathurst's version of the *Shepheardes Calender* in 1653, or the appearance of words from Spenser in John Ray's *A Collection of English Words not generally used* (1674) and Thomas Jackson does make an explicit complaint to that effect.[77] Hughes in fact shows in his emendations that he did not exactly understand the old words, but a failure of exact understanding seldom provokes general consternation. Spenser's language is so often attacked simply because it is that feature of his writing most susceptible of attack. Dillingham notes in his preface to Bathurst that the *Shepheardes Calender* in English is a poem '*cum barba*,' and Fanshawe echoes him, again comparing the original with the fluency of Bathurst's Latin, that it is 'a Poem, which the Author made it his businesse to cloathe in rugged English'.[78] Neither Dillingham nor Evelyn is really unsympathetic – most critics of their time were. They are generously represented on the following pages, and elaborate summary here is unnecessary.

Not only Spenser's archaism is open to attack, but his choice of stanza in the *Faerie Queene* – where the archaism is a little less pressingly obvious. Many would still regard it as unfortunate. Harvey thought the Alexandrine a grace in each stanza of the poem (No. 132a), as did Gill (No. 147), and even later Phillips (No. 173). Harvey may have pronounced it trippingly on the tongue (No. 132a); but there is no evidence to suggest that Gill or Phillips did. Harington found it twisted his mouth, Lisle found it tended to irregularity. D'Avenant sees that it forced Spenser into the use of abnormal forms (No. 88), and Hughes agrees. Among those who do object there is a strong possibility that their central ground of complaint is the inappropriateness of the stanza for epic. It is after all only another symptom of Spenser's lamentable dependence on the Italians. This feeling is however differently rationalized. Hughes finds that the stanza tends to monotony (No. 159), while Dennis finds it tends to the lyrical (No. 166b). Both statements might be true: the different emphasis derives from the preoccupation of one with the narrative, and of the other with abstract questions of genre.

When one considers what baneful influence Spenser's mannerisms could exert, it is possible to sympathize with the complaints. Edmund Bolton finds that he cannot allow the use of Spenser 'for practick English' (No. 146). Fatuous in isolation, the remark takes on meaning when one sees just how often he was so recommended. Spenser was very self-consciously a stylist and some at least of his mannerisms were recognized as widely useful and adaptable. Webbe offers the *Shepheardes Calender* as a model for the practising poet, as does Fraunce the

23

Faerie Queene. Spenser contributes about a tenth of the quotations in Bodenham's *Belevedere*, and that the reader may see to what end, I have included Bodenham's preface in this book (No. 144). Spenser's work is dredged till mid-century for illustrations of rhetorical categories, or for incidental beauties, or for fine commonplaces. Robert Allott's *Englands Parnassus* (1600), Daniel Tuvill's *The Dove and the Serpent* (1614), and Joshua Poole's *The English Parnassus* (1651) may be added to those from which passages appear in this book.

VII

FOREIGN RECEPTION

In spite of the hopes of Digby (No. 71a), who thought that if Spenser were known then the English language would be studied, and Fanshawe, who thought that Bathurst's version of the *Shepheardes Calender* would 'doe more honour to England Abroad', Spenser seems to have been little known on the Continent.[79] But that is a fate that he shares at this time with all writers in English, and indeed with the English language. The difficulty of the language may have contributed not a little to the general ignorance of its poetry. Marville de Vigneul writes in 1702: '*Le stile des Anglois est un stile long, ennuyeux, embarasse, tres difficile à traduire en Latin, en Italien, & en Francois.*'[80] Theodore Parrhase writes in 1699 that even the Northern nations boast of having poets equal to the French, '*mais c'est de quoi je ne saurois juger.*'[81] The Continent's sense of its own cultural superiority may be another factor. A writer in the *Journal de la Republique des Lettres* asks: '*Qui est-ce, hors de l'Angleterre, qui ait oui parler de Spenser, de Milton, de Ben Jonson, de Shakespeare?*' Few indeed. Guy Miège in the *Etat Présent de l'Angleterre* names Spenser as an English poet, but he had known Marvell and (rare thing) took an interest in English affairs.[82] The abbé Fraguier in 1707 had been stimulated at least to want to read Spenser, but had difficulty in getting hold of a copy.[83] It is not, I think known if he did.

Dr van Dorsten of the Sir Thomas Browne Institute has been able to disclose to me no early references to Spenser in Dutch or in Dutch writers. Even if Sidney's early fame was not always specifically literary, the contrast is remarkable.[84] Only it would seem with the anglophile van Effen is there any attempt to write on Spenser and even then the attempt is not spectacular. We are told that he is thought highly of in England, but that his language is difficult.[85] In Germany, where Sidney's *Arcadia* enjoyed a considerable reputation, Spenser did not fare much better. Weckherlin's prefatory poem to *Öden und Gesänge* (1618) may be an imitation of Spenser's lines 'To his Booke' in front of the *Shepheardes Calender*. Other apparent borrowings can be taken to a common source. The notion that Valentin Lober adapts that same piece in his *Teutschender Owenus*, is to me suspect. Von Hofmannswaldau tells us that Spenser, Drayton, Jonson, Quarles and Donne are artistically superior to Chaucer and Robert of Gloucester; and Morhof quotes Rymer on Spenser – the only account of any substance.[86]

VIII

LIVES

'Nobody can write the life of a man, but those who have eat and drunk and lived in social intercourse with him.' So Dr Johnson, quoted by Helen Darbishire, to illustrate Milton's good fortune in having had contemporaries willing to be his biographers.[87] Camden is the only one of Spenser's biographers who can ever have done any of those things with him, and Camden never really saw it as his business to write Spenser's biography: the notices he gives of Spenser's life are always part of more comprehensive projects. A. C. Judson points to the obvious inadequacy of the early lives, and laments the fact that neither Harvey nor Bryskett saw fit to devote their leisure to writing better ones.[88] The fact is they did not. It is furthermore unfortunate that none of the seventeenth-century writers who give notices of Spenser's life were prepared to devote energy and industry, failing intimacy with their subject, to their projects. The lives as well as being deficient in detail are deficient in accuracy: their writers are happy to perpetrate legend, and the extent to which each later life (Ware's excepted) is blindly dependent on the earlier must surprise even the cynical. Hughes is the first biographer, not reporting what he knows to be the case, who has made any attempt to evaluate the facts and pseudo-facts available to him.

I have arranged the accounts chronologically, since this is the most intelligible way of making the relation to one another obvious. The lives of Camden, Ware, Fuller, Aubrey, Phillips, that of 1679, and that by Winstanley are discussed by A. C. Judson. The accounts by Johnston, Sandys, and Blount are wholly derivative.

IX

CRITICISM SINCE 1715

Johnson reports in his *Life of Hughes* that the editions of 1715 failed to attract a greater public to Spenser. The completion by the end of the 1750s of editions by Thomas Birch (1751), John Upton (1758), and Richard Church (1758) indicate a change. Some thirty editions of the *Works* as a whole appeared between that date and the end of the nineteenth century, of which the most important are those by H. J. Todd (1805), J. P. Collier (1862), and A. B. Grosart (1882–4). The first American edition was by G. S. Hillard (Boston, 1839). The most important editions prepared in the twentieth century are those by J. C. Smith and E. de Selincourt (Oxford, 1909–10 and reprinted in the Oxford Standard Authors Series, 1912), and the *Variorum Spenser* (Baltimore, 1932–49). Since the late eighteenth century there seems at least to have been a market for scholarly editions. The work of the *Spectator* writers and of Hughes had, however, made Spenser common property, and that fact is reflected in the number of selections and adaptations which appeared, perhaps a little tardily, from the end of the eighteenth century: *Una and Arthur, An Allegorical Romance* (1779) leads naturally through one Mrs Peabody's *Holiness* (Boston, 1836) to M. H. Towry's *Spenser for Children* (1885). If Shakespeare deserved Charles and Mary Lamb or Dr Bowdler, then Spenser deserved Mrs Peabody or M. H. Towry. The poet Yeats's selections from Spenser (1906), perhaps the most famous of a long line, represent only a slightly more worthy manifestation of his broader fame. Outside the English-speaking world too, Spenser's popularity is evident. Attempts at translation were made in the *Teutscher Merkur* (1788) and the *Deutche Monatsschrift* (1795). And T. J. Mathias, an Englishman and an editor of Gray, imported Spenser to Italy with *Il Cavaliero della Croce Rossa* (Naples, 1827).

The terms on which Spenser is widely accepted are for a long time those of Hughes. Thomas Warton, generally accepted as the most considerable of Spenser's eighteenth-century critics, duplicates much of what Hughes had already said. But he is subtler and more inventive, and also more discriminating. Hughes had maintained the regularity of Book I of the *Faerie Queene* as 'an entire Work of it self'; Warton points to the damaging consequences to the later Books of their mutual independence. However, while being less complacent than Hughes about what he regards as Spenser's deficiencies, Warton resorts to the same sort of solutions: while the *Faerie Queene* is 'destitute of that arrangement and oeconomy which epic severity requires', it remains 'the careless exhuberance of a warm imagination and a strong sensibility'; and if 'the critic is not satisfied, yet the reader is transported'.[89] The progress of this suspension of critical standards is briefly interrupted by Upton, and the *Preface* to his editions of the *Faerie Queene* (1758) is noteworthy for marking a regression from Hughes's solutions and a return to the spirit of Digby. It is too easy to ridicule the *Preface*, which maintains at least a Homeric unity for the *Faerie Queene*: Upton was probably more in touch with what Spenser wanted his readers to believe about the *Faerie Queene* than any critic since Digby or any critic after himself. The notes in his edition display learning of astounding breadth and quality. Indeed, the quality of learning and perception in those notes has made more than one reader of the *Variorum Spenser* wish for more of Upton and less of almost anyone else. There is a strong case for reprinting everything Upton said about Spenser. But Upton's *Preface* and Upton's notes (except in so far as they are useful to source hunters) were largely forgotten. He may still be generally accounted only a superior Jortin, whose uninspired *Remarks on Spenser's Poems* were published in 1734.

Instead it is to Hurd that the glory had gone.[90] Hurd it was who confirmed Hughes's intuition of the compatibility of Spenser's poem with the structure of a Gothic cathedral. The trouble, at least until very recently, with most modern accounts of Gothic is that they incorporate complacently the neo-classical objections to Gothic. Hurd is relatively free from this complacency. But his attempt to establish a rule of Gothic unity, 'a unity of design [i.e. intention] and not of action' failed. This he himself recognized. For he could not square the evident classical pretensions of the poem with its evident romantic variety, and is obliged to admit that confusion and perplexity attend the whole.

With perplexity and confusion on his head, Spenser enters the nineteenth century. Hazlitt is the most notorious of Spenser Romantic critics: 'if [readers] do not meddle with the allegory, the allegory will not meddle with them.'[91] That Coleridge should have in the same year objected to Hazlitt's procedure (and Coleridge is not free in any case from the English Romantic bias) signifies nothing for the immediate history of Spenser's critical fortunes.[92] James Russel Lowell, who has written, it must be admitted, one of the most sensitive essays ever to appear on Spenser, follows Hazlitt: 'whoever can tolerate music and painting and poetry all in one, whoever wishes to be rid of thought and to let the busy anvils of the brain be silent for a time, let him read in the *Faerie Queene*'.[93] It was to that pass that Hughes, without intending anything of this kind, led.

Dowden's reply to Lowell owns a spiritual debt to Coleridge and Ruskin, and restores the notion that the useful may also be beautiful:[94] 'Spenser's conception of life was puritan in its seriousness.' Mueller recommends the essays by Lowell and Dowden as those seminal for all future criticism of Spenser.[95]

The bulk, range, and quality of Spenser criticism in this century make summary description impossible. There are always those among Spenser's readers who will find it in themselves to admire the poet for Lowell's reasons. But with very few exceptions they have been silenced by the extraordinary sophistication of those whom Mueller would regard as the heirs of Dowden: he cites as products of Dowden's spirit W. L. Renwick's *Edmund Spenser: An Essay on Renaissance Poetry* (1925), B. E. C. Davis's *Edmund Spenser: A Critical Study* (1933), W. B. C. Watkin's *Shakespeare and Spenser* (Princeton, 1950). Spenser's seriousness is now taken for granted, and even if the memory of Lowell now and again mitigates the astringency of their conclusions, the authors even of general studies no longer pretend otherwise. Where and how this seriousness operates are still matters of contention. That is, what is now at issue is the consistency of Spenser's poetry, the connexion between its meaning and its structure. The contention is not always fully rational, and disagreements over principles are not always distinguished from distaste for particular applications of principles. For example, the exaggerations in Lilian Winstanley's exposition of historical and topical allusion in her editions of Book II (1914) and Book I (1915) of the *Faerie Queene* quite illogically damaged the reputation of her method. The sanity of the exposition in Paul McLane's *Spenser's Shepheardes Calender: A Study in Elizabethan Allegory* (Notre Dame, 1961) may restore it. Resistance to historical allegorism is more recently paralleled by that to numerological and iconographical criticism as it appears in Kent Heiatt's treatment of the *Epithalamion* in *Short Time's Endless Monument* (New York, 1960) or Alastair Fowler's of the *Faerie Queene* in *Spenser and the Numbers of Time* (1964). Both books, the latter more ambitiously, not only make clear the complexity of Spenser's system of reference, but reveal in Spenser's poetry a structure strict beyond all modern expectations. What reasoned grounds there are for objection to such criticism is not clear. No critic of Spenser, not even Ruskin, ever believed in the exclusive value of the 'discovered' part of an allegorical equivalence. The appreciation of Spenser's pictorialism has in any case given way to the study of Spenser's iconographies. Thomas P. Roche's *The Kindly Flame* (Princeton, 1964), and Rosemond Tuve's *Allegorical Imagery* (Princeton, 1966) combine a resistance to referential notions of allegory with a sensitivity to precise signification. Even a critic so insistent of the quality of surface in the *Faerie Queene* as is Paul Alpers in *The Poetry of Edmund Spenser*, does not deny the relevance of 'allegorical encounters and emblematic figures'. Sometimes the debate seems to be between those who make their reservations explicit and those who do not; it is in any case peripheral to the substance of the contribution made by those engaged in it.

NOTES

1 *The Critics of Edmund Spenser* (Syracuse, 1959), p. 1.
2 In Webbe's *Discourse* (1586) Spenser is identified as the author, but only covertly; and Whetstone, in *Sir Philip Sidney* (1587) imagines that the author is Sidney. For information on editions of Spenser, see Francis R. Johnson, *A Critical Bibliography of the Works of Edmund Spenser* (Baltimore, 1933).
3 See headnote to No. 1.
4 The story of Sidney's reading the Despair canto is first repeated by Aubrey, in his *Life of Sidney*.
5 *The Evolution of the 'Faerie Queene'* (Chicago, 1942).
6 For the view that Spenser as well as Ponsonby was involved in the publication of the volume, see the edition of W. I. Renwick (1928), pp. 179–80.
7 See *Poets on Fortune's Hill* (1952), pp. 33–6.
8 See Eleanor Rosenberg, *Leicester, Patron of Letters* (New York, 1955), pp. 346–8.
9 In *Two Centuries of Spenser Scholarship* (Baltimore, 1936).
10 Wurtsbaugh, p. 5.
11 Wurtsbaugh, p. 11.
12 *Life of Hughes* in *Lives of the Poets* (1784).

13 That is, the reprint of Hughes in 1750, the edition of Thomas Birch (1751), an anonymous edition in 1758, and in the same year those by John Upton and Richard Church.

14 See G. Agnelli and G. Ravegnani, *Gli Annali delle edizioni Ariostee* (Bologna, 1933).

15 The *Shakespeare Allusion Book*, rev. J. M. Munro, re-issued with preface by Sir Edmund Chambers (1932), p. xxxiii.

16 See G. E. Bentley, *Shakespeare and Jonson* (Chicago, 1945), I. 7. Bentley has at least established Jonson's reputability. Reviews by, for example, Baldwin Maxwell, *PQ*, XXIV (1945), 91–3, or Alfred Harbage, *MLN*, LX (1945), 414–17, damage his wider conclusions.

17 *Dialogus de Oratoribus* xiii; quoted R. D. Williams, 'Changing Attitudes to Virgil: A study in the History of Taste from Dryden to Tennyson', in *Virgil*, ed. D. R. Dudley (1969), p. 120.

18 See H. E. Cory, *The Critics of Edmund Spenser, University of California Publications in Modern Philology*, II (1911), 81–182.

19 For a general account, see Charles R. Baskerville, 'The Early Fame of *The Shepheardes Calender*', *PMLA*, XXVIII (1913), 291–313.

20 B.M. MS. Harleian 367, fol. 129.

21 *John of Bordeaux* was edited for the Malone Society in 1936 by W. L. Renwick. See pp. 43–4.

22 *Parthenophil and Parthenope* (1593), ii. 8.

23 *Chloris* (1596), sig. A2.

24 The address to Cupid is in the *The Affectionate Shepheard* (1594), *The Shepheards Content*, st. 33. For his avowal that he imitates Cupid, see *Cynthia* (1595), sig. A4^v.

25 *Ellis Catalogue* 204, item 330.

26 This is hardly the place to go into the vexed question of relations between *Tamburlaine* and the *Faerie Queene*. But see T. W. Baldwin, 'Spenser's Borrowings from Marlowe', *ELH*, IX (1942), 157–87, and for the other point of view. C. B. Watkins, 'The Plagiarist: Spenser or Marlowe?' *ELH*, XI (1944), 249–65.

27 *Poemata* (1605), sig. E6^v: '*siue canis siluas, Spencere, uel horrida belli . . .*'. There is perhaps a pun on *silvas*.

28 *The First Commentary on the 'Faerie Queene'*, ed. Graham Hough (priv. publ.). The copy is in the hands of Lord Bessborough.

29 See the unsigned note, 'MS Notes to Spenser's *Faerie Queene*', *N&Q*, CCII (1957), 509–15; and Alastair Fowler, 'Oxford and London Marginalia to *The Faerie Queene*', *N&Q*, CCVI (1961), 416–19. An article on Sir Walter Ralegh's marginalia on Spenser is forthcoming in *The Library*: Dr Oakeshott, who owns the copy and has written the article, informs me that the notes are mainly topical.

30 See F. I. Carpenter, *A Reference Guide to Edmund Spenser* (Chicago, 1923), p. 240.

31   *Shakespeare Allusion Book*, p. xxvi.

32   *The Critics of Edmund Spenser*, p. 98. For general accounts of Spenser's influence, see also H. E. Cory, *Spenser, the School of the Fletchers and Milton, University of California Publications in Modern Philology*, II (1911), 311–73; and Douglas Bush, *English Literature in the Earlier Seventeenth Century* (Oxford, 1945), pp. 76–103. Recently published is Joan Grundy's *The Spenserian Poets* (1969).

33   *Historial and Poetical Medley* (1737), p. xii.

34   In the prefatory poem 'In Autorem', in Bedell's *A Protestant Memorial* (1713), sig. C.

35   On Niccols, see Dorothy F. Atkinson, *Edmund Spenser: A Bibliographical Supplement* (Baltimore, 1937), p. 172.

36   On the Fletchers, see Cory, *Spenser, the School. of the Fletchers and Milton*, pp. 314–31.

37   *Sir Philip Sidney's Ourania* (1606), sigs. B2ᵛ–B3.

38   That is, by T. K. Dunseath, *Spenser's Allegory of Justice* (Princeton, 1968).

39   Bush, p. 76.

40   See Rosemary Freeman, *English Emblem Books* (1948), p. 71.

41   The first masque to show signs of Spenser's influence seems to be the *Masque of Proteus* (1594) – see *Gesta Grayorum*, ed. W. W. Greg, Malone Society Publications (1915), p. xxi. On the debt to Spenser of *Lingua* (1607), see M. P. Tilley, '*Lingua* and the *Faerie Queene*', *MLN*, XLII (1927), 150–7. The influence persists up to Shirley.

42   *The Critics of Edmund Spenser*, p. 96.

43   *A Method of Trauell* (1605), sig. C.

44   *Epicedium* (1603), sig. B3.

45   Bodleian MS. Rawlinson D 679, preliminary leaf.

46   *An Apologie for Womenkinde* (1605), sigs. A4ᵛ–B.

47   In John Gower's *Pyromachia* (1635), sig. F4.

48   John Taylor, *A Brown Dozen of Drunkards* (1648), p. 16.

49   See Leicester Bradner, 'The Latin Translations of Spenser's *Shepheardes Calender*', *MP*, XXXIII (1935–6), 26.

50   *Greenes Ghost Havnting Coniecatchers* (1602), sigs. E4, E4ᵛ, F, etc.

51   *Nero Caesar* (1624), p. 161.

52   *England, Wales, Scotland and Ireland Described* (1627), sig. A3ᵛ.

53   In prefatory poem to Cartwright's *Comedies . . .* (1651), sig. ★★★2.

54   *The First Part of the Return from Parnassus* (1606), II.1180 3; and *Pasquils Palinodia* (1619), sig. A3.

55   The best and fullest account of the Italian debates on heroic poetry is in Bernard Weinberg, *A History of Literary Criticism in the Italian Renaissance*, 2 vols. (Chicago, 1961).

56   Compare *Three Parnassus Plays*, ed. J. B. Leishman (1949), pp. 54–5. Gullio prefers Shakespeare to Chaucer and Spenser, but what one makes of that preference is certainly open to dispute.

57 Sir Thomas Herbert, *Memoirs of the Two Last Years of . . . King Charles I* (1702), p. 43.

58 *Pleasant Notes upon Don Quixot* (1654), p. 21. Gayton however thinks this also of *Gondibert*.

59 See Gervase Markham, *The English Arcadia* (1607), sig. A2; E.G.'s poem is among the prefatory matter of Martin Llewellyn's *Men Miracles* (1646), sig. A5.

60 *A Treatise of Religion and Learning* (1656), p. 160.

61 *A Reference Guide*, p. 242.

62 R.H., *Arraignment of the Whole Creature* (1631), p. 186.

63 *Vindex Anglicus* (Oxford, 1644), sig. A3.

64 *A Poem to the Queen . . .* (Oxford, 1691), sig. D2.

65 *The Mourning Muse of Alexis* (1695), in *Works*, ed. M. Summers (1923), IV. 39.

66 *The Guardian*, 15 April 1713; see also the number for 17 April.

67 Letter to Hughes, 7 October 1715. See *The Correspondence*, ed. George Sherburn (Oxford, 1956), I. 316.

68 *A Full Enquiry into the True Nature of Pastoral* (1717); repr. Augustan Reprint Society (1948), pp. 39–40. The genius for pastoral imagery in Spenser and Ovid is displayed in the *Metamorphoses* of the one and in the *Faerie Queene* of the other.

69 *Poems and Letters*, ed. H. M. Margoliouth (Oxford, 1927), I. 185.

70 *The Immortality of Poesie*, in N. Tate's collection, *Poems by Several Hands* (1695), p. 91.

71 *Athenian Mercury* XII. 1 (24 October 1693).

72 In edition by Hugh Macdonald (1937), p. 38.

73 *Works of Virgil* (1697), p. 240.

74 *A Tracte containing the Rules of curious painting and carving* (1598), p. 84.

75 *Observations, Anecdotes . . .*, ed. J. M. Osborn (Oxford, 1966), I.182.

76 In *The Guardian* No. 152.

77 *Works* (1673), III.746 (written *c.* 1620).

78 Dillingham's prefatory epistle to Bathurst's *Calendrium Pastorale* (1653), sig. A3^v; for Fanshawe, see W. E. Simeone, 'A Letter from Richard Fanshawe to John Evelyn', *N&Q*, CXCVI (1951), 315–16.

79 See the note by Simeone.

80 *Mélanges d'Histoire et de Litterature* (Rotterdam, 1702), p. 28.

81 *Parrhasiana* (Amsterdam, 1699), pp. 6–8.

82 Quoted G. Ascoli, *La Grande Bretagne devant l'Opinion Francaise au XVIIe Siècle* (Paris, 1930), II. 120. Guy Miège is quoted there also; for his relations with Marvell, see P. Legouis, *André Marvell* (Paris and London, 1928), p. 248.

83 See Ascoli, II. 121.

84 For an account of Sidney in Holland, see Jan A. van Dorsten, *Poets Patrons and Professors* (1962).

85 W. J. B. Pienaar, *English Influences in Dutch Literature* (Cambridge, 1929), p. 225.

86 The information on Germany is taken from G. Waterhouse, *The Literary Relations of England and Germany in the Seventeenth Century* (Cambridge, 1914).

87 *The Early Lives of Milton* (1932), p. vii.

88 'The Seventeenth-Century Lives of Edmund Spenser', *HLQ*, X (1946–7), 35–48.

89 *Observations on the Fairy Queen of Edmund Spenser* (1754), revised and enlarged in 2 vols. (1762).

90 Richard Hurd, Letters on *Chivalry and Romance* (1762), VIII, in *Works* (1810), IV. 296–306.

91 William Hazlitt, *Lectures on the English Poets* (1818), in *Complete Works*, ed. P. P. Howe (1930–4), V.38.

92 *Literary Remains*, ed. A. N. Coleridge (1836–9), I. 89–97.

93 *Literary Essays* (1890), IV. 353.

94 Dowden's reply was first printed in A. B. Grosart's edition of Spenser's *Works* (priv. publ., 1882–4), I. 304–39. Ruskin's essay forms Appendix Z to *The Stones of Venice* in *Works*, ed. E. T. Cook and A. Wedderbury (1904), XI. 251–2.

95 Mueller, p. 16.

THE PERIOD 1579–1600

I. E.K.

1579

The most widely accepted identification of E.K. is as Edward Kirke (1553–1613) of Pembroke Hall and then Caius College, Cambridge. The identification with Spenser himself, or with Harvey, is now discountenanced. More recently, Paul McLane (in *Spenser's Shepheardes Calender* [Notre Dame, 1961]) has proposed for consideration the poet and friend of Sidney, Fulke Greville (1554–1628). That suggestion has at least the merit of being interesting, since something is known of Fulke Greville, and nothing of Edward Kirke (though see René Graziani, 'Verses by E.K.', *N&Q*, CCXIV [1969], 21). E.K. was also engaged to write a gloss on the *Dreames* (see No. 2a).

(a) The epistle *To the most excellent and learned . . . Mayster Gabriell Harvey* in *The Shepheardes Calender* (1579), sigs. ¶ij–¶iijᵛ (repr. in all editions of Spenser):

Uncovthe vnkiste, Sayde the olde famous Poete Chaucer: whom for his excellencie and wonderfull skil in making, his scholler Lidgate, a worthy scholler of so excellent a maister, calleth the Loadestarre of our Language: and whom our Colin clout in his Aeglogue calleth Tityrus the God of shepheards, comparing hym to the worthiness of the Roman Tityrus Virgile. Which prouerbe, myne owne good friend Ma. Haruey, as in that good old Poete it serued well Pandares purpose, for the bolstering of his baudy brocage, so very well taketh place in this our new Poete, who for that he is vncouthe (as said Chaucer) is vnkist, and vnknown to most men, is regarded but of few. But I dout not, so soone as his name shall come into the knowledg of men, and

35

his worthines be sounded in the tromp of fame, but that he shall be not onely kiste, but also beloued of all, embraced of the most, and wondred at of the best. No lesse I thinke, deserueth his wittinesse in deuising, his pithinesse in vttering, his complaints of loue so louely, his discourses of pleasure so pleasantly, his pastorall rudenesse, his morall wisenesse, his dewe obseruing of Decorum euerye where, in person-ages, in seasons, in matter, in speach, and generally in al seemely simplycitie of handeling his matter, and framing his words: the which of many thinges which in him be straunge, I know will seeme the straungest, the words them selues being so auncient, the knitting of them so short and intricate, and the whole Periode and compasse of speache so delightsome for the roundnesse, and so graue for the straungenesse. And firste of the wordes to speake, I graunt they be something hard, and of most men vnused, yet both English, and also vsed of most excellent Authors and most famous Poetes. In whom whenas this our Poet hath bene much traueiled and throughly redd, how could it be, (as that worthy Oratour sayde) but that walking in the sonne although for other cause he walked, yet needes he mought be sunburnt; and hauing the sound of those auncient Poetes still ringing in his eares, he mought needes in singing hit out some of theyr tunes. But whether he vseth them by such casualtye and custome, or of set purpose and choyse, as thinking them fittest for such rusticall rudenesse of shepheards, eyther for that theyr rough sounde would make his rymes more ragged and rustical, or els because such olde and obsolete wordes are most vsed of country folke, sure I think, and think I think not amisse, that they bring great grace and, as one would say, auctoritie to the verse. For albe amongst many other faultes it specially be obiected of Valla against Liuie, and of other against Saluste, that with ouer much studie they affect antiquitie, as coueting thereby credence and honor of elder yeeres, yet I am of opinion, and eke the best learned are of the lyke, that those auncient solemne wordes are a great ornament both in the one and in the other; the one labouring to set forth in hys worke an eternall image of antiquitie, and the other carefully dis-coursing matters of grauitie and importaunce. For if my memory fayle not, Tullie in that booke, wherein he endeuoureth to set forth the paterne of a perfect Oratour, sayth that ofttimes an auncient worde maketh the style seeme graue, and as it were reuerend: no otherwise then we honour and reuerence gray heares for a certein religious regard, which we haue of old age, yet nether euery where must old words be stuffed in, nor the commen Dialecte and maner of speaking so corrupted therby, that as in old buildings it seme disorderly and ruinous. But all as in most exquisite pictures they vse to blaze and portraict not onely the daintie lineaments of beautye, but also rounde about it to shadow the rude thickets and craggy clifts, that by the basenesse of such parts, more excellency may accrew to the principall; for oftimes we fynde ourselues, I knowe not how, singularly delighted with the shewe of such naturall rudenesse, and take great pleasure in that disorderly order. Euen so doe those rough and harsh termes enlumine and make more clearly to appeare the brightnesse of braue and glorious words. So oftentimes a dischorde in Musick maketh a comely concordaunce: so great delight tooke the worthy Poete Alceus to behold a blemish in the ioynt of a wel shaped body. But if any will rashly blame such his purpose in choyse of old and vnwonted words, him may I more iustly blame and condemne, or of witlesse headinesse in iudging, or of heedelesse hardinesse in condemning for not marking the compasse of hys bent, he wil iudge of the length of his cast. For in my opinion it is one special prayse, of many whych are dew to this Poete, that he hath laboured to restore, as to theyr rightfull heritage such good and naturall English words, as haue ben long time out of vse and almost cleane disherited. Which is the onely cause, that our Mother tonge, truely of it self is both ful enough for prose and stately enough for verse, hath long time ben counted most bare and barrein of both. which default when as some endeuoured to salue and recure, they patched vp the holes with peces and rags of other languages, borrowing here of the French, there of the Italian, euery where of the Latine, not weighing how il those tongues accorde with themselues, but much worse with ours: So now they haue made our English tongue, a gallimaufray or hodgepodge of al other speches. Other some not so wel seene in the English tonge as perhaps in other languages, if them happen to here an olde word albeit very naturall and significant, crye out streight way, that we speak no English, but gibbrish, or rather such, as in old time Euanders mother spake. whose first shame is, that they are not ashamed, in their own mother tonge straungers to be counted and alienes. The second shame no lesse then the first, that what so they vnderstand not, they streight way deeme to be sencelesse, and not at al to be vnderstode. Much like to the Mole in Aesopes fable, that being blynd her selfe, would in no wise be perswaded, that any beast could see. The last more shameful then both, that of their owne country and natural speach, which together with their Nources milk they sucked, they haue so base

37

regard and bastard judgement, that they will not onely themselues not
labor to garnish and beautifie it, but also repine, that of other it should
be embellished. Like to the dogge in the maunger, that him selfe can
eate no hay, and yet barketh at the hungry bullock, that so faine would
feede: whose currish kind though it cannot be kept from barking, yet
I conne them thanke that they refrain from byting.

Now for the knitting of sentences, whych they call the ioynts and
members thereof, and for al the compasse of the speach, it is round
without roughnesse, and learned wythout hardnes, such indeede as may
be perceiued of the leaste, vnderstoode of the moste, but iudged onely
of the learned. For what in most English wryters vseth to be loose, and
as it were vngyrt, in this Authour is well grounded, finely framed, and
strongly trussed vp together. In regard wherof, I scorne and spue out
the rakehellye route of our ragged rymers (for so themselues vse to
hunt the letter) which without learning boste, without iudgement
iangle, without reason rage and fome, as if some instinct of Poeticall
spirite had newly rauished them aboue the meanenesse of commen
capacitie. And being in the middest of all theyr brauery, sodenly
eyther for want of matter, or of ryme, or hauing forgotten theyr
former conceipt, they seeme to be so pained and traueiled in theyr
remembrance, as it were a woman in childebirth or as that same Pythia,
when the traunce came vpon her.

Os rabidum fera corda domans &c.
[Virgil, *Aeneid* VI. 80]

Nethelesse let them a Gods name feede on theyr owne folly, so they
seeke not to darken the beames of others glory. As for Colin, vnder
whose person the Author selfe is shadowed, how furre he is from such
vaunted titles and glorious showes, both him selfe sheweth, where he
sayth.

Of Muses Hobbin. I conne no skill. And,
Enough is me to paint out my vnrest, &c.
[*June* 65–79]

And also appeareth by the basenesse of the name, wherein, it seemeth,
he chose rather to vnfold great matter of argument couertly, then
professing it, not suffice thereto accordingly. Which moued him rather
in Aeglogues, then other wise to write, doubting perhaps his habilitie,
which he little needed, or mynding to furnish our tongue with this
kinde, wherein it faulteth, or following the example of the best and most

auncient Poetes, which deuised this kind of wryting, being both so base for the matter, and homely for the manner, at the first to trye theyr habilities: and as young birdes, that be newly crept out of the nest, by little first to proue theyr tender wyngs, before they make a greater flyght. So flew Theocritus, as you may perceiue he was all ready full fledged. So flew Virgile, as not yet well feeling his winges. So flew Mantuane, as being not full somd. So Petrarque. So Boccace; So Marot, Sanazarus, and also diuers other excellent both Italian and French Poetes, whose foting this Author euery where followeth, yet so as few, but they be wel sented can trace him out. So finally flyeth this our new Poete, as a bird, whose principals be scarce growen out, but yet as that in time shall be hable to keepe wing with the best.

Now as touching the generall dryft and purpose of his Aeglogues, I mind not to say much, him selfe labouring to conceale it. Onely this appeareth, that his vnstayed yougth had long wandred in the common Labyrinth of Loue, in which time to mitigate and allay the heate of his passion, or els to warne (as he sayth) the young shepheards .s. his equalls and companions of his vnfortunate folly, he compiled these xij. Aeglogues, which for that they be proportioned to the state of the xij. monethes, he termeth the SHEPHEARDS CALENDAR, applying an olde name to a new worke. Hereunto haue I added a certain Glosse or scholion for the exposition of old wordes and harder phrases: which maner of glosing and commenting, well I wote, wil seeme straunge and rare in our tongue: yet for somuch as I knew many excellent and proper deuises both in wordes and matter would passe in the speedy course of reading, either as vnknowen, or as not marked, and that in this kind, as in other we might be equal to the learned of other nations, I thought good to take the paines vpon me, the rather for that by meanes of some familiar acquaintance I was made priuie to his counsell and secret meaning in them, as also in sundry other works of his. Which albeit I know he nothing so much hateth, as to promulgate, yet thus much haue I aduentured vpon his frendship, him selfe being for long time furre estraunged, hoping that this will the rather occasion him, to put forth diuers other excellent works of his, which slepe in silence, as his Dreames, his Legendes, his Court of Cupide, and sondry others; whose commendations to set out, were verye vayne; the thinges though worthy of many, yet being knowen to few. These my present paynes if to any they be pleasurable or profitable, be you iudge, mine own good Maister Haruey, to whom I have both in respect of your worthinesse generally, and otherwyse vpon some particular and special considerations voued this my labour, and the maydenhead of this our commen frends Poetrie, himselfe hauing already in the beginning dedicated it to the Noble and worthy Gentleman, the right worshipfull Ma. Phi. Sidney, a special fauourer and maintainer of all kind of learning. Whose cause I pray you Sir, yf Enuie shall stur vp any wrongful accusasion, defend with your mighty Rhetorick and other your rare gifts of learning, as you can, and shield with your good wil, as you ought, against the malice and outrage of so many enemies, as I know wilbe set on fire with the sparks of his kindled glory. And thus recommending the Author vnto you, as vnto his most special good frend, and my selfe vnto you both, as one making singuler account of two so very good and so choise frends, I bid you both most hartely farwel, and commit you and your most commendable studies to the tuicion of the greatest.

Your owne assuredly to
be commaunded E. K.

(b) *The generall argument of the whole booke*, in *The Shepheardes Calender* (1579), sigs. ¶iiij–¶iij^v (repr. in all editions of Spenser):

Little I hope, needeth me at large to discourse the first Originall of Aeglogues, hauing alreadie touched the same. But for the word Aeglogues I know is vnknown to most, and also mistaken of some the best learned (as they think) I wyll say somewhat thereof, being not at all impertinent to my present purpose.

They were first of the Greekes the inuentours or them called Aeglogaj as it were αἴγον or αἰγονόμων λόγοι that is Goteheards tales. For although in Virgile and others the speakers be more shepheards, then Goteheards, yet Theocritus in whom is more ground of authoritie, then in Virgile, this specially from that deriuing, as from the first head and welspring the whole Inuencion of his Aeglogues, maketh Goteheards the persons and authors of his tales. This being, who seeth not the grossenesse of such as by colour of learning would make vs beleeue that they are more rightly termed Eclogai, as they would say, extraordinary discourses of vnnecessarie matter, which difinition albe in substance and meaning it agree with the nature of the thing, yet nowhit answereth with the ἀνάλυσις and interpretation of the word. For they be not termed Eclogues, but Aeglogues. which sentence this authour very well obseruing, vpon good iudgement, though indeede few Goteheards haue to doe herein, nethelesse doubteth not to cal them by the vsed and best knowen name. Other curious discourses hereof I reserue to greater occasion. These xij. Aeclogues euery where answering to the seasons of the twelue monthes may be well deuided into three formes or ranckes. For eyther they be Plaintiue, as the first, the sixth, the eleuenth, and the twelfth, or recreatiue, such as al those be, which conceiue matter of loue, or commendation of special personages, or Moral: which for the most part be mixed with some Satyricall bitter-nesse, namely the second of reuerence dewe to old age, the fift of coloured deceipt, the seuenth and ninth of dissolute shepheards and pastours, the tenth of contempt of Poetrie and pleasant wits. And to this diuision may euery thing herein be reasonably applyed: a few onely except, whose speciall purpose and meaning I am not priuie to. And thus much generally of these xij. Aeclogues. Now will we speake particularly of all, and first of the first. Which he calleth by the first monethes name Ianuarie: wherein to some he may seeme fowly to haue faulted, in that he erroniously beginneth with that moneth, which beginneth not the yeare. For it is wel known, and stoutly mainteyned with stronge reasons of the learned, that the yeare beginneth in March, for then the sonne reneweth his finished course, and the seasonable spring refresheth the earth, and the pleasaunce thereof being buried in the sadnesse of the dead winter now worne away, reliueth. This opinion maynteine the olde Astrologers and Philosophers, namely the reuerend Andalo, and Macrobius in his holydayes of Saturne, which accoumpt also was generally obserued both of Grecians and Romans. But sauing the leaue of such learned heads, we maintaine a custome of coumpting the seasons from the moneth Ianuary, vpon a more speciall cause, then the heathen Philosophers euer coulde conceiue, that is, for the incarna-tion of our mighty Sauiour and eternall redeemer the L. Christ, who as then renewing the state of the decayed world, and returning the compasse of expired yeres to theyr former date and first commence-ment, left to vs his heires a memoriall of his birth in the ende of the last yeere and beginning of the next. Which reckoning, beside that eternall monument of our saluation, leaneth also vpon good proofe of special iudgement. For albeit that in elder times, when as yet the coumpt of the yere was not perfected, as afterwarde it was by Iulius Caesar, they began to tel the monethes from Marches beginning, and according to the same God (as is sayd in Scripture) comaunded the people of the Iewes to count the moneth Abib, that which we call March, for the first moneth, in remembraunce that in that moneth he brought them out of the land of Aegipt: yet according to tradition of latter times it hath bene otherwise obserued, both in gouernment of the church, and rule of Mightiest Realmes. For from Iulius Caesar who first obserued the leape yeere which he called Bissextilem Annum, and brought in to a more certain course the odde wandring dayes which of the Greekes were called ὑπερβαίνοντες. Of the Romanes intercalares (for in such matter of learning I am forced to vse the termes of the learned) the monethes haue bene nombred xij. which in the first ordinaunce of Romulus were but tenne, counting but CCCiiij. dayes in euery yeare, and beginning with March. But Numa Pompilius, who was the father of al the Romain ceremonies and religion, seeing that reckoning to agree neither with the course of the sonne, nor of the Moone, therevnto added two monethes, Ianuary and February: wherin it seemeth, that wise king minded vpon good reason to begin the yeare at Ianuarie, of him therefore so called *tanquam Ianua anni* the gate and entraunce of the yere, or of the name of the god Ianus, to which god for that the old Paynims attributed the byrth and beginning of all creatures new comming into the worlde, it seemeth that he therfore to him assigned the beginning and first entraunce of the yeare. Which account for the most part hath hetherto continued. Notwithstanding that the Aegiptians beginne theyr yeare at September, for that according to the opinion of the best Rabbins, and very purpose of the scripture selfe, God made the worlde in that moneth, that is called of them Tisri. And therefore he commanded them, to keepe the feast of Pauilions in the end of the yeare, in the xv. day of the seuenth moneth, which before that time was the first.

But our Authour respecting nether the subtiltie of thone parte, nor the antiquitie of thother, thinketh it fittest according to the simplicitie of commen vnderstanding, to begin with Ianuarie, wening it perhaps no decorum, that Shepheard should be seene in matter of so deepe insight, or canuase a case of so doubtful iudgement. So therefore beginneth he, and so continueth he throughout.

2. Edmund Spenser

1580–90

Spenser's comment on his own work is extraordinarily limited. The first two pieces printed here illustrate his interest in experiment with quantitative verse, under the influence of friends both at Penshurst and Cambridge. Compare Harvey, No. 132b. The third is the Letter to Ralegh, too rarely taken seriously.

(a) From *Three Proper, and wittie familiar Letters* . . . (1580); (repr. in most editions of Spenser):

Loe here I let you see my olde vse of toying in Rymes, turned into your artificial straightnesse of Verse, by this *Tetrasticon*. I beseech you tell me your fancie, without parcialitie.

> See yee the blindefouled pretie God, that feathered Archer,
>   Of Louers Miseries which maketh his bloodie Game?
> Wote ye why, his Moother with a Veale hath coouered his Face?
>   Trust me, least he my Looue happely chaunce to beholde.

Seeme they comparable to those two, which I translated you *ex tempore* in bed, the last time we lay togither in Westminster?

> That which I eate, did I ioy, and that which I greedily gorged,
>   As for those many goodly matters leaft I for others.

I would hartily wish, you would either send me the Rules and Precepts of Arte, which you obserue in Quantities, or else followe mine, that *M. Philip Sidney* gaue me, being the very same which *M. Drant* deuised, but enlarged with *M. Sidneys* own iudgement, and augmented with my Obseruations, that we might both accorde and agree in one: leaste we ouerthrowe one an other, and be ouerthrown of the rest. Truste me, you will hardly beleeue what great good liking and estimation Maister *Dyer* had of youre *Satyricall Verses*, and I, since the viewe thereof, hauing before of my selfe had speciall liking of *Englishe*

Versifying, am euen nowe aboute to giue you some token, what, and howe well therein I am able to doe: for, to tell you trueth, I minde shortely at conuenient leysure, to sette forth a Booke in this kinde, whyche I entitle, *Epithalamion Thamesis*, whyche Booke I dare vndertake wil be very profitable for the knowledge, and rare for the Inuention, and manner of handling. For in setting forth the marriage of the Thames: I shewe his first beginning, and offspring, and all the Countrey, that he passeth thorough, and also describe all the Riuers throughout Englande, whyche came to this Wedding, and their righte names, and right passage, &c. A worke beleeue me, of much labour, wherein notwithstanding Master *Holinshed* hath muche furthered and aduantaged me, who therein hath bestowed singular paines, in searching oute their firste heades, and sourses: and also in tracing, and dogging oute all their Course, til they fall into the Sea.

> O Tite, siquid, ego,
> Ecquid erit pretij?
> [Cicero, *De Senectute* i.1]

But of that more hereafter. Nowe, my *Dreames*, and *dying Pellicane*, being fully finished (as I partelye signified in my laste Letters) and presentlye to bee imprinted, I wil in hande forthwith with my *Faery Queene*, whyche I praye you hartily send me with al expedition: and your frendly Letters, and long expected Iudgement wythal, whyche let not be shorte, but in all pointes suche, as you ordinarilye vse, and I extraordinarily desire. . . . I take best my *Dreames* should come forth alone, being growen by meanes of the Glosse, (running continually in maner of a Paraphrase) full as great as my *Calendar*. Therein be some things excellently, and many things wittily discoursed of E.K. and the pictures so singularly set forth, and purtrayed, as if *Michael Angelo* were there, he could (I think) nor amende the best, nor reprehende the worst. I know you woulde lyke them passing wel. Of my *Stemmata Dudleiana*, and especially of the sundry Apostophes therein, addressed you knowe to whome, muste more aduisement be had, than so lightly to sende them abroade: howbeit, trust me (though I doe neuer very well,) yet in my owne fancie, I neuer dyd better . . .

(b) From *Two Other very Commendable Letters* . . . (1580); repr. in most editions of Spenser:

But I am, of late, more in loue wyth my Englishe Versifying, than with

Ryming: which I should haue done long since, if I would then haue followed your councell. *Sed te solum iam suspicabar cum Aschamo sapere: nunc Aulam video egregios alere poetas Anglicos* . . . Truste me, your Verses I like passingly well . . . And nowe requite I you with the like, not with the verye beste, but with the verye shortest, namely with a fewe *Iambickes*: I dare warrant, they be precisely perfect for the feete (as you can easily iudge) and varie not one inch from the Rule. . . .

[quotes *Iambicum Trimetrum*]

(c) *A Letter of the Authors expounding his whole intention* . . ., in *The Faerie Queene* (1590), pp. 591–595 (repr. in all editions of Spenser):

To the Right noble, and Valourous, Sir Walter Raleigh knight, Lo. Wardein of the Stanneryes, and her Maiesties liefetenaunt of the County of Cornewayll. Sir knowing how doubtfully all Allegories may be construed, and this booke of mine, which I haue entituled the Faery Queene, being a continued Allegory, or darke conceit, I haue thought good aswell for auoyding of gealous opinions and misconstructions, as also for your better light in reading thereof, (being so by you commanded,) to discouuer unto you the general intention and meaning, which in the whole course thereof I haue fashioned, without expressing of any particular purposes or by-accidents therein occasioned. The generall end therefore of all the booke is to fashion a gentleman or noble person in vertuous and gentle discipline: Which for that I conceiued shoulde be most plausible and pleasing, being coloured with an historicall fiction, the which the most part of men delight to read, rather for variety of matter, then for profite of the ensample: I chose the historye of king Arthure, as most fitte for the excellency of his person, being made famous by many mens former workes, and also furthest from the daunger of envy, and suspition of present time. In which I haue followed all the antique Poets historicall, first Homere, who in the Persons of Agamemnon and Vlysses hath ensampled a good gouernour and a vertuous man, the one in his Ilias, the other in his Odysseis: then Virgil, whose like intention was to doe in the person of Aeneas: after him Ariosto comprised them both in his Orlando: and lately Tasso disseuered them againe, and formed both parts in two persons, namely that part which they in Philosophy call Ethice, or vertues of a priuate man, coloured in his Rinaldo: The other named Politice in his Godfredo. By ensample of which excellente Poets, I labour to pourtraict in Arthure, before he was king, the image of a braue knight, perfected in

C

45

the twelve private morall vertues, as Aristotle hath deuised, the which is the purpose of these first twelve bookes: which if I finde to be well accepted, I may be perhaps encoraged, to frame the other part of polliticke vertues in his person, after that hee came to be king. To some I know this Methode will seeme displeasaunt, which had rather haue good discipline deliuered plainly in way of precepts, or sermoned at large, as they use, then thus clowdily enwrapped in Allegoricall deuises. But such, me seeme, should be satisfide with the use of these dayes, seeing all things accounted by their showes, and nothing esteemed of, that is not delightfull and pleasing to commune sence. For this cause is Xenophon preferred before Plato, for that the one in the exquisite depth of his iudgement, formed a Commune welth such as it should be, but the other in the person of Cyrus and the Persians fashioned a gouernement such as might best be: So much more profitable and gratious is doctrine by ensample, then by rule. So haue I laboured to doe in the person of Arthure: whome I conceiue after his long educa-tion by Timon, to whom he was by Merlin deliuered to be brought up, so soone as he was borne of the Lady Igrayne, to haue seene in a dream or vision the Faery Queen, with whose excellent beauty rauished, he awaking resolued to seeke her out, and so being by Merlin armed, and by Timon throughly instructed, he went to seeke her forth in Faerye Land. In that Faery Queene I meane glory in my generall intention, but in my particular I conceiue the most excellent and glorious person of our soueraine the Queene, and her kingdome in Faery land. And yet in some places els, I doe otherwise shadow her. For considering she beareth two persons, the one of a most royall Queene or Empresse, the other of a most vertuous and beautiful Lady, this latter part in some places I doe express in Belphoebe, fashioning her name according to your owne excellent conceipt of Cynthia, (Phoebe and Cynthia being both names of Diana.) So in the person of Prince Arthure I sette forth magnificence in particular, which vertue for that (according to Aristotle and the rest) it is the perfection of all the rest, and conteineth in it them all, therefore in the whole course I mention the deedes of Arthure applyable to that vertue, which I write of in that booke. But of the xii. other vertues, I make xii. other knights the patrones, for the more variety of the history: Of which these three bookes contayn three. The first of the knight of the Red-crosse, in whome I expresse Holynes: The seconde of Sir Guyon, in whome I sette forth Temperaunce: The third of Britomartis a Lady knight, in whome I picture Chastity. But because the beginning of the whole worke seemeth abrupte and as depending upon other antecedents, it needs that ye know the occasion of these three knights seuerall aduentures. For the Methode of a Poet historical is not such, as of an Historiographer. For an Historiographer discourseth of affayres orderly as they were donne, accounting as well the times as the actions, but a Poet thrusteth into the middest, euen where it most concerneth him, and there recoursing to the thinges forepaste, and diuining of thinges to come, maketh a pleasing Analysis of all. The beginning therefore of my history, if it were to be told by an Historiographer, should be the twelfth booke, which is the last, where I deuise that the Faery Queene kept her Annuall feaste xii. dayes, uppon which xii. seuerall dayes, the occasions of the xii. seuerall aduentures hapned, which being undertaken by xii. seuerall knights, are in these xii. books seuerally handled and discoursed. The first was this. In the beginning of the feast, there presented him selfe a tall clownishe younge man, who falling before the Queen of Faries desired a boone (as the manner then was) which during that feast she might not refuse: which was that hee might haue the atchieuement of any aduenture, which during that feaste should happen, that being graunted, he rested him on the floore, unfitte through his rusticity for a better place. Soone after entred a faire Ladye in mourning weedes, riding on a white Asse, with a dwarfe behind her leading a warlike steed, that bore the Armes of a knight, and his speare in the dwarfes hand. Shee falling before the Queene of Faeries, complayned that her father and mother an ancient King and Queene, had bene by an huge dragon many years shut up in a brasen Castle, who thence suffred them not to yssew: and therefore besought the Faery Queene to assygne her some one of her knights to take on him that exployt. Presently that clownish person upstarting, desired that aduenture: whereat the Queene much wondering, and the Lady much gainesaying, yet he earnestly importuned his desire. In the end the Lady told him that unlesse that armour which she brought, would serue him (that is the armour of a Christian man specified by Saint Paul v. Ephes.) that he could not succeed in that enterprise, which being forthwith put upon him with dewe furnitures thereunto, he seemed the goodliest man in al that company, and was well liked of the Lady. And eftesoones taking on him knighthood, and mounting on that straunge Courser, he went forth with her on that aduenture: where beginneth the first booke, vz.

A gentle knight was pricking on the playne &c.

The second day ther came in a Palmer bearing an Infant with bloody hands, whose Parents he complained to haue bene slayn by an Enchauntresse called Acrasia: and therfore craued of the Faery Queene, to appoint him some knight, to performe that aduenture, which being assigned to Sir Guyon, he presently went forth with that same Palmer: which is the beginning of the second booke and the whole subiect thereof. The third day there came in, a Groome who complained before the Faery Queene, that a vile Enchaunter called Busirane had in hand a most faire Lady called Amoretta, whom he kept in most grieuous torment, because she would not yield him the pleasure of her body. Whereupon Sir Scudamour the louer of that Lady presently tooke on him that aduenture. But being unable to performe it by reason of the hard Enchauntments, after long sorrow, in the end met with Britomartis, who succoured him, and reskewed his loue.

But by occasion hereof, many other aduentures are intermedled, but rather as Accidents, then intendments. As the loue of Britomart, the ouerthrow of Marinell, the misery of Florimell, the vertuousnes of Belphoebe, the lasciuiousnes of Hellenora, and many the like.

Thus much Sir, I have briefly ouerronne to direct your understanding to the wel-head of the History, that from thence gathering the whole intention of the conceit, ye may as in a handfull gripe al the discourse, which otherwise may happily seeme tedious and confused. So humbly craning the continuance of your honorable fauour towards me, and th'eternall establishment of your happiness, I humbly take leaue.

23. Ianuary. 1589.
Yours most humbly affectionate.
Ed. Spenser.

3. Gabriel Harvey

1580–93

Gabriel Harvey (1545–1630) migrated from Christ's College to Pembroke a year after Spenser's admission there as a sizar (1569). He was probably most generally known to his contemporaries in the context of the controversy with Nashe, but to us as the friend and intimate of Spenser. He has been identified, I think improbably, with E.K. For an account of his relations with Spenser see Mary Parmenter, 'Colin Clout and Hobbinoll: A Reconsideration of the Relationship of Edmund Spenser and Gabriel Harvey', Johns Hopkins University Ph.D. Dissertation, 1933. In view of his close association with Spenser, I have been less selective of his remarks than is in general my rule. See also No. 132.

(a) From the *Marginalia*, ed. G. C. Moore Smith (Stratford-upon-Avon, 1913): To 1542 edition of Quintilian's *Institutes*; Moore Smith, p. 122:

The three brightest talents of Britain have been Chaucer, More, and Jewel. To those I would add three more now flourishing: Heywood, Sidney, and Spenser.[1]

Ibid., p. 161; To 1572 edition of Twine's translation of Dionysius Periegetes, *The Surueye of the World*:

M. Digges hath the whole Aquarius of Palingenius bie hart: & takes mutch delight to repeate it often.
    M. Spenser conceiues the like pleasure in the fourth day of the first Weeke of Bartas. Which he esteemes as the proper profession of *Urania*.

Ibid., p. 162; on the same:

---

[1] *Tria viuidissima Britanorum ingenia, Chaucerus, Morus, Juellus: Quibus addo tres florentissimas indoles, Heiuodum, Sidneium, Spencerum.*

49

I have often marvelled that Chaucer and Lydgate were such good astronomers in those days, while modern poets are so ignorant of astronomy – apart from Buckley, Sidney (?), Blagrave, and a very few others, sons of Urania.

Spenser himself is ashamed, though he is not completely ignorant of the globe and the astrolabe, of the difficulty he has with astronomical rules, tables, and instruments.[1]

Ibid., pp. 231–3; to Speght's 1598 edition of Chaucer:

Not manie Chawcers, or Lidgates, Gowers, or Occleues, Surries, or Heywoods, in those days: & how few Aschams, or Phaers, Sidneys, or Spensers, Warners or Daniels, Siluesters, or Chapmans, in this pregnant age. . . .

And now translated Petrarch, Ariosto, Tasso, & Bartas himself deserue curious comparison with Chaucer, Lidgate, & owre best Inglish, auncient and moderne. Amongst which, the Countesse of Pembroke's *Arcadia*, & the *Faerïe Queene* are now freshest in request: & *Astrophil*, and *Amyntas* ar none of the idlest pastimes of sum fine humanists. . . .

Amaryllis, & Sir Walter Raleighs *Cynthia*, how fine and sweet inuentions? Excellent matter of emulation for Spencer, Constable, France, Watson, Daniel, Warner, Chapman, Siluester, Shakespeare, & the rest of owr florishing metricians.

(b) From *Three Proper, and wittie, familar Letters* (1580); repr. in *Variorum Spenser: Prose Works*, pp. 459–60:

Commende mee to thine owne good selfe, and tell thy dying Pellicane, and thy Dreames from me, I wil nowe leaue dreaming any longer of them, til with these eyes I see them forth indeede: And then againe, I imagine your *Magnificenza*, will hold vs in suspense as long for your nine Englishe *Commoedies* and your Latine *Stemmata Dudleiana*: whiche two shal go for my money, when all is done: especiallye if you woulde but bestow one seuennights pollishing and trimming vppon eyther. Whiche I praye thee hartily doe, for my pleasure, if not for their sake, nor thine owne profite.

(c) *Ibid;* repr. *Variorum Spenser: Prose Works*, pp. 471–2:

[1] *Saepe miratus sum, Chaucerum, et Lidgatum tantos fuisse in diebus illis astronomos. Hodiernos poetas tam esse ignaros astronomiae: praeter Buclaeum, Astrophilum, Blagravum: alios perpaucos, Uraniae filios. Pudet ipse Spenserum, etsi Sphaerae, astrolabijque non plane ignarum; suae in astronomicis Canonibus, tabulis, instrumentisque imperitiae.*

Extra iocum, I like your *Dreames* passingly well and the rather, bicause they sauour of that singular extraordinarie veine and inuention, whiche I euer fancied moste, and in a manner admired onelye in *Lucian,* *Petrarche, Aretine, Pasquill,* and all the most delicate, and fine conceited Grecians and Italians: (for the Romanes to speake of, are but verye Ciphars in this kinde:) whose chiefest endeuour, and drifte was, to haue nothing vulgare, but in some respecte or other, and especially in *liuely Hyperbolicall Amplifications,* rare, queint, and odde in euery pointe, and as a man would saye, a degree or two at the leaste, aboue the reache, and compasse of a common Schollers capacitie. In whiche respecte notwithstanding, as well for the singularitie of the manner, as the Diunitie of the matter, I hearde once a Diuine, preferre *Saint Iohns Reuelation* before al the veriest *Maetaphysicall Visions,* and iollyest conceited *Dreames* or *Extasies,* that euer were diused by one or other, howe admirable, or superexcellent soeuer they seemed otherwise to the worlde. And truely I am so confirmed in this opinion, that when I bethinke me of the verie notablest, and most wonderful Propheticall, or Poetical Vision, that euer I read, or hearde, me seemeth the proportion is so vnequall, that there hardly appeareth anye semblaunce of Comparison: no more in a manner (specially for Poets) than doth betweene the incomprehensible Wisedom of God, and the sensible Wit of Man. But what needeth this digression betweene you and me? I dare saye you wyll holde your selfe reasonably wel satisfied, if youre *Dreames* be but as well esteemed of in Englande, as *Petrarches Visions* be in Italy: whiche I assure you, is the very worst I wish you. But, see, how I haue the Arte *Memoratiue* at commaundement. In good faith I had once againe nigh forgotten your *Fairie Queene*: howbeit by good chaunce, I haue nowe sent hir home at the laste, neither in better nor worse case, than I founde hir. And must you of necessitie haue my Iudgement of hir in deede? To be plaine, I am voyde of al iudgement, if your *Nine Comoedies,* wherevnto in imitation of *Herodotus,* you giue the names of the *Nine Muses,* (and in one mans fansie not vnworthily) come not neerer *Ariostoes Comoedies,* eyther for the finenesse of plausible Elocution, or the rarenesse of Poetical Inuention, than that *Eluish Queene* doth to his *Orlando Furioso,* which notwithstanding, you wil needes seeme to emulate, and hope to ouergo, as you flatly professed your self in one of your last Letters. Besides that you know, it hath bene the vsual practise of the most exquisite and odde wittes in all nations, and specially in *Italie,* rather to shewe, and aduaunce themselues that way, than any other: as namely, those three notorious dyscoursing heads,

Bibiena, Machiauel, and *Aretine* did, (to let *Bembo* and *Ariosto* passe) with
the great admiration, and wonderment of the whole countrey: being
in deede reputed matchable in all points, both for conceyt of Witte, and
eloquent decyphering of matters, either with *Aristophanes* and *Menander*
in Greek, or with *Plautus* and *Terence* in Latin, or with any other, in
any other tong. But I wil not stand greatly with you in your owne
matters. If so be the *Faerye Queene* be fairer in your eie than the *Nine
Muses,* and *Hobgoblin* runne away with the Garland from *Apollo*: Marke
what I saye, and yet I will not say that I thought, but there an End for
this once, and fare you well, till God or some good Aungell putte you
in a better minde.

(d) *To the Learned Shepheard*, from the commendatory verses on *The
Faerie Queene* (1590), pp. 597–8; repr. *Variorum Spenser*, III. 186:

> Collyn I see by thy new taken taske,
>   some sacred fury hath enricht thy braynes,
> That leades thy muse in haughtie verse to maske,
>   and loath the layes that longs to lowly swaynes.
> That lifts thy notes from Shepheardes vnto kings,
> So like the liuely Larke that mounting sings.
>
> Thy louely Rosolinde seemes now forlorne,
>   and all thy gentle flockes forgotten quight,
> Thy chaunged hart now holdes thy pypes in scorne,
>   those prety pypes that did thy mates delight.
> Those trustie mates, that loued thee so well,
> Whom thou gau'st mirth: as they gaue thee the bell.
>
> Yet as thou earst with thy sweete roundelayes,
>   didst stirre to glee our laddes in homely bowers:
> So moughtst thou now in these refyned layes,
>   delight the dainty eares of higher powers.
> And so mought they in their deepe skanning skill
> Alow and grace our Collyns flowing quill.
>
> And fare befall that *Faerie Queene* of thine,
>   in whose faire eyes loue linckt with vertue sits:
> Enfusing by those bewties fiers deuine,
>   such high conceites into thy humble wits,

As raised hath poore pastors oaten reede,
From rusticke tunes, to chaunt heroique deedes.

So mought thy *Redcrosse* knight with happy hand
   victorious be in that faire Ilands right:
Which thou doest vaile in Type of Faery land
   Elyzas blessed field, that *Albion* hight.
That shieldes her friends, and warres her mightie foes,
Yet still with people, peace, and plentie flowes.

But (iolly Shepheard) though with pleasing style,
   thou feast the humour of the Courtly traine:
Let not conceipt thy setled sence beguile,
   ne daunted be through enuy or disdaine.
Subiect thy dome to her Empyring spright,
From whence thy Muse, and all the world takes light.

(e) From *Foure Letters and Certaine Sonnets* (1592), p. 7; repr. A. B. Grosart, *The Works of Gabriel Harvey*, The Huth Library (1884), I. 164:

I must needs say, Mother-Hubbard in heat of choller, forgetting the pure sanguine of her sweete Faery Queene, wilfully ouer-shott her malcontented selfe: as elsewhere I haue specified at larg, with the good leaue of vnspotted friendshipp. Examples in some ages doe exceedingmuch hurt. *Salust*, and *Clodius* learned of *Tully*, to frame artificial Declamations, & patheticall Inuectiues against *Tully* himselfe, and other worthy members of that most-florishing State: if mother Hubbard in the vaine of *Chawcer*, happen to tel one Canicular Tale; father *Elderton*, and his sonne *Greene*, in the vaine of *Skelton*, or *Scoggin*, will counterfeit an hundred dogged Fables, Libles, Calumnies, Slaunders, Lies for the whetstone, what not & most currishly snarle, & bite where they should most-kindly fawne, and licke. Euery priuate excesse is daungerous: but such publike enormities, incredibly pernitious, and insupportable: and who can tell, what huge outrages might amount of such quarrellous, and tumultous causes?

(f) *Ibid.*, pp. 48–9; repr. Grosart, I. 217–18:

Good sweete Oratour, be a deuine Poet indeede: and vse heauenly Eloquence indeede: and employ thy golden talent with amounting

vsance indeede: and with heroicall Cantoes honour right Vertue, &
braue valour indeede: as noble Sir Philip Sidney and gentle Maister
Spencer haue done, with immortall Fame. . . . Such liuely springes
of streaming Eloquence: & such right-Olympicall hilles of amountinge
witte: I cordially recommend to the deere Louers of the Muses: and
namely to the professed Sonnes of the-same; *Edmond Spencer, Richard
Stanihurst, Abraham France, Thomas Watson, Samuell Daniell, Thomas
Nash,* and the rest.

(g) *Ibid.,* p. 59; repr. Grosart, I. 234:

[Many contemporary writers] are fine men, & haue many sweete
phrases: it is my simplicity, that I am so slenderly acquainted with that
dainty stile: the only new fashion of current Eloquence in Esse: far
surpassing the stale vein of *Demosthenes,* or *Tully: Iewel,* or *Harding:
Whitgift,* or *Cartwright: Sidney,* or *Spencer.*

(h) *Ibid.,* p. 66 (Sonnet X: *A more particular Declaration of his Intention*);
repr. Grosart, I. 244:

> Yet let Affection interpret selfe:
> *Arcadia* braue, and dowty *Faery Queene*
> Cannot be stain'd by *Gibelin,* or *Guelph,*
> Or goodliest Legend, that Witts eye hath seene.
> The dainty Hand of exquisitest Art,
> And nimble Head of pregnantest receit,
> Neuer more finely plaid their curious part,
> Then in those liuely Christals of conceit.

(i) From *A New Letter of Notable Contents* (1593), sig. A4ᵛ; repr.
Grosart, I. 266:

Is not the Prose of *Sir Philip Sidney* in his sweet Arcadia, the embrodery
of finest *Art* and daintiest Witt? Or is not the Verse of M. *Spencer* in
his braue Faery Queene, the Virginall of the diuinest Muses, and
gentlest Graces? Both delicate Writers: alwaies gallant, often braue,
continually delectable, sometimes admirable. What sweeter tast of
Suada, than the Prose of the One: or what pleasanter relish of the
Muses, then the Verse of the Other?

(j) From *Pierces Superorogation or A New Prayse of The Olde Asse* (1593), p. 15; repr. Grosart, II. 50:

But euen since that flourishing transplantation of the daintiest, and sweetest lerning, that humanitie euer tasted; Arte did but springe in such, as Sir Iohn Cheeke, and M. Asham & witt budd in such as Sir Phillip Sidney, & M. Spencer; which were but the violetes of March, or the Primeroses of May.

(k) *Ibid.*, p. 46; repr. Grosart, II. 93:

Petrarck was a delicate man, and with an elegant iudgement gratiously confined Loue within the limits of Honour; Witt within the boundes of Discretion; Eloquence within the termes of Ciuility: as not many yeares sithence an Inglishe Petrarck did, a singular Gentleman, and a sweete Poet, whose verse singeth, as valour might speake, and whose ditty is an image of the Sun, voutsafing to represent his glorious face in a clowde.

(l) *Ibid.*, p. 173, repr. Grosart, II. 266:

Come diuine Poets, and sweet Oratours, the siluer streaming fountaines of flowingest witt, and shiningest Art: come Chawcer, and Spencer; More, and Cheeke; Asham and Astely; Sidney, and Dier.

4. William Webbe

1586

William Webbe (1568–91) was educated at St John's in Cambridge, where he knew both Spenser and Harvey, though clearly not well. It is not the least importance of the *Discourse* however, that it reflects the sort of critical notions with which Spenser grew up. Apart from the more general comment printed here, lines from the *Shepheardes Calender* are used by Webbe to illustrate 'the different sortes of verses'.

A Discourse of English Poetrie (1586), sig. Biii; repr. G. Gregory Smith, *Elizabethan Critical Essays* (Oxford, 1904), I. 232:

Wherevnto I doubt not equally to adioyne the authoritye of our late famous English Poet, who wrote the *Shepheards Calender*, where lamenting the decay of Poetry, at these dayes, saith most sweetely to the same.

> Then make thee winges of thine aspyring wytt,
> And whence thou camest flye back to heauen apace. &c.
> [*October* ll. 83–84]

Whose fine poeticall witt, and most exquisite learning, as he shewed aboundantly in that peace of worke, in my iudgement inferiour to the workes neither of *Theocritus* in Greeke, nor *Virgill* in Latine, whom hee narrowly immitateth: so I nothing doubt, but if his other workes were common abroade, which are as I thinke in *the* close custodie of certaine his friends, we should haue of our own Poets, whom wee might matche in all respects with the best. And among all other his workes whatsoeuer, I would wysh to haue the sight of hys *English Poet*, which his freend *E.K.* did once promise to publishe, which whether he performed or not, I knowe not, if he did, my happe hath not beene so good as yet to see it.

Sigs. C iiii^v-D; repr. Smith, I. 245–6:

This place haue I purposely reserued for one, who if not only yet in my iudgement principally deserueth the tytle of the rightest English Poet, that euer I read: that is, the Author of the *Sheepeheardes Kalendar*, intituled to the woorthy Gentleman Master *Philip Sydney*: whether it was Master *Sp.* or what rare Scholler in Pembrooke Hall soeuer, because himself and his freendes, for what respect I knowe not, would not reueale it, I force not greatly to sette downe: sorry I am that I can not find none other with whom I might couple him in this *Catalogue*, in his rare gyft of Poetry: although one there is, though nowe long since, seriously occupied in grauer studies, (*Master Gabriell Haruey*) yet, as he was once his most special freende and fellow Poet, so because he hath taken such paynes, not onely in his Latin Poetry (for which he enioyed great commendations of the best both in iudgement and dignity in thys Realme) but also to reforme our English verse, and to beautify the same with braue deuises, of which I thinke the cheefe lye hidde in hatefull obscurity: therefore wyll I aduenture to sette them together, as two of the rarest witts, and learnedest masters of Poetrie in England. Whose worthy and notable styl in this faculty, I would wysh if their high dignities and serious businesses would permit, they would styll graunt to bee a furtheraunce to that reformed kinde of Poetry, which Master *Haruey* did once beginne to ratify . . .

As for the other Gentleman, if it would please him or hys freendes to let those excellent *Poemes*, whereof I know he hath plenty, come abroad, as his *Dreames*, his *Legends*, his Court of *Cupid*, his *English Poet* with other: he should not onely stay the rude pens of my selfe and others, but also satisfye the thirsty desires of many which desire nothing more, then to see more of hys rare inuentions.

Sigs. Eiiii-F; repr. Smith, I. 263–5:

But nowe yet at *the* last hath England hatched vppe one Poet of this sorte, in my conscience comparable with the best in any respect: euen Master *Sp*: Author of the *Sheepeheardes Calender*, whose trauell in that peece of English Poetrie, I thinke verely is so commendable, as none of equall iudgement can yeelde him lesse prayse for his excellent skyll, and skylfull excellency shewed foorth in the same, then they would to eyther *Theocritus* or *Virgill*, who in my opinion, if the coursenes of our speeche (I meane the course of custome which he woulde not infringe) had beene no more let vnto him, then theyr pure natiue tongues were vnto them, he would haue (if it might be) surpassed them. What one thing is there in them so worthy admiration, whereunto we may not adioyne some thing of his, or equall desert? Take *Virgil* and make some little comparison betweene them, and iudge as ye shall see cause.

Virgill hath a gallant report of *Augustus* couertly comprysed in the first *Aeglogue*: the like is in him, of her Maiestie, vnder the name of *Eliza*. *Virgill* maketh a braue coloured complaint of vnstedfast freendshyppe in the person of *Corydon*: the lyke is him in his 5. *Aeglogue*. Agayne behold the pretty Pastorall contentions of *Virgill* in the third *Aeglogue*: of his in *the* eight *Eglogue*. Finally, either in comparison with them or respect of hys owne great learning, he may well were the Garlande, and steppe before ye best of all English Poets that I haue seene or hearde: for I thinke no lesse deserueth (thus sayth *E.K.* in hys commendations) hys wittinesse in deuising, his pithinesse in vttering, his complaintes of loue so louely, his discourses of pleasure so pleasantly, his Pastrall rudenes, his Morrall wysenesse, his due obseruing of *decorum* euery where, in personages, in season, in matter, in speeche, and generally in all seemely simplicity, of handling hys matter and framing hys wordes. The occasion of his worke is a warning to other young men, who being intangled in loue and youthful vanities, may learne to looke to themselves in time, and to auoyde inconueniences which may breede if they be not in time preuented. Many good Morrall lessons are therein contained, as the reuerence which young men owe to the aged in the second *Eglogue*: the caueate or warning to beware a subtill professor of freendshippe in the fift *Eglogue*: the commendation of good pastors, and shame and disprayse of idle and ambitious Goteheardes in the seauenth, the loose and retchlesse lyuing of Popish Prelates in the ninth. The learned and sweet complaynt of the contempt of learning vnder the name of Poetry in the tenth. There is also much matter vttered somewhat couertly, especially ye abuses of some whom he would not be too playne withall: in which, though it be not apparent to euery one, what hys speciall meaning was, yet so skilfully is it handled, as any man may take much delight at hys learned conueyance, and picke out much good sence in the most obscurest of it. Hys notable prayse deserued in euery parcell of that worke, because I cannot expresse as I woulde and as it should: I wyll cease to speake any more of, the rather because I neuer hearde as yet any that hath reade it, which hath not with much admiration commended it. One only thing therin haue I hearde some curious heades call in question: *viz:* the

motion of some vnsauery loue, such as in the sixt *Eglogue* he seemeth to
deale withall, which (say they) is skant allowable to English eares, and
might well haue beene left for the Italian defenders of loathsome beast-
lines, of whom perhappes he learned it: to thys obiection I haue often
aunswered (and I thinke truely) that theyr nyce opinion ouershooteth
the Poets meaning, who though hee in that as in other thinges immitateth
the auncient Poets, yet doth not meane, no more did they before hym,
any disordered loue, or the filthy lust of the deuillish *Pederastice* taken
in the worse sensce, but rather to shewe howe the dissolute life of young
men intangled in loue of women, doo neglect the freendshyp and
league with their olde freendes and familiers. Why (say they) yet he
shold gyue no occasion of suspition, nor offer to the viewe of Christians, any token of such filthinesse, howe good soeuer hys meaning
were: wherevnto I oppose the simple conceyte they haue of matters
which concerne learning or wytt, wylling them to gyue Poets leaue
to vse theyr vayne as they see good: it is their foolysh construction, not
hys wryting that is blameable. Wee must prescrybe to no wryters,
(much lesse to Poets) in what sorte they should vtter theyr conceyts.

5. Thomas Nashe

1589–96

Thomas Nashe (1567–1601), educated at St John's College, Cambridge, enjoyed the friendship of Lodge, Daniel Marlowe, and of course Greene, along with the enmity of Harvey (*q.v.*). His controversy with Harvey did not affect at all his judgment of Spenser whom he consistently and extravagantly admired. His tendentious representation of relations between Spenser and Harvey (not reprinted here) has however infected many modern accounts of the friendship; it should be ignored. See however K. B. Harder, 'Nashe and Spenser'. *Vanderbilt Studies in the Humanities*, II (1955).

(a) From the epistle *To the Gentlemen Students of both Universities* prefatory to Greene's *Menaphon* (1589), sigs. A2-A2ᵛ; repr. *Works o, Thomas Nashe*, ed. R. B. McKerrow (1910), III. 323:

As for Pastorall Poemes, I will not make the comparison [with the works of foreign, particularly Italian, writers], least our countrimens credit should be discountenanst by the contention, who although they cannot fare, with such inferior facilitie, yet I knowe would carrie the bucklers full easilie, from all forreine brauers, if their *subiectum circa quod*, should sauor of anything haughtie: and should the challenge of deepe conceit, be intruded by any forreiner, to bring our english wits, to the tutchstone of Arte, I would preferre, diuine Master *Spencer*, the miracle of wit to bandie line for line for my life, in the honor of *England*, against *Spaine*, *France*, *Italie*, and all the worlde. Neither is he, the only swallow of our summer.

(b) From *Pierce Penilesse His Svpplication to the Diuell* (1592). pp. 39–40; repr. McKerrow, I. 234–4:

And here (heauenlie *Spencer*) I am most highly to accuse thee of forgetfulnes, that in that honourable Catalogue of our English *Heroes*, which insueth the conclusion of thy famous Fairie Queene, thou wouldest let so speciall a piller of Nobilitie [the Earl of Derby?] passe vnsaluted. The verie thought of his farre deriued discent, and extra-ordinarie parts wherewith hee asto[ni]eth the world, and drawes all harts to his loue, would haue inspired thy forewearied *Muse* with new furie to proceede to the next triumphs of thy statelie Goddesse, but as I in fauor of so rare a Scholer, suppose with this counsaile, he refraind his mention in this first part, that he might with full saile proceede to his due commendations in the second. Of this occasion long since I happened to frame a Sonnet, which being wholy intended to the reuer-ence of this renoumed Lord, (to whom I owe all the vtmost powers of my loue and deutie) I meante heere for variety of stilr to insert[.]

> Perusing yesternight with idle eyes,
>   The Fairy Singers stately tuned verse:
> And viewing after Chap-mans wonted guise,
>   What strange contents the title did rehearse.
> I streight leapt ouer to the latter end,
>   Where like the queint Comaedians of our time,
> That when their Play is doone do fall to ryme,
>   I found short lines, to sundry Nobles pend.
> Whom he as speciall Mirrours singled fourth,
>   To be the Patrons of his Poetry;
> I read them all, and reuerenc't their worth,
>   Yet wondred he left out thy memory.
> But therefore gest I he supprest thy name,
>   Because few words might not comprise thy fame.

Beare with mee gentle Poet, though I conceiue not aright of thy purpose, or be too inquisitiue into the intent of thy obliuion: for how euer my coniecture may misse the cushion, yet shall my speech sauour of friendship, though it be not allied to Iudgement.

(c) From *Have With You to Saffron-Waldon* (1596), sig. Q4ᵛ; repr. McKerrow, III. 107–8:

Hereby hee thought to conny catch the simple world, and make them beleeue, that these and these great men, euerie waye sutable to Syr *Thomas Baskeruile*, Master *Bodley*, Doctor *Andrewes*, Doctor *Doue*,

Clarencius and Master *Spencer*, had separately contended to outstrip *Pindarus* in his *Olympicis*, and sty aloft to the highest pitch. . . . Doctour Doue and Clarencius, I turne loose to bee their owne Arbitratours and Audocates; the one being eloquent enough to defend himselfe, and the other a Vice roy & next Heyre apparant to the King of Heralds, able to emblazon him in his right colours, if hee finde hee hath sustained any losse by him: as also in like sort Master *Spencer*, whom I do not thrust in the lowest place because I make the lowest valuation of, but as wee vse to set *Summ' tot'* alway underneath or at the bottome, he being the *Sum' tot'* of whatsoeuer can be said of sharpe inuention and schollership.

6. George Puttenham

1589

George Puttenham (d. 1590) spent his days at Oxford in the study of poetry. Of all the Elizabethan 'arts', Puttenham's is the most ambitious and the most comprehensive. It will be noticed that he is still unaware of the true authorship of the *Shepheardes Calender*.

From *The Arte of English Poesie* (1589), p. 51; repr. in the edition of Gladys Willcock and Alice Walker (Cambridge, 1936), pp. 62–3:

That for Tragedie, the Lord of Buckhurst & Maister Edward Ferrys . . . do deserue the hyest price. . . . For Eglogue and pastorall Poesie, Sir *Philip Sydney* and Maister *Challenner*, and that other Gentleman who wrate the late *shepheardes Callender*.

7. Anonymous commendatory verses

The verses below are signed Ignoto, which rather blocks any attempt to discover their authorship.

Commendatory verse from *The Faerie Queene* (1590), p. 600 (repr. in all editions):

> To looke vpon a worke of rare deuise
> The which a workman setteth out to view,
> And not to yield it the deserued prise,
> That vnto such a workmanship is dew,
>   Doth either proue the iudgement to be naught
>   Or els doth shew a mind with enuy fraught.
>
> To labour to commend a peece of worke,
> Which no man goes about to discommend,
> Would raise a iealous doubt that there did lurke,
> Some secret doubt, whereto the prayse did tend.
>   For when men know the goodnes of the wyne,
>   T'is needlesse for the hoast to haue a sygne.
>
> Thus then to shew my iudgement to be such
> As can discerne of colours blacke, and white,
> As alls to free my minde from enuies tuch,
> That neuer giues to any man his right,
>   I here pronounce this workmanship is such,
>   As that no pen can set it forth too much.
>
> And thus I hang a garland at the dore,
> Not for to shew the goodnes of the ware:
> But such hath beene the custome heretofore,
> And customes very hardly broken are.
>   And when your tast shall tell you this is trew,
>   Then looke you giue your hoast his vtmost dew.

8. H.B., Commendatory verses

1590

As John Worthington says (No. 95), it needs some Oedipus to discover the identities of the contributors of the commendatory verses to the *Faerie Queene*. Carpenter's *Reference Guide*, p. 87, suggests in explanation of H.B. the following: Henry Bosvill, Sir Henry Brouncker, Henry Bedingfield, Sir Henry Bagnall, Hugh Beeston, Henry Boughton, and Sir Henry Bromly.

Commendatory verse from *The Faerie Queene* (1590), p. 598 (repr. in all editions):

> Graue Muses march in triumph and with prayses,
> Our Goddesse here hath giuen you leaue to land:
> And biddes this rare dispenser of your graces
> Bow downe his brow vnto her sacred hand.
> Desertes findes dew in that most princely doome,
> In whose sweete brest are all the Muses bredde:
> So did that great *Augustus* erst in Roome
> With leaues of fame adorne his Poets hedde.
> Faire be the guerdon of your *Faery Queene*,
> Euen of the fairest that the world hath seene.

9. W.L., Commendatory verses

1590

Carpenter's *Reference Guide*, p. 87, offers the following interpretations of the initials: William Lawson, William Lee, William Leigh, William Leighton, William Lewin, William Lawes, William Lombard, and ('the best guess') William Lyon.

Commendatory Verse from *The Faerie Queene* (1590), p. 599 (repr. in all editions):

> When stout *Achilles* heard of *Helens* rape
> And what reuenge the States of Greece deuisd:
> Thinking by sleight the fatall warres to scape,
> In womans weedes him selfe he then disguisde:
> But this deuise Vlysses soone did spy,
> And brought him forth, the chaunce of warre to try.

> When *Spencer* saw the fame was spredd so large,
> Through Faery land of their renowned Queene:
> Loth that his Muse should take so great a charge,
> As in such haughty matter to be seene,
> To seeme a shepeheard then he made his choice,
> But *Sydney* heard him sing, and knew his voice.

> And as *Vlysses* brought faire *Thetis* sonne
> From his retyred life to menage armes:
> So *Spencer* was by *Sidneys* speaches wonne,
> To blaze her fame not fearing future harmes:
> For well he knew, his Muse would soone be tyred
> In her high praise, that all the world admired,

> Yet as *Achilles* in those warlike frayes,
> Did win the palme from all the *Grecian* Peeres:

SPENSER

So *Spencer* now to his immortall prayse,
Hath wonne the Laurell quite from all his feres.
What though his taske exceed a humaine witt,
He is excus'd, sith *Sidney* thought it fitt.

10. Sir Walter Ralegh, Commendatory verses

1590

Sir Walter Ralegh (1552?–1618), probably educated at Oriel College, met Spenser either through Sidney or in Ireland. See Walter Oakeshott's *The Queen and the Poet* (1960) for an account of their relations. Dr Oakeshott is in possession of Ralegh's annotated copy of the 1609 Folio, which will be described in a forthcoming article in the *Library*.

(a) *A Vision vpon this conceipt of the Faery Queene* from the commendatory verses to *The Faery Queene* (1590), p. 596:

Me thought I saw the graue, where *Laura* lay,
Within that Temple, where the vestall flame
Was wont to burne, and passing by that way,
To see the buried dust of liuing fame,
Whose tombe faire loue, and fairer vertue kept,
All suddeinly I saw the Faery Queene:
At whose approch the soule of *Petrarke* wept,
And from thenceforth those graces were not seene.
For they this Queene attended, in whose steed
Obliuion laid him downe on *Lauras* herse:
Hereat the hardest stones were seene to bleed,

66

And grones of buried ghostes the heuens did perse.
Where *Homers* spright did tremble all for griefe,
And curst th'accesse of that celestiall theife.

(b) *Another of the same, ibid:*

The prayse of meaner wits this worke like profit brings,
As doth the Cuckoes song delight when *Philumena* sings.
If thou hast formed right true vertues face herein:
Vertue her selfe can best discerne, to whom they written bin.

If thou hast beauty praysd, let her sole lookes diuine
Iudge if ought therein be amis, and mend it by her eine.
If Chastitie want ought, or Temperaunce her dew,
Behold her Princely mind aright, and write thy Queene anew.

Meane while she shall perceiue, how far her vertues sore
Aboue the reach of all that liue, or such as wrote of yore:
And thereby will excuse and fauour thy good will:
Whose vertue can not be exprest, but by an Angels quill.
Of me no lines are lou'd, nor letters are of price,
Of all which speak our English tongue, but those of thy deuice.

11. R.S., Commendatory verses

1590

Carpenter's *Reference Guide*, p. 87, proposes the following explanations of the initials: Robert Sackville, Sir Richard Smyth, Robert Sidney, Richard Stapleton. But a letter by C. M. Millican to the *TLS*, 7 August 1937, p. 576, suggests Robert Salter, chaplain to Lord Sheffield, as the most likely author of the lines. See also No. 69.

Commendatory Verse from *The Faerie Queene* (1590), p. 598 (repr. in all editions):

> Fayre *Thamis* streame, that from *Ludds* stately towne,
> Runst paying tribute to the Ocean seas,
> Let all thy Nymphes and Syrens of renowne
> Be silent, whyle this Bryttane *Orpheus* playes:
> Nere thy sweet bankes, there liues that sacred crowne,
> Whose hand strowes Palme and neuer-dying bayes,
> Let all at once, with thy soft murmuring sowne
> Present her with this worthy Poets prayes.
> For he hath taught hye drifts in shepeherdes weedes,
> And deepe conceites now singes in *Faeries* deedes.

12. William Vallans

William Vallans (flor. 1578–90) was an antiquarian and a friend of Camden (*q.v.*) *A Tale of Two Swannes* is, as a poetical exercise, modelled on the lost *Epithalmion Thamesis*, or on the 'Marriage of the Medway and Thames' in *Faerie Queene* IV. ix. Spenser's reference to the lost poem is in the first of *Three Proper and Wittie familiar Letters*, which explains that the poem is the result of a collaboration with Holinshed, presumably the other of 'those worthy Poets'.

From *A Tale of Two Swannes. Wherein is comprehended the original and increase of the riuer Lee commonly called Ware-riuer: together with the antiquitie of sundrie places and townes seated vpon the same* (1590), sig. A2:

Yet hereby I would animate, or encourage those worthy Poets, who haue written *Epithalamion Thamesis*, to publish the same: I haue seen it in Latine verse (in my iudgement) wel done, but the Author I know not for what reason doth suppresse it: That which is written in English, though long since it was promised, yet is it not perfourmed: so as it seemeth, some vnhappy Star enuieth *the* sight of so good a work: which once set abroad, such trifles as these would vanish, and be ouershadowed, much like the Moon and other starres, which after the appearing of the Sunne are not to be seene at all.

13. Thomas Watson

1590

Thomas Watson (1557–92) left Oxford without a degree to study law in London. His inclination was always to poetry and he was fortunate enough to meet during his travels on the Continent a future patron in Walsingham, for whom the elegy below. Harvey commends Watson in the third of the *Foure Letters* (*q.v.*) for his 'studious endeavours in enriching and polishing his native tongue' ranking him with Spenser, Stanyhurst, Fraunce, Daniel, and of all people (as Nashe himself pointed out) Nashe. In *Colin Clout* Spenser commends him as the 'noblest swaine,/That euer piped in an oaten quill'.

See William Kingsler, 'Spenser and Thomas Watson', *MLN*, LXIX (1954), 484–7.

An Eglogue Vpon the death of the Right Honorable Sir Francis Walsingham in *Meliboeus Thomae Watsoni, siue Ecloga in Obitum F. Walsinghami* (1590), sigs. C3ᵛ-C4; repr. in *Poems*, ed. Edward Arber (1870), p. 173:

> Yet lest my homespun verse obscure hir worth,
>   sweet *Spencer* let me leaue this taske to thee,
> Whose neuerstooping quill can best set forth
>   such things of state, as passe my Muse, and me.
>
> Thou *Spencer* art the alderliefest swaine,
>   or haply if that word be all to base,
> Thou art *Apollo* whose sweet hunnie vaine
>   amongst the Muses hath a chiefest place.
> Therefore in fulnes of thy duties loue,
>   calme thou the tempest of *Dianaes* brest,
> Whilst shee for *Meliboeus* late remoue
>   afflicts hir mind with ouerlong vnrest.

70

Tell hir forthwith (for well she likes thy vaine)
that though great *Meliboeus* be swaie:
Yet like to him there manie still remaine,
which will vphold hir countrie from decaie.

[Watson's own Latin reads:]

Sed quid eam refero, quae nostro carmine maior,
Est cantanda tuo, dulcis Spencere cothurno,
Cuius inest numeris Hiblaei copia mellis.
Tu quoque nobiscum (quoniam tu noster Apollo)
Lugentem solare Deam, quoties Meliboei
Tristia lacrymulis preciosis funera deflet.
Dic illi (tu namque potes foelice camaena)
Arcades innumeros, quanquam Meliboeus obiuit,
Praestantes superesse viros, similes Meliboei.
Damoetam memora, quo non praeclarior alter,
Non quisquam ingenio melior, non promptior ore,
Ille est Damaetas, qui iuris corrigit iram,
Quem vocat Hattonum Triuiae venerabile Numen.

14. John Florio

1591

John Florio (1553?–1625), after serving as tutor in modern languages to the son of the Bishop of Durham, entered the Southampton circle in London. The passage printed below, though admittedly tendentious, is illuminatingly alien in its bias.

From *Florios Second Frutes* (1591), The Epistle Dedicatorie, sigs. A3-A3ᵛ:

The maiden-head of my industrie I yeelded to a noble Mecenas (renoumed Lecester) the honour of England, whom though like Hector euery miscreant Mirmidon dare strik being dead, yet sing *Homer* or *Virgil*, write frend or foe, of *Troy*, or *Troyes* issue, that *Hector* must have his desert, the General of his Prince, the Paragon of his Peeres, the watchman of our peace,

> *Non so se miglior Duce o Caualliero.* [*Triumphus Fame* i. 99]

as *Petrarke* hath in his triumph of fame; and to conclude, the supporter of his friends, the terror of his foes, the *Britton* Patron of the Muses.

> *Dardanias light, and Troyans faithfulst hope.* [*cf. Aeneid VI.* 875–7]

But nor I, nor this place may halfe suffice for his praise, which the sweetest singer of all our westerne shepheards hath so exquisitely depainted, that as Achilles by Alexander was counted happy for hauing such a rare emblazoner of his magnanimitie, as the Meonian Poete; so I account him thrice-fortunate in hauing such a herauld of his vertues as Spenser; Curteous Lord, Curteous Spenser, I knowe not which hath perchast more fame, either he in deseruing so well of so famous a scholler, or so famour a scholler in being so thankfull without hope of requitall to so famous a Lord.

15. Sir John Harington

Harington (1574–1612), was educated at Christ's College, Cambridge, and Lincoln's Inn. As a godson of Queen Elizabeth, he began from his first time in London to frequent the court. The first of the passages below is ironically illuminated by the story about Harington's expulsion from court for having circulated among the ladies his translation of just this canto of the *Furioso*. The disclaimer in the second passage is lightly intended: as an allegorizer of Ariosto, Harington must know that Spenser intends both the senses he pretends not to be able to distinguish between. (In the context, perhaps it should be said, a Spenserian allusion is more likely than a Biblical one.)

(a) From *Orlando Furioso in English Heroical Verse* (1591), p. 373:

The hosts tale in the xxvviij book of this worke, is a bad one: M. *Spencers* tale of the squire of Dames, in his excellent Poem of the Faery Queene, in the end of vij. Canto of the third booke, is to the like effect, sharpe and well conceyted; In substance thus, that his Squire of dames could in three yeares trauell, find but three women that denyed his lewd desire: of which three, one was a courtesan, that reiected him because he wanted coyne for her: the second a Nun, who refused him because he would not sweare secreacie; the third a plain countrie Gentlewoman, that of good honest simplicitie denyed him.

(b) From *Of Monsters. To my Lady Rogers*, in *The Most Elegant and Wittie Epigrams of Sir Iohn Harington, Knight, Digested Into Foure Bookes: Three whereof neuer before published* (1618; this epigram does not appear in the first edition of 1615), sig. G8ᵛ; repr. in *Letters and Epigrams of Sir John Harington*, ed. N. E. McClure (Philadelphia, 1930), pp. 224–5:

> Strange-headed Monsters, Painters haue described.
> To which the Poets strange parts haue ascribed, . . .

73

On what seu'n-headed beast the Strumpet sits,
That weares the scarfe, sore troubleth many wits,
Whether seu'n sinnes be meant, or else seu'n hils,
It is a question fit for higher skils.

16. Samuel Daniel

1592–99

Samuel Daniel (1562–1619), educated at Magdalen Hall, Oxford, entered the service of the Countess of Pembroke as tutor to William Herbert and so joined the Wilton circle. Early he showed promise as a poet, and Spenser in Colin Clout is able to speak of him as

> A new shepheard late up sprang,
> The which doth all afore him far surpasse;
> Appearing well in that well tuned song,
> Which late he sung unto a scornfull lasse.

The compliment is returned less unambiguously. It is clear from what is printed below that Daniel thought highly of Spenser, but it is clear also that both as love poets and as historical poets their aims were distinct.

(a) From *Delia. Contayning certayne Sonnets: with the complaint of Rosamond* (1592), Sonnet XLVI, sig. G3ᵛ; repr. in *Complete Works*, ed. A. B. Grosart (1885), I. 73:

> Let others sing of Knights and Palladines,
> In aged accents, and vntimely words:
> Paint shadowes in imaginary lines,
> Which well the reach of their high wits records.

74

(b) From *Delia and Rosamond augmented. Cleopatra* (1594), *To the Right Honourable, The Lady Marie, Countess of Pembroke,* sig. H7; repr. in Grosart, III. 26–7:

> Whereby great SYDNEY & our SPENCER might,
> With those *Po*-singers beeing equalled,
> Enchaunt the world with such a sweet delight,
> That theyr eternall songs (for euer read,)
> May shew what great ELIZAS raigne hath bred.
> What musique in the kingdome of her peace,
> Hath now beene made to her, and by her might,
> Whereby her glorious fame shall neuer cease.

(c) From *The Poeticall Essayes* (1599), *The Civill Wars of England, The Fowrth Booke,* stanzas 5–6, p. 69; repr. Grosart, II. 175:

> Why do you seeke for fained *Palladins*
> Out of the smoke of idle vanitie,
> That maie giue glorie to the true dissignes
> Of *Bourchier, Talbot, Neuile, Willoughby?*
> Why should not you striue to fill vp your lines
> With wonders of your owne, with veritie?
> T'inflame their offspring with the loue of Good
> And glorious true examples of their bloud.
>
> O what eternall matter here is found!
> Whence new immortal *Iliads* might proceed,
> That those whose happie graces do abound
> In blessed accents here maie haue to feed
> Good thoughts, on no imaginary ground
> Of hungrie shadowes which no profit breed:
> Whence musicke like, instant delight may grow,
> But when men all do know they nothing know.

(d) From *The Poeticall Essayes* (1599), *Mvsophilvs. Containing A generall defence of all learning,* sig. C4ᵛ; repr. Grosart, I. 239:

> How many thousands neuer heard the name
> Of *Sydney,* or of *Spencer,* or their bookes?
> And yet braue fellowes, and presume of fame
> And seem to beare downe all the world with lookes:

What then shall they expect of meaner frame,
On whose indeuors few or none scarse looks?

(e) *Ibid.*, sig. F2; repr. Grosart, I. 254:

> And do not thou contemne this swelling tide
> And streame of words that now doth rise so hie
> Aboue the vsuall banks, and spread so wide
> Ouer the borders of antiquitie:
> Which I confesse comes euer amplifide
> With th'abounding humours that do multiplie.

17. Thomas Churchyard

1593, 1595

Thomas Churchyard (1520?–1604) is very much the survival of an earlier age – which is the tenor of Drayton's condemnation of him in the *Epistle to Henry Reynolds*, but even in old age he was receptive enough to fall under Spenser's influence. The interest of the two pieces below is only general, but more exact testimony to the extent of Spenser's reputation could scarcely be found than these words of an older poet overtaken by a younger.

(a) *A newe Kinde of a Sonnet* from *Churchyards Challenge* (1593), sig. **v; repr. in Sir Samuel Egerton Brydges, *Censura Literaria* (1805–9), II. 303–9:

> In writing long, and reading works of warre,
> That *Homer* wrote and *Vergils* verse did show:
> My muse me led in ouerweening farre,
> When to their Stiles my pen presumde to goe.

Ouid himselfe durst not haue vaunted so,
Nor *Petrarke* graue with *Homer* would compare:
Dawnt durst not think his sence so hye did flow,
As *Virgils* works that yet much honord are.
Thus each man saw his iudgement hye or low,
And would not striue or seeke to make a iarre:
Or wrastle where they haue an ouerthrow.
So that I finde the weakenes of my bow,
Will shoot no shaft beyond my length I troe:
For reason learnes and wisdome makes me know.
Whose strength is best and who doth make or marre:
A little Lamp may not compare with Starre.
A feeble head where no great gifts doo grow:
Yeelds vnto skill, whose knowledge makes smal shew.
Then gentle works I sweetly thee beseech:
Call *Spenser* now the spirit of learned speech.

(b) From *A Praise of Poetrie, some notes thereof drawen out of the Apologie, the noble minded Night, sir Phillip Sidney wrate, in A Musicall Consort of Heauenly harmonie (compounded out of many parts of Musicke) called Churchyards Charitie* (1595), sig. G3ᵛ:

> In Spensers morall *Fairie Queene*
> And Daniels rosie mound
> If they be throwly waid and seen
> Much matter may be found.

18. Michael Drayton

1593–1627

Michael Drayton (1563–1631) combined a sort of literary profes-
sionalism with more traditional poetic ambitions (a mixture
extraordinary in his age). He was a friend of Francis Beaumont,
William Browne, and Drummond of Hawthornden, all of them
nothing as poets if not respectable. He also acquired the services of
the antiquary Selden as commentator on his *Poly-Olbion*. In the
circumstances, he could have hitched his wagon to no better star
than Spenser's. I have included in this section passages from
Selden's notes to *Poly-Olbion*.

(a) From *The Third Eclog* in *Idea. The Shepheards Garland* (1593),
p. 13; repr. in *Works*, ed. J. W. Hebel (Oxford, 1931–41), I. 55:

> In thy sweete son so blessed may'st thou bee,
> For learned *Collin* laies his pipes to gage,
> And is to fayrie gone a Pilgrimage:
>   the more our mone.

(b) From *Endimion and Phoebe. Ideas Latamus* (1595), sig. G^v; repr. Hebel,
I. 155:

> Deare *Collin*, let my Muse excused be,
> Which rudely thus presumes to sing by thee,
> Although her straines be harsh untun'd & ill,
> Nor can attayne to thy divinest skill.

(c) From the epistle *To the Reader* in *The Barrons Wars in the raigne o
Edward the second* (1603), sig. A3^v; repr. Hebel, II. 5:

The Italians vse Cantos, & so our first late great Reformer Ma.
Spenser, that I assume another name for the sections in this volum
cannot be disgratious, nor vnauowable.

(d) From the epistle *To the Reader* in *Poems Lyrick and pastorall. Odes, Eclogs, The man in the Moone* (1605), sig. A4ᵛ; repr. Hebel, II. 346:

And would at this time also gladly let thee vnderstand, what I thinke aboue the rest of the last Ode of the twelue, or if thou wilt Ballad in my Book; for both the great master of Italian rymes *Petrarch*, & our *Chawcer* & other of the vper house of the muses, haue thought their Canzons honoured in the title of a Ballade, which, for that I labour to meet truely therein with the ould English garb, I hope as able to iustifie as the learned *Colin Clout* his Roundelaye.

(e) From the epistle *From the Author of the Illustrations* in *Poly-Olbion* (1612), sig. A2ᵛ; repr. Hebel, IV. ix:

Concerning the Arcadian deduction of our *British* Monarchy . . . no Relation was extant, which is now left to our vse. How then are they, which pretend Chronologies of that Age without any Fragment of Authors before *Gildas? . . .* For my part, I beleeue much in them as I do the finding of Hiero's Shipmast in our Mountaines . . . or that *Iulius Caesar* built *Arthurs Hoffen* in *Stirling* Shirifdome; or, that *Britons* were at the Rape of *Hesione* with *Hercules*, as our excellent wit *Ioseph of Excester* . . . singeth: which are euen warrantable, as *Ariosto's* Narrations of Persons and Places in his *Rowlands*, *Spensers* Elfin Story, or *Rablais* his strange discoueries.

(f) From the *Illustrations, ibid.*, p. 12; repr. Hebel, IV. 85:

Some account him St. George an allegory of our Sauiour Christ; and our admired Spencer hath made him an embleme of Religion.

Ibid., p. 71; repr. Hebel, IV. 89:

Merlin's buriall (in supposition as vncertaine as his birth, actions, and all of those too fabulously mixt stories) and his *Lady* of the *Lake* it is by liberty of profession laid in *France* by that *Italian* [*Orland. Furios.* canto 3. See Spencers *Faery Q. lib.* 3. *cant.* 3.] Ariosto: which perhaps is credible as som more of his attributes, seeing no perswading authority, in any of them, rectifies the vncertainty.

Ibid., p. 84; repr. Hebel, IV. 108:

79

SPENSER

His Mother (a Nun, daughter to *Pubidius* K. of Mathraual, and cald Matilda, as by [Spensers *Faery Q. lib.* 3. cant. 3.] Poeticall authority onely I finde iustifiable.)

Ibid., p. 123; repr. Hebel, IV. 154:

Vnto this referre that suppos'd prophecie of Merlin:

> *Doctrinae studium quod nunc viget ad vada Boum*
> *Ante finem secli celebrabitur ad vada Saxi.*

Which you shall have *Englished* in that solemnized Marriage of Thames and Medway, by a most admired Muse of our Nation, thus with advantage: [quotes *Faerie Queene* IV. xi. 35]

Ibid., p. 165; repr. Hebel, IV. 210:

Hence questionles was that Fiction of the Muses best pupil, the noble *Spenser*, [*Faery Q. lib.* 1. *Cant.* 9 *Stanz.* 4.] in supposing *Merlin* vsually to visit his old *Timon*, whose dwelling he places

> low in a valley greene

Ibid., p. 183; repr. Hebel, IV. 323–4:

Personating the *Genius* of *Verlam*, that euer famous [In his *Ruines of Time.*] *Spenser* sung

> I was that Citie . . .

As vnder the *Romans*, so in the *Saxon* times afterward it endured a second Ruine: and, out of its corruption, after the Abbey erected by K. *Offa*, was generated that of Saint *Albons*; whither, in later times most of the stone workes and whatsoeuer fit for building was by the Abbots translated. So that

> Now remaines no Memorie . . .

. . . *Gildas*, speaking of S. *Albons* martyrdome and his miraculous passing through the Riuer at *Verlamcestre*, calls it *inter ignotum trans Thamesis fluvii alueum*: so by collection they guest that *Thames* had been his full course this way, being thereto further mou'd by Anchors and such like here digd vp. This coniecture hath been followed by the [Spenser] Noble Muse thus in the person of *Verlam*.

[quotes *RT* 134–40, 148–54]

g) From the Epistle *To the Reader*, prefatory to *The Legends of Robert Duke of Normandie* . . ., in *Poems* (1619), p. 312; repr. Hebel, II. 382:

The word LEGEND, so called of the Latine Gerund, *Legendum*, and signifying, by the Figure *Hexoche*, things specially worthy to be read, was anciently vsed in an Ecclesiasticall sense, and restrained therein to things written in Prose, touching the Liues of Saints. Master EDMUND SPENSER was the very first among vs, who transferred the vse of the word LEGEND, from Prose to Verse: nor that vnfortunately; the Argu- of his Bookes being of a kind of sacred Nature, as comprehending in them things as well Diuine as Humane. And surely, that excellent Master, knowing the weight and vse of Words, did completely answer the *Decorum* of a LEGEND, in the qualitie of his Matter, and meant to giue it a kind of Consecration in the Title. To particularize the Lawes of this Poeme, were to teach the making of a Poeme; a Worke for a Volume, not an Epistle. But the principall is, that being a *Species* of an *Epick* or Heroick Poeme, it eminently describeth the act or acts of some one or other eminent Person; not with too much labour, compasse, or extension, but roundly rather, and by way of Briefe, or *Compendium*.

(h) From the epistle *To the Reader of his Pastorals*, prefatory to *Pastorals. Contayning Eglogves, ibid.*, p. 432; repr. Hebel, II. 518:

Master EDMVND SPENSER had done enough for the immortalitie of his Name, had he only giuen vs his *Shepheards Kalender*, a Master piece if any. The *Colin Clout* of SKOGGAN, vnder King HENRY the Seuenth, is prettie: but BARKLEY's *Ship of Fooles* hath twentie wiser in it. SPENSER is the prime *Pastoralist* of England.

(i) From the *Epistle to Henry Reynolds* in *The Battails of Agincourt . . . The Shepheards Sirens . . . Elegies vpon sundry occasions* (1627), pp. 205–6; repr. Hebel, III. 228:

> Graue morrall *Spencer* after these came on
> Then whom I am perswaded there was none
> Since the blind *Bard* his Iliads vp did make,
> Fitter a taske like that to vndertake,
> To set down boldly, brauely to inuent,
> In all high knowledge, surely excellent.

19. Thomas Lodge

1593, 1596

Thomas Lodge (1558–1625) was educated, as Spenser was, at Merchant Taylors' School, and then at Trinity College, Oxford, and Lincoln's Inn. He joined the literary society of London and was acquainted with such figures as Greene, Barnabe Rich, Daniel, Drayton, Lyly, and Watson. The influence of Spenser on Lodge's verse is deep and pervasive, and Lodge's indebtedness is in part acknowledged by his dedication of the First Eclogue in *A Fig for Momus* to 'reuerend Colin'.

---

a) From *The Induction* to *Phillis: Honoured with Pastorall Sonnets, Elegies, and amorous delights* (1593), sig. A4ᵛ; repr. *Complete Works*, ed. Edmund Gosse (Glasgow, 1883), II. 6:

> As moderne Poets shall admire the same,
> *I* meane not you (you neuer matched men)
> Who brought the Chaos of our tongue in frame,
> Through these Herculean labours of your pen:
>   I meane the meane, I meane no men diuine,
>   But such whose fathers are but waxt like mine.
>
> Goe weeping Truce-men in your sighing weedes,
> Vnder a great *Mecaenas* I haue past you:
> *If* so you come where learned *Colin* feedes
> His louely flocke, packe thence and quickly haste you;
>   You are but mistes before so bright a sunne,
>   Who hath the Palme for deepe inuention wunne.

(b) From *Wits Miserie, and the Worlds Madness* (1596), p. 57; repr. Gosse, IV. 63:

Diuine wits, for many things as sufficient as all antiquity (I speake it not on slight surmise, but considerate iudgement) to you belongs the death that doth nourish this poison: to you the paine, that endure reproofe. LILLY, the famous for facility in discourse: SPENCER, best read in ancient Poetry: DANIEL, choise in word, and inuention: DRAITON, diligent and formall: TH. NASH, true English Aretine.

20. I.O.

1594

The verses below are taken from *The Lamentation of Troy, for the death of Hector. Whervnto is annexed an Olde womans Tale in hir solitarie Cell* (1594). Nothing is known of the author, apart from his initials.

(a) From *The Lamentation of Troy, The Prologue*, sig. A3ᵛ; repr. Sir Egerton Brydges, *Censura Literaria* (1805–9), II. 349:

Yet had she [Troy's ghost] rather Spencer would haue told them,
For him she calde that he would helpe t'vnfold them.
But when she saw he came not at hir call
She kept hir first man that doth shew them all.

(b) *Ibid.*, sig. B2; repr. Brydges, II. 349:

O then good *Spencer* the only *Homer* liuing,
Deign for to write with thy fame-quickeninge quill:
And though poore *Troy* due thanks can not be giuing,
The Gods are iust and they that giue them will.
    Write then O *Spencer* in thy Muse so trim,
    That he in thee and thou maiest liue in him.

Although thou liuest in thy *Belphaebe* faire,
And in thy *Cynthia* likely art to shine,
So long as *Cynthia* shineth in the ayre:
Yet liue and shine in this same Sunne of mine.
O liue in him that whilom was my Sun,
But now his light and so my life is done.

21. E.C.

1595

Nothing is known of E.C., the author of *Emaricdulfe*. The editor of the Roxburghe Club reprint, is unable even to identify him.

Sonnet 40 in *Emaricdulfe* (1595), sig. C7ᵛ; repr. *A Lamport Garland*, Roxburghe Club Publications 109 (1881).

Some bewties make a god of flatterie,
And scorne *Eliziums* eternall types,
Nathes, I abhorre such faithles prophesie,
Least I be beaten with thy vertues stripes,
Wilt thou suruiue another world to see?
Delias sweete Prophet shall the praises singe
Of bewties worth exemplified in thee,
And thy names honour in his sweete tunes ring:
Thy vertues *Collin* shall immortalize,
Collin chast vertues organ sweetst esteem'd,
When for *Elizas* name he did comprise
Such matter as inuentions wonder seem'd.
Thy vertues hee, thy bewties shall the other,
Christen a new, whiles I sit by and wonder.

22. William Covell

1595

William Covell (d. 1614), a Fellow of Queens' College, Cambridge, was the author of a number of theological tracts.

From *Polimanteia . . . Whereunto is added England to Her Three Daughters, Cambridge, Oxford, Innes of Court, and to all the rest of her inhabitants* (Cambridge and London, 1595), sigs. Q^v-R2^v; repr. Sir Egerton Brydges, *The British Bibliographer* (1810), I. 281–4:

So onely without compare, eternallie should you [Cambridge] liue; for in your children shall the loue-writing muse of diuine *Sydnay*, and the pure flowing streame of Chrystallin *Spenser* suruiue onely: write then of *Elizas* raigne, a taske onely meete for so rare a pen.

23. Thomas Edwards

1595

Thomas Edwards (*flor.* 1595) is known only as the author of *Cephalus and Procris*; *Narcissus* (1595). The name is a common one, and the *DNB* lists five possible identifications of our author. It would be foolhardy on my part to risk commitment to any one of them. Edwards is enthusiastic for Spenser, whose influence is pervasive in his own verse.

(a) From *Cephalus and Procris* (1595), sig. B2ᵛ; repr. in edition of W. E. Buckley, Roxburghe Club Publications, 105 (1882), p. 12:

> Heroicke Parramore of Fairie land,
> That stately built, with thy immortal hand,
> A golden, Angellike, and modest Aulter,
> For all to sacrifice on, none to alter.
> Where is that vertuous Muse of thine become?

(b) *Ibid.*, sig. D2-D2ᵛ; Buckley, pp. 27-8:

> But what is more in vse, or getteth praise,
> Then sweete Affection tun'd in homely layes?
> Gladly would our *Cephalian* muse haue sung
> All of white loue, enamored with a toungue,
> That still *Styll* musicke sighing teares together,
> Could one conceite haue made beget an other,
> And so haue ransackt this rich age of that,
> The muses wanton fauourites haue got [.]
> Heauens-gloryfier, with thy holy fire,
> O thrise immortall quickener of desire,
> That scorn'st this vast and base prodigious clime,
> Smyling at such as beg in ragged rime,

86

Powre from aboue, or fauour of the prince,
Distilling wordes to hight the quintessence
of fame and honor: such I say doest scorne,
Because thy stately verse was Lordly borne,
Through all *Arcadia*, and the *Fayerie* land
And hauing smale true grace in Albion,
Thy natiue soyle, as thou of sight deserued'st,
Rightly adornes one now, that's richly serued:
O to that quick sprite of thy smooth-cut quill,
Without surmise of thinking any ill
*I offer vp in duetie and in zeale,
This dull conceite of mine, and do appeale,
With reuerence to thy [affection.]
On will I put that breast-plate and there on,
Riuet the standard boare in spite of such:
As thy bright name condigne or would but touch[.]
Affection is the whole Parenthesis,
That here I strecke, which from our taske doth misse.

(c) *Ibid.*, sig. H3ᵛ; Buckley, p. 62:

Collyn was a mighty swaine,
In his power all do flourish,
We are shepheards but in vaine,
   There is but one tooke the charge,
By his toile we do nourish,
   And by him are inlarg'd.

He vnlockt *Albions* glorie,
He twas tolde of *Sidneys* honor,
Onely he of our stories,
   Must be sung in greatest pride,
In an Eglogue he hath wonne her,
   Fame and honor on his side.

* *He thinkes it the duetie of eueryone that sailes, to strike main-top, before that great & mighty Poet* COLLYN.

24. Joshua Sylvester

1595, 1605

Joshua Sylvester (1563–1618) emerges from unpromising beginnings as the English Bartas and in that capacity exercises such literary influence on the English seventeenth century as can hardly be exaggerated. Sylvester's name is often cited alongside Spenser's, and Dryden (No. 100) confesses to having preferred the former poet in his youth.

(a) From *The Epistle Dedicatorie To ... M. Anthonie Bacon*, in *The First Day of The Worldes Creation: Or of the first weeke of that most Christian Poet, W. Salustius, Lord of Bartas* (1595), sig. A2:

· .. this most Christian Poet, and noble *Frenchman Lord of Bartas*, might haue been naturalized among vs, either by a generall act of a Poeticall Parliament: or haue obtained a kingly translator for his weeke (as he did for his Furies:) or rather a diuine *Sidney*, a stately *Spencer*, or a sweet *Daniell* for an interpreter thereof.

(b) From *Bartas. His Deuine Weekes & Workes Translated* (1605), *Eden*, pp. 272–3; repr. *Complete Works*, ed. A. B. Grosart (1880), p. 99:

> Let This [work] prouoke our modern wits to sacre
> Their wondrous gifts to honour thee their Maker:
> That our mysterious ELFINE oracle,
> Deepe, Morall, graue, inuentions miracle:
> My deere sweet Daniel, sharpe-conceipted briefe,
> Ciuill, sententious, for pure accents chiefe:
> And our new *Naso*, that so passionates
> Th'heroicke sighes of loue-sick Potentates:
> May change their subiect, and aduance their wings
> Vp to these higher and more holy things.

25. Charles Fitzgeoffrey

1596

Charles Fitzgeoffrey (1575–1638) made his name early as a poet with *Sir Francis Drake* (1596). Francis Meres calls him 'that high touring Falcon', but the high flying was not long sustained. He finished his days as a divine and is not remembered as a poet. See also No. 39.

From *Sir Francis Drake* (Oxford, 1596), sigs. B5-B5ᵛ; repr. in *Poems*, ed. A. B. Grosart, Occasional Issues, XVI (1881), 21–2:

> Then you, sweete-singing Sirens of these times,
> Deere darlings of the *Delian* Deitie,
> That with your Angels-soule-inchauntinge rimes
> Transport *Pernassus* in *Britainie*,
> With learnings garland crowninge Poesie;
>   Sdaine not that our harsh plaints should beate your eares:
>   Arts want may stop our tongues, but not our teares.

> SPENSER, whose hart inharbours *Homers* soule,
> If *Samian* Axioms be autenticall:
> DANIEL, who well mayst *Maro's* text controule,
> With proud *Plus ultra* true note marginall:
> And golden-mouthed DRAYTON musicall,
>   Into whose soule sweete SIDNEY did infuse
>   The essence of his Phoenix-feather'd Muse:

> Types of true honour, *Phoebus Tripodes*,
> Hell-charminge *Orphei*, *Sirens* of the sense,
> Wits substance, *Ioues* braine-borne *Pallades*,
> Soules *Manna*, heauens *Ambrosian* influence,
> True centers of renownes circumference,
>   The gracefull *Graces* faire triplicitie,
>   Of moderne Poets rarest trinarie.

Imbath your Angel-feathers loftie quill
In fluent amber-dropping *Castalie*,
That liquid gold may from your pen distill,
Encarving characters of memorie,
In brasen-leavd bookes of eternitie:
  Be DRAKES worth royalized by your wits,
  That DRAKES high name may coronize your writs.

Let famous RED CROSSE yeld to famous DRAKE,
And good SIR GVION give to him his launce;
Let all the MORTIMERS surrender make
To one that higher did his fame advance;
Cease LANCASTERS, & YORKES iars to enhaunce;
  Sing all, and all to few to sing DRAKES fame;
  Your Poems neede no laurell saue his name.

26. Joseph Hall

1597–c. 1610

Joseph Hall (1574–1656), educated in the Puritan atmosphere of Emmanuel College, Cambridge, early developed his talents as a satirist. The extracts printed below surprisingly perhaps, indicate almost unqualified approval for the very different mode of the *Faerie Queene*. Their tone, and Hall's general indebtedness to Spenser, is crystallized in another line from *Virgidemiarum*:

> At *Colins* feet I throw my yeelding reed.

Both the authorship and the dating of the last two pieces is doubtful. For comment see *The Collected Poems*, ed. A. Davenport (Liverpool, 1949), which includes also discussion of Hall on Spenser (pp. xlii–xliii). Against Davenport, I prefer a date of 1610 for the Bodleian MS. piece.

(a) From *His Defiance of Enuy* in *Virgidemiarum, Six Bookes. First thre Bookes, Of Tooth-lesse Satyrs* (1597), sig. A5; repr. in *Complete Poems*, ed. A. B. Grosart, Occasional Issues, IX (1879), p. 7:

> . . . Or scoure the rusted swords of Eluish knights,
> Bathed in Pagan blood: or sheath them new
> In misty morall Types: or tell their fights,
> Who mighty Giants, or who Monsters slew.
>   And by some strange inchanted speare and shield,
>   Vanquisht their foe, and wan the doubtfull field.

> Maybe she [his Muse] might in stately *Stanzaes* frame
> Stories of Ladies, and aduenturous knights:
> To raise her silent and inglorious name,
> Vnto a reach-lesse pitch of Prayses hight.

(b) From *Virgidemiarum*, Lib. I, sat. 4, p. 11; repr. Grosart, p. 27:

But let no rebell *Satyre* dare traduce
Th' eternall *Legends* of thy *Faery Muse*,
Renowmed *Spencer:* whom no earthly wight
Dares once to emulate, much lesse dares despight.
Salust of *France*, and *Tuscan Ariost*,
Yeeld vp the *Lawrell girlond* ye haue lost:
And let all others willow weare with mee,
Or let their vnd[e]seruing *Temples* bared bee.

(c) Prefactory poem to William Bedell's *A Protestant Memorial, or, the Shepherd's Tale of the Pouder-Plott. A Poem in Spenser's Style* (written *c.* 1605, first published 1713):

Willy, thy rhythmes so sweetly runn & rise,
And answer rightly to thy tunefull reed,
That (so mought both our fleecy cares succeed)
I ween (nor is it any vaine device)
    That Collin dying his immortal muse
    Into thy learned breast did late infuse.

Thine be his verse, not his reward be thine,
Ah me! that after unbeseeming care,
And secret want, *which* bred his last misfare,
His relicks deare obscurely tombed lien
    Under unwriten stones, that who goes by
    Cannot once read, Lo Here doth Collin ly.
Not all the shepheards of his Calendar
(Yet learned shepheards all, & seen in song)
Theire deepest layes & dittyes deep among,
More lofty song did ever make or leare
    Then this of thine. Sing on; thy task shall be
    To follow him, while others follow thee.

(d) Poem from Bodleian MS Wood D 32, fol. 260 (*c.* 1610):

One fayre Par-royal hath our Iland bred
    Whereof one is a liue and 2 are dead
Sidney *the* Prince of prose & sweet conceit
Spenser of numbers & Heroick Ryme
Iniurious Fate did both their liues defeate

For war & want slew both before their time
  Now tho they dead lodge in a princely roome
  One wants a verse, *the* other wants a toome

  Camden thou liuest alone of all the three
  For Roman stile & Englishe historye
Englande made them thou makest England knowen
So well art thou *the* prince of all *the* payre
Sithence thou hast an Englande of thine owne
Less welthy, but a fruitfull and more fayre
  Nor is thine Englande moated with *the* maine
  But doth our seas, & firmed lands contain.

27. Richard Barnfield

1598

Richard Barnfield (1574–1627), educated at Brasenose College, Oxford, was a friend of Thomas Watson, Francis Meres, and Michael Drayton, a group of which he is the least articulate enthusiast of Spenser. As a poet he is himself heavily indebted to Spenser: he commends his own. *Cynthia* (1595) in a prefactory epistle (sig. A4^v) 'if for no other cause, yet, for that it is the first imitation of the verse of that excellent Poet, Maister *Spencer*, in his *Fayrie Queene*'. The two fragments quoted below are of no specific interest, but serve to illustrate one dominant emphasis in contemporary criticism of Spenser.

(a) *To his friend Maister R.L. In praise of Musique and Poetrie*, in *Poems: in diuers humors* (1598), sig. E2; repr. *Some Longer Elizabethan Poems*, ed. A. H. Bullen (Westminster, 1903), p. 264:

> Dowland to thee is deare; whose heauenly tuch
> Vpon the Lute, doeth rauish humaine sense:
> *Spenser* to mee; whose deepe Conceit is such,
> As passing all Conceit, needs no defence.

(b) From *A Remembrance of some English Poets*, in *Poems*, sig. E2^v; repr· Bullen, p. 265:

> Liue *Spenser* euer, in thy *Fairy Queene*:
> Whose like (for deepe Conceit) was neuer seene.
> Crownd mayst thou bee, vnto thy more renowne,
> (As King of Poets) with a Lawrell crowne.

28. Richard Carew

1595, 1598

Richard Carew (1555–1620) was educated at Christ Church, where he was a younger contemporary of Sir Philip Sidney. Better known as an antiquary than anything else, he became an active member of the Society of Antiquaries in 1589. The *Survey of Cornwall* (Cornwall was his native county) secured his reputation in this field. His enthusiasm for Spenser as a descriptive poet, if the author of the second of these two pieces is indeed Carew, may derive from his antiquarian interests. The comparison of Spenser with Lucan in the first piece is ambiguously complimentary: compare Sidney on Lucan in his *Apology for Poetry*. For another notice by Carew on Spenser, see No. 145.

(a) From *The Excellencie of the English tongue by R.C. of Antony Esquire to W.C.* (written *c.* 1595), in Camden's *Remaines, concerning Britaine* (1614), p. 44. The text here is reprinted from G. Gregory Smith, *Elizabethan Critical Essays* (Oxford, 1904, II. 293):

Will you read Virgill? take the Earle of Surrey, *Catullus?* Shakespeare and Barlowe's fragment, Ouid? Daniell, Lucan? Spencer, Martial? Sir Iohn Davies and others: will you haue all in all for Prose and verse? take the miracle of our age Sir Philip Sidney.

(b) From *A Herrings Tale* (1598), sig. B4ᵛ:

> But neither can I tell, ne can I stay to tell,
> This pallace architecture, where perfections dwell:
> Who list such know, let him *Muses despencier* reede,
> Or thee, whom *England* sole did since the conquest breed,
> To conquer ignorance, *Sidney* like whom endite,
> Euen *Plato* would, or *Ioue* (they say) like Plato write.

[On the authorship of this piece, which is uncertain, see *CBEL* I. 826.]

29. Francis Meres

1598

Francis Meres (1565–1647), educated at Pembroke College, Cambridge, was by the late 1590s mixing in London literary circles where he enjoyed some reputation as a poet. *Palladis Tamia. Wits Treasury. Being the Second part of Wits Common wealth* was published in 1598 and, as the title indicates, was a continuation of *Politeuphuia: Wits Commonwealth*, published in 1597 and largely the work of Nicholas Ling. *Palladis Tamia* was reissued twice in the seventeenth century, first (confusingly) as *Wits Commonwealth* (1634), and then as *Wits Academy* (1636).

From *Palladis Tamia* (1598), fol. 278^v:

And our famous English Poet *Spenser*, who in his *Sheepeheards Calendar* samenting the decay of Poetry at these dayes, saith most sweetly to the lame.

> *Then make thee wings of thine aspiring wit*
> *And whence thou camest fly backe to heauen apace, &c.*
> [*October* ll. 83–4]

Ibid., fol. 280:

As the Greeke tongue is made famous and eloquent by *Homer, Hesiod, Euripedes, Aeschilus, Sophocles, Pindarus, Phocylides,* and *Aristophanes;* and the Latine tongue by *Virgill, Ouid, Horace, Silius Italicus, Lucanus, Lucretius, Ausonius* and *Claudianus:* so the English tongue is mightily enriched and georgeouslie inuested in rare ornaments and resplendent abiliments by sir *Philip Sidney, Spencer, Daniel, Drayton, Warner, Shakespeare, Marlow* and *Chapman.*

Ibid., fol. 280^v:

As Sextus Propertius saide; *Nescio quid magis nascitur Iliade* [*Elegies* II.

xxxiv. 66]: so I say of *Spencers Fairy Queene*, I knowe not what more excellent or exquisite Poem may be written.

As *Achilles* had the aduantage of *Hector*, because it was his fortune to be extolled and renowned by the heauenly verse of *Homer*: so *Spensers Elisa the Fairy Queen* hath the aduantage of all the Queenes in the worlde, to bee eternized by so diuine a Poet.

As *Theocritus* is famoused for his *Idyllia* in *Greeke*, and *Virgill* for his *Eclogs* in *Latine*: so Spencer their imitatour in his *Shepheardes Calender*, is renowned for the like argument, and honoured for fine Poeticall inuention, and most exquisit wit.

Ibid., fols. 282–282ᵛ:

And as Horace saith of his; *Exegi monumentum aere perennius; Regalique situ pyramidum altius: Quod non imber edax; Non Aquilo impotens possit diruere; aut innumerabilis annorum series & fuga temporum:* [*Odes* III. xxx. 1–5] so say I seuerally of sir *Philip Sidneys, Spencers, Daniels, Draytons, Shakespeares,* and *Warners workes:*

> *Non Iouis ira: imbres: Mars: ferrum: flamma, senectus,*
> *Hoc opus vnda: lues: turbo: venena ruent.*
> *Et quanquam ad pulcherrimum hoc opus euertendum tres illi Dij*
> *conspirabunt, Cronus, Vulcanus, & pater ipse gentis;*
> *Non tamen annorum series, non flamma, nec ensis,*
> *Aeternum potuit hoc abolere Decus.*
> [cf. Ovid, *Metamorphoses* XV. 871–2]

Ibid., fols. 282ᵛ–3:

As *Homer* and *Virgil* among the Greeks and Latines are the chiefe Heroick Poets: so *Spencer* and *Warner* be our chiefe heroicall Makers.

As *Pindarus, Anacreon* and *Callimachus* among the Greekes; and *Horace* and *Catullus* among the Latines are the best Lyrick Poets: so in this faculty the best among our Poets are *Spencer* (who excelleth in all kinds) *Daniell, Drayton, Shakespeare, Bretton.*

Ibid., fols. 283ᵛ–4:

As these are famous among the Greeks for Elegie, *Melanthus*... *Pigres Halicarnassus;* and these among the Latines, *Mecaenas*... *Clodius Sabinus:* so these are the most passionate among vs to bewaile and bemoane the perplexities of Loue, *Henrie Howard* Earle of Surrey, sir

Thomas Wyat the elder, sir Francis Brian, sir *Philip Sidney*, sir *Walter Rawley*, sir *Edward Dyer*, *Spencer*, *Daniel*, *Drayton*, *Shakespeare*, *Whetstone*, *Gascoyne*, *Samuell Page* sometimes fellowe of *Corpus Christi* Colledge in Oxford, *Churchyard*, *Bretton*.

As *Theocritus* in Greeke, *Virgil* and *Mantuan* in Latine, *Sanazar* in Italian, and the authour of *Amyntae Gaudia* and *Walsinghams Melibaeus* are the best for pastorall: so amongst vs the best in this kind are sir *Philip Sidney*, master *Challener*, *Spencer*, *Stephen Gosson*, *Abraham Fraunce*, and *Barnefield*.

30. Thomas Speght

1598

Of Thomas Speght (*flor. c.* 1600) surprisingly little is known. A schoolmaster of antiquarian interests, he is made famous by his edition of Chaucer.

From *The Workes of our Antient and Learned English Poet, Geffrey Chavcer, newly Printed* (1598), sigs. Ciii–Ciii^v:

And as for men of later time, not onely that learned gentleman M. William Thynne, in his Epistle Dedicatorie to the Kings Maiestie, but also two of the purest and best writers of our daies: the one for Prose, the other for Verse, M. *Ascham* and M. *Spenser*, haue deliuered most worthy testimonies of their approouing of him. . . .

Master *Spenser* in his first Eglogue of his *Shepheardes Kalender*, calleth him *Titirus*, the god of Shepheards, comparing him to the worthinesse of the Roman Titirus Virgil. In his *Faerie Queene* in his discourse of friendship, as thinking himselfe most worthy to be Chaucers friend, for his like naturall disposition that Chaucer had, hee sheweth that none that liued with him, nor none that came after him, durst presume to reuiue Chaucers lost labours in that vnperfite tale of the Squire, but only himselfe: which he had not done, had he not felt (as he saith) the infusion of Chaucers owne sweete spirite, suruiuing within him. And a little before he termeth him, Most renowned and heroicall Poet: and his Writings, The workes of heauenly wit: concluding his commendation in this manner:

> Dan Chaucer, Well of English vndefiled,
> On Fames eternal beadrole worthy to be filed.
> I follow here the footing of thy feet,
> That with thy meaning so I may the rather meet.

And once againe I must remember M. *Camdens* authority, who as it were reaching one hand to Maister *Ascham*, and the other to Maister *Spenser*, and so drawing them togither vttereth of him these words:

De Homero nostro Anglico illud vere asseram, quod de Homero eruditus ille Italus dixit:

> ... *Hic ille est, cuius de gurgite sacro*
> *Combibit arcanos vatum omnis turba furores.*
> [*Britannia* (1586), p. 199]

OBITUARY VERSE

31. John Weever

1599–1601

John Weever (1576–1632), educated at Queens' College, Cambridge, combined strong antiquarian interests with a leaning to poetry. Of his many references to Spenser I include here only the most specific. It is worth noting that Weever often has recourse to *Ruines of Time* in his late work *Ancient Funerall Monuments* (1631).

(a) *In Obitum Ed. Spencer Potae presantiss.*, *Epigrammes in the oldest cut, and newest fashion* (1599), sig. G.3; repr. in edition of R. B. McKerrow (1911), p. 101:

> *Colin*'s gone home, the glorie of his clime,
> The Muses Mirrour, and the Shepheards Saint;
> *Spencer* is ruin'd of our latter time
> The fairest ruine, Faëries foulest want:
> When his *Time ruines* did our ruine show,
> Which by his ruine we vntimely know:
> Spencer therefore thy *Ruines* were cal'd in,
> Too soone to sorrow least we should begin.

(b) From *Favnus and Melliflora or, The Original of our English Satyres* (1600), sig. F2ᵛ; repr. in edition of A. Davenport (Liverpool, 1948), p. 42:

> By some great power or heauenly influence,
> The Faeries proued full stout hardy knights,
> In iusts, in tilts, in turnaments, and fights,
> As *Spencer* shewes. But *Spencer* now is gone,
> You Faery Knights, your greatest losse bemone.

(c) From *The Mirror of Martyrs, or The Life and death of . . . Sir Iohn Old-castle, Knight Lord Cobham* (1601), sig. B5ᵛ; repr. Roxburgh Club Publications (1873), p. 194:

> But how he courted, how himselfe hee carri'd,
> And how the fauour of this *Nimph* he wonne,
> And with what pompe *Thames* was to *Medway* marri'd.
> Sweete Spenser shewes (O griefe that Spenser's gone!)
>   With whose life heavens a while enricht vs more,
>   That by his death wee might be euer pore.

32. William Alabaster

1600

William Alabaster (1567–1640), Fellow of Trinity College, Cambridge, enjoyed, as the author of the tragedy *Roxana*, considerable reputation as a Latin poet. As the author of the *Eliseis*, he enjoyed the special regard of Spenser (see *Colin Clout* II. 40 ff.)

From *Epigrammata* (1600), Bodleian MS. Rawlinson D. 293, fol. 19ᵛ:

If, passerby, you ask who it is is buried here, then you deserve to find out. Spenser is buried here. If you persist and ask who he was, you are not worthy to know the answer.[1]

---

[1] *Hoc qui sepulchro conditur siquis fuit*
Quaeris viator, dignus es qui rescias.
Spencerus istic conditur, si quis fuit
Rogare pergis, dignus es qui nescias.

33. Nicholas Breton

1600

Nicholas Breton (1545–1626), one of the more prolific of the Elizabethan lyrists, was educated at Oxford.

An Epitaph vpon Poet Spencer, in *Melancholike humours, in verses of diuerse natures* (1600), sigs. F3–F4; repr. in G. B. Harrison's edition (1929), pp. 44–6:

> Movrnfvll Muses, sorrowes minions,
> Dwelling in despaires opinions,
> Yee that neuer thought inuented,
> How a heart may be contented
> (But in torments alle distressed,
> Hopelesse how to be redressed,
> All with howling and with crying,
> Liue in a continuall dying)
>   Sing a Dirge on *Spencers* death,
>   Till your soules be out of breath.
>
> Bidde the Dunces keepe their dennes,
> And the Poets breake their pennes:
> Bidde the Sheepheards shed their teares,
> And the Nymphes go teare their haires:
> Bidde the Schollers leaue their reeding,
> And prepare their hearts to bleeding:
> Bidde the valiant and the wise,
> Full of sorrowes fill their eyes;
>   All for griefe, that he is gone,
>   Who did grace them euery one.
>
> Fairy Queene, shew fairest Queene,
> How her faire in thee is seene.

102

Sheepheards Calender set downe,
How to figure best a clowne.
As for Mother *Hubberts* tale,
Cracke the nut, and take the shale:
And for other workes of worth,
(All too good to wander forth)
   Grieue that euer you were wrot,
   And your Author be forgot.

Farewell Arte of Poetry,
Scorning idle foolery;
Farewell true conceited reason,
Where was neuer thought of treason:
Farewell iudgement, with inuention,
To describe a hearts intention:
Farewell wit, whose sound and sense
Shewe a Poets excellence:
   Farewell all in one togither,
   And with *Spencers* garland, wither.

And, if any Graces liue,
That will vertue honour giue,
Let them shewe their true affection,
In the depth of griefes perfection,
In describing forth her glory,
When she is most deepely sory;
That they all may wish to heere,
Such a song, and such a quier,
   As, with all the woes they haue,
   Follow *Spencer* to his graue.

34. John Chalkhill

c. 1600

Of John Chalkhill (*flor. c.* 1600) little is known beyond the possibility that he was coroner for Middlesex, and the fact that he was an acquaintance both of Spenser and of Isaak Walton, who edited his *Thealma and Clearchus* in 1678. Imitation of Spenserian mannerisms is pervasive in the poem, but the only overt mention of Spenser is contained in the lines printed below.

From *Thealma and Clearchus. A Pastoral History, in smooth and easie Verse. Written long since, By John Chalkhill, Esq; An Acquaintance and Friend of Edmund Spenser* (1683), p. 3; repr. in G. Saintsbury, *Minor Poets of the Caroline Period* (1906), II. 374:

> Close by the River, was a thick-leav'd Grove,
> Where Swains of old sang stories of their Love;
> But unfrequented now since *Collin* di'd,
> *Collin* that King of Shepherds, and the pride
> Of all *Arcadia*.

35. I.F.

1600

See also entries under John Weever, No. 31.

From prefatory material to Weever's *Favnus and Melliflora* (1600), sig· A4; repr. in the edition by A. Davenport (Liverpool, 1948), p. 5:

> If for to write of Loue, and Loues delights,
> Be not fit obiects for the grauer sights,
> Then stil admired *Chaucer*, thou maist rue
> And write thy auncient stories all anew:
> And that same Fayry Muse may rise againe,
> To blot those works that with vs do remaine.

36. Hugh Holland

c. 1600

Hugh Holland (d. 1633) moved from Westminster School, where he was taught by Camden, to Trinity College, Cambridge, where he was elected to a Fellowship. He contributed a commendatory sonnet to the First Folio of Shakespeare, and according to Edward Phillips in *Theatrum Poeticum* (*q.v.*) he was as a poet rated by some next to Sidney and Spenser – how is quite obscure. A variant of the first couplet in the quatrain printed below is quoted by Manningham in his *Diary* (B.M. MS. Harleian 5353, fol. 2).

On Spencer the Poett, in B.M. Add. MS. 21433, fol. 177ᵛ:

>He was and is, see then where lyes the odds
>Once God of Poetts, now Poet of the Gods
>And though lyne of life begone aboute
>The life yet of his lyne shall neuer out.

37. Francis Thynne

1600

Francis Thynne (1545?–1608), son of Chaucer's editor, was himself an amateur of literary studies. His earlier controversy with Speght (*q.v.*) was resolved in a form of collaboration with him. *Emblemes and Epigrames* is at points Spenserian in both diction and inspiration.

From *Emblemes and Epigrames*, Huntingdon MS. Ellesmere 34/B/12, fol. 53ᵛ (Epigram 38); repr. in edition of F. J. Furnivall, *EETS*, O.S., LXIV (1876), p. 71:

> *Spencers fayrie Queene*
> Renowmed Spencer, whose heavenlie sprite
> ecclipseth the sonne of former poetrie:
> in whome the muses harbor with delighte,
> gracinge thy verse with Immortalitie,
> Crowning thy fayrie Queene with deitie,
> the famous *Chaucer* yealds his Lawrell crowne
> vnto thy sugred penn for thy renowne.
>
> Noe cankred envie cann thy fame deface,
> nor eatinge tyme consume thy sacred vayne,
> no carping zoilus cann thy verse disgrace,
> nor scoffinge Momus taunt the with disdaine.
> since thy rare worke eternall praise doth gayne.
> then live thou still, for still thy verse shall live,
> to vnborne poets which light and life will give.

38. Francis Beaumont

after 1600

Francis Beaumont (1584–1616) the dramatist and collaborator with Fletcher, left Oxford without a degree to study law at the Inner Temple. His acquaintance included Jonson and Drayton. The piece below, if it is indeed by Beaumont, is either precocious or, despite its sense, written after Spenser's death. Though not properly speaking obituary at all, it is printed among a series of epitaphs by Beaumont's first editor, who I cannot but feel was guided by a sound sense of tone.

On Mr. Edm. Spenser, Famous Poet, in *Poems* (1653), sig. M2; repr. in Alexander Chalmers, *English Poets* (1810), VI. 204:

> At *Delphos* shrine, one did a doubt propound,
>   Which by th'Oracle must be released,
> Whether of Poets were the best renow'nd:
> Those that survive, or they that are deceased?
>   The Gods made answer by divine suggestion,
>   While *Spencer* is alive, it is no question.

39. Charles Fitzgeoffrey

1601

See headnote to No. 25.

(a) From *Affaniae: sive Epigrammatum Libri tres, Ejusdem Cenotaphia* (Oxford, 1601) sig. D5; repr. in *Poems*, ed. A. B. Grosart Occasional Issues, XVI (Manchester, 1881), p. xix. [The translation printed below is Grosart's (from p. xxiii)]:

> *To Edmund Spenser*
> Our Virgil in Dan Chaucer dost thou see?
> Badly! if aught can badly come from thee:
> Chaucer our Ennius, thou our Virgil be![1]

(b) *Ibid.*, sig. D5–D5ᵛ; repr. Grosart, p. xix. [The translation is my own]:

On the same
If fertile England can number three hundred poets, why cannot she number two Spensers? That is my question. And the answer comes from our English Apollo (Spenser bids us use that honourable title): Greece, they say, bore only one Homer, nor Rome herself two Virgils.[2]

(c) *Ibid.*, sig. D6; repr. Grosart, p. xiv. [The translation is my own]:
To Samuel Daniel

---

[1] *Nostrū* Maronē EDMONDE CHAVCERUM *vocas?*
  Male hercle! si tu quidpiā potes male;
  Namq; ille noster Ennius, *sed* Maro.

[2] *Tercentum numeret cum fertilis* Anglia *Vates,*
  Spenseros nequeat cur numerare duos?
  Sig ego; sic contra vati Thamisinus Apollo
  (SPENSERVS *tituli iussit honore frui*)
  Graecia Maeoniden tantum dare dicitur vnum,
  Virgiliosq; tulit Roma nec ipse duos.

If one wanted Spenser to be our Virgil, you Daniel would be our
British Ovid. If he were rather to be our British Phoebus, you Daniel
would be our Virgil. No poet is greater than Phoebus. If there were, it
would be Spenser, and you Daniel would be our Phoebus. And if
Phoebus wished to sing in English, he could hardly do so, but by using
your tongue.[1]

(d) *Ibid.*, sig. N2–N2^v; repr. Grosart, p. xix. [The translation is Grosart's
(p. xxiii)]:

> *To Edmund Spenser*
> While England of her poet proudly boasts,
> And singly challenges the world's wide coasts,
> And thou, O Tasso, tacitly dost yield,
> And men see Bartas, worsted, quit the field,
> And Ariosto's lips in silence sealed;
> Not only o'er the earth does Envy reign
> But scales the heavens and puts the gods to pain:
> From thee thy poet Spenser, lo, they snatch,
> England, because his skill they cannot match.
> Great bard, for thee not realms of earth have striven,
> Thy rivals are the very gods of heaven.[2]

(e) *Ibid.* sig. N2^v; repr. Grosart p. xx. [The translation is Grosart's
(p. xxiii)]:

> [1] Spenserum *si quis nostrum velit esse Maronem,*
> Tu DANIELE *mihi* Naso *Britannus eris.*
> Sin illum potius Phaebum *velit esse Britannum*
> Tum DANIELE *mihi tu* Maro *noster eris.*
> Nil Phaebo *vlterius; si quid foret, illud haberet*
> Spenserus, Phaebus *tu* Daniele *fores.*
> Quippe loqui Phaebus *cuperet si more Britanno*
> Haud scio quo poterat, ni velit ore tuo.
>
> [2] *Dum tumet inq; suo nimis* Anglia *vate superbit*
> Atq; omnes mundi provocat vna sinus,
> Et tu Tasso *taces nec tu* Bartasse *triumphas*
> Vlterius, caepit teq; Arioste *pudor,*
> Non tantum invidiam populis movet omnibus audax
> Sed coelum invasit livor, agitq; Deos:
> Spenserumq; *tibi Superi rapuere poetam,*
> Anglia, *cum vatem non habuere parem,*
> Quantus erat, pro quo non tantum regna, sed ipsos
> Rivales meruit patria habere Deos?

On his grave next to Chaucer in Westminster
Spenser lies here, who after Chaucer comes
In age, in tomb contiguous, art superior.[1]

40. William Basse

1602

William Basse (d. 1653) is perhaps most famous as the author of the
epitaph on Shakespeare contributed to the 1640 Folio. He appears
in the piece below as a thorough-going disciple of Spenser – as he
puts it in the verse epistle *To the Reader* prefacing the *Pastoral
Elegies* one 'nursed vp in *Colins* lore'.

From *Three Pastoral Elegies: Anander Anetor and Muridella* (1602),
sig. E3ᵛ (Elegie 3); repr. *Poetical Works* ed. R. W. Bond (1893) pp.
73–4:

> Whilome when I was *Collins* loued boy
> (Ah *Collin* for thee *Collin*, weep I now,)
> For thou art dead, ah, that to me didst ioy,
> As *Coridon* did to *Alexis* vow.
> But (as I sed,) when I was *Collins* boy,
> This deare young boy, and yet of yeares inow,
> To leade his willing heard along the plaine,
> I on his pipe did learne this singing veine.
> And oh, (well mote he now take rest therfore,)
> How oft in pray'rs and songs he pray'd and sung,
> That I (as had himselfe full long before,)

---

[1] Spenserus *cubat hic*, Chaucero *aetate priori*
Inferior, tumulo proximus, arte prior.

Mought liue a happy shepheard and a young;
And many vowes, and many wishes more,
When he his Pipe into my bosome flung:
And said, though *Collin* ne're shall be surpast,
Be while thou liu'st, as like him as thou maist.

Much was my deare therefore when *Collin* died,
When we (alacke) were both agreed in griefe:
He for his infant swaine that me affide,
Yet happed not to liue to see my priefe.
And I that to his gouernance had tide
My bounden youth, in loosing such a chiefe:
And how wou'd he haue sung, and with what grace?
Ananders Loue, and *Muridellaes* Face.

He wou'd haue blazed in eternall note.

41. John Ross

c. 1605

From *Parerga* (1605?), Folger MS. 800.1, p. 49:

On Edw. [sic] *Spenser, the modern poet, an Epitaph, 1599*
Spenser, you sang of many and no one sings of you. But this is not
because no one wants to do so, but because no one can do so.[1]

---

[1] In *Edw: Spenseram* [sic] *poetam modernum, Epitaph:* 1599
> *Tu multos, te nemo canit (Spensere) sed est hoc,*
> *Non quia nemo velit, sed quia nemo potest.*

42. William Warner

1606

William Warner (1558–1609) left Oxford without a degree and made his name in London as a translator and a historical poet. He knew Drayton.

To the Reader, in *A Continuance of Albions England* (1606), sig. A2 (Spurgeon 1.178):

> The *Musists*, though themselves they please,
> Their Dotage els finds Meede nor Ease:
> Vouch't *Spencer* in that Ranke preferd,
> *Per Accidens*, only interr'd
> Nigh Venerable *Chaucer*, lost,
> Had not kinde *Brigham* reard him Cost,
> Found next the doore Church-outed neere,
> And yet a Knight, Arch-Lauriat Heere.

THE PERIOD 1600-1660

(See Introduction pp. 10–18)

43. William Camden

1600, 1605

William Camden (1551–1623) after a rather irregular under-graduate career at Oxford, where he knew both Carew and Sidney, moved to London and as a teacher at Westminster School began the antiquarian work which was to make him famous. See also No. 168.

(a) From *Britannia* (1600), p. 379:

Here we should mention the chief of English poets, Geoffrey Chaucer, and the one who came nearest him of English poets in happiness of genius and the rich vein of poetry – Edmund Spenser.[1]

(b) From *Certaine Poems, . . . and Epitaphs of the English Nation in former Times* appended to *Remaines concerning Britaine* (1605), p. 8:

These may suffice for some Poeticall descriptions of our auncient Poets, if I would come to our time, what a world could I present to you out of Sir *Philipp Sidney, Ed. Spencer, Samuel Daniel, Hugh Holland, Ben: Iohnson, Th. Campion, Mich. Drayton, George Chapman, Iohn Marston, William Shakespeare,* & other most pregnant witts of these our times, whom succeeding ages may iustly admire.

---

[1] *Quique minime tacendus Poetarum Anglorum princeps Galfredus Chaucer; & qui ad illum ingenij faelicitate, & diuite Poeseos vena proxime accessit Edm. Spencerus.*

44. George de Malynes

1601

George de Malynes (*flor.* 1586–1641) is best known as a writer on economics. The extracts below, though they have no necessary reference to Spenser, are most probably influenced by de Malynes's reading of the *Faerie Queene*.

From *Saint George for England, allegorically described* (1601), sigs. A2–A3:

The inuented historie of S. *George* (right honorable and my singular good Lord) howsoeuer heretofore abused, may conueniently be applied to these our dayes of her Maiesties most happy gouernement, wherein the beames of the Orientall starre of Gods most holy word appeare vnto vs most splendent and transparent, to the singular comfort of all faithfull. For whereas vnder the person of the noble champion Saint *George* our Sauiour Christ was prefigured, deliuering the Virgin (which did signifie the sinfull soules of Christians) from the dragon or diuels power: So her most excellent Maiesty by aduancing the pure doctrine of *Christ Iesvs* in all truth and sincerity, hath (as an instrument appointed by diuine prouidence) bene vsed to performe the part of a valiant champion, deliuering an infinite number out of the diuels power, whereunto they were tied with the forcible chaines of darknesse.

Ibid., sig. E2:

She came accompanied with a Lambe representing her innocencie.

Ibid., sig. E4–E4ᵛ:

And the greater was the exployt of Saint George in deliuering her, who like a valiant champion being arriued into this Iland, and vnderstanding of the danger she was in, came with a Princely resolution to deliuer her, mounted on a pyball horse of seuerall colours, armed like a conqueror, to fight the combat with the shield of faith, hauing on the breast-plate of righteousnesse, the helmet of salvation, his loynes girt about with verity, and being adorned with the liuery of the Crosse, did with the sword of the Spirit destroy this monster.

45. The Author of the *Returne from Parnassus*

1602

The lines printed below are taken from the Second Part of *The Returne from Parnassus: or The Scourge of Simony*, of unknown authorship, but first produced in St John's College, Cambridge, in 1602. This second part was printed in 1606. The *Pilgrimage to Parnussus*, first acted *c.* 1598, and the first part of the trilogy to which this play belongs, also contains many echoes of Spenser and one or two explicit references which suggest a quarrel between the partisans of Spenser and those of Shakespeare. The three plays can be found together under the title *The Three Parnassus Plays*, ed. J. B. Leishman (1949) in which edition see further comment.

From *The Returne from Parnussus* I. ii (in 1606 ed., sig. B^v; Leishman, pp. 236–8):

Ingenioso: [Reads the names of the most famous poets, beginning with *Edmund Spencer.*] Good men and true, stand togither: heare your censure, what's thy judgement of *Spencer?*

> *Iudicio:* A sweeter swan then euer song in Poe,
> A shriller Nightingale then euer blest
> The prouder groues of selfe admiring Rome.
> Blith was each vally, and each sheapeard proud,
> While he did chaunt his rural minstralsye.
> Attentiue was full many a dainty eare.

Nay hearers hong vpon his melting tong,
While sweetly of his Faiery Queene he song.
While to the waters fall he tun'd [her] fame,
And in each barke engrau'd Elizaes name.
And yet for all this, vnregarding soile
Vnlac't the line of his desired life,
Denying mayntenance for his deare reliefe.
Carelesses [ere] to preuent his exequy,
Scarce deigning to shut vp his dying eye.

Ingenioso: Pity it is that gentler witts should breed,
Where thickskin chuffes laugh at a schollers need.
But softly may our [Homer's] ashes rest,
That lie by mery *Chaucers* noble chest.

46. William Harbert

1604

William Harbert (*flor.* 1604) was educated at Christ Church, and may be identified with the friend of Raleigh who accompanied him on his last voyage.

From the epistle *To The Maiestie of King Iames, Monarch of all Britayne* in *A Prophesie of Cadwallader last King of the Britaines* (1604), sig. H2ᵛ:

Albions Moeonian, Homer, natures pride,
Spenser the Muses sonne and sole delight:
If thou couldst through *Dianas* kingdome glide,
Passing the Pallace of infernall night,
(The Sentinels that keepes thee from the light)
Yet couldst thou not his retchlesse worth comprise,
Whose minde containes a thousand purities.

47. Sir John Roe

c. 1605

Sir John Roe (1581–1608) was educated at Queen's College, Oxford. For an account of him and his relations with Donne, see Donne's *Poems*, ed. Sir Herbert Grierson (Oxford, 1912), II. cxxix–cxxxv.

From *To Sir Nicholas Smith* first published in the seventh edition of John Donne's *Poems* (1669), p. 138; repr. Grierson, I. 401:

> Here sleeps House by famous Ariosto,
> By silver-tongu'd Ovid, and many moe,
> Perhaps by golden-mouth'd Spencer too pardie,
> (Which builded was some dozen Stories high)
> I had repair'd.

48. Lodowick Bryskett

1606

Lodowick Bryskett (*flor.* 1571–1611) was educated at Trinity College, Cambridge. It was probably first in Ireland that he met Spenser. Both knew Sidney however, who may have established contact between them. Bryskett's testimony is especially valuable, for Spenser was active in composing the *Faerie Queene* during the time of their friendship, and it is to Bryskett that Spenser makes his apology in *Amoretti* 33 for the delayed progress of the poem. Bryskett is also a contributor to Spenser's collection of elegies on Sidney published along with *Colin Clout* under the title *Astrophel* (1595). The *Discourse* is an adaptation of Giraldi, and is cast in the form of a dialogue.

From *A Discourse of Civill Life: Containing the Ethike part of Morall Philosophie. Fit for the instructing of a Gentleman in the course of a vertuous life* (1606), pp. 25–8:

Yet is there a gentleman in this company whom I haue had often a purpose to intreate, that as his leisure might serue him, he would vouchsafe to spend some time with me to instruct me in some hard points which I cannot of my selfe vnderstand: knowing him to be not onely perfect in the Greek tongue, but also very well read in Philosophie, both morall and naturall. Neuertheles such is my bashfulnes, as I neuer yet durst open my mouth to disclose this my desire vnto him, though I have not wanted some hartning thereunto from himselfe. For of loue and kindnes to me, he encouraged me long sithens to follow the reading of the Greeke tongue, and offered me his helpe to make me vnderstand it. But now that so good an opportunitie is offered vnto me, to satisfie in some sort my desire; I thinke I should commit a great fault, not to my selfe alone, but to all this company, if I should not enter my request thus farre, as to moue him to spend this time which we haue now destined to familiar discourse and conuersation, in declaring vnto vs the great benefites which men obtaine by the knowledge of Morall Philosophie, and in making vs to know what the same is, what be the parts thereof, whereby vertues are to be distinguished from vices: and finally that he will be pleased to run ouer in such order as he shall thinke good, such and so many principles and rules thereof, as shall serue not only for my better instruction, but also for the contentment and satisfaction of you al. For I nothing doubt, but that euery one of you will be glad to heare so profitable a discourse, and thinke the time very wel spent, wherein so excellent a knowledge shal be reuealed vnto you, from which euery one may be assured to gather some fruit as wel as my self. Therefore (said I) turning my selfe to M. *Spenser*, It is you sir, to whom it pertaineth to shew your selfe courteous now vnto vs all, and to make vs all beholding vnto you for the pleasure and profit which we shall gather from your speeches, if you shall vouchsafe to open vnto vs the goodly cabinet, in which this excellent treasure of vertues lieth locked vp from the vulgar sort. And thereof in the behalfe of all, as for my selfe, I do most earnestly intreate you not to say vs nay. Vnto which wordes of mine euery man applauding most with like words of request, and the rest with gesture and countenances expressing as much, M. *Spenser* answered in this maner.

Though it may seeme hard for me to refuse the request made by you all, whom, euery one alone, I should for many respects be willing to gratifie: yet as the case standeth, I doubt not but with the consent of the most part of you, I shall be excused at this time of this taske which would be laid vpon me. For sure I am, that it is not vnknowne vnto you, that I haue already vndertaken a work tending to the same effect, which is in *heroical verse*, vnder the title of a *Faerie Queene*, to represent all the moral vertues, assigning to euery vertue, a Knight to be the patron and defender of the same, in whose actions and feates of arms and chiualry, the operations of that vertue, whereof he is the protector, are to be expressed, and the vices and unruly appetites that oppose themselues against the same, to be beaten down & ouercome. Which work, as I haue already well entred into, if God shall please to spare me life that I may finish it according to my mind, your wish (M. *Bryskett*) will be in some sort accomplished, though perhaps not so effectually as you could desire. And the same may very well serue for my excuse, if at this time I craue to be forborne in this your request, since any discourse, that I might make thus on the sudden in such a subject, would be but simple, and little to your satisfactions. For it would require good aduisement and premeditation for any man to vndertake the declaration of these points that you have proposed, containing in effect the Ethicke part of Morall Philosophie. Whereof since I haue taken in hand to discourse at large in my poeme before spoken, I hope the expectation of that work may serue to free me at this time from speaking in that matter, notwithstanding your motion and all your intreaties. But I will tell you, how I thinke by himselfe he may very well excuse my speech, and yet satisfie all you in this matter. I haue seene (as he knoweth) a translation made by himselfe out of the Italian tongue, of a dialogue comprehending all the Ethicke part of Moral Philosophy, written by one of those three he formerly mentioned, and that is by *Giraldi* vnder the title of a dialogue of ciuil life. If it please him to bring vs forth that translation to be here read among vs, or otherwise to deliuer to vs, as his memory may serue him, the contents of the same; he shal (I warrant you) satisfie you all at the ful, and himselfe wil haue no cause but to thinke the time well spent in reuiewing his labors, especially in the company of so many his friends, who may thereby reape much profit, and the translation happily fare the better by some mending it may receiue in the perusing, as all writings also may do by the often examination of the same. Neither let it trouble him, that I so turne ouer to him againe the taske he wold haue put me to: for it falleth out fit for him to verifie the principall part of all this Apologie, euen now made for himselfe: because thereby it will appeare that he hath not withdrawne himself from seruice of the State, to liue idle or wholly priuate to himselfe, but hath spent some time in doing that which may greatly benefit others, and hath serued not a little to the bettering of his owne mind, and increasing of his knowledge, though he for modesty pretend much ignorance, and pleade want in wealth, much like some rich beggars, who either of custom, or for couetousnes, go to begge of others those things whereof they haue no want at home.

With this answer of M. *Spensers*, it seemed that all the company were wel satisfied: for after some few speeches, whereby they had shewed an extreme longing after his worke of the *Faerie Queene*, whereof some parcels had bin by some of them seene, they all began to presse me to produce my translation mentioned by M. *Spenser*, that it might be perused among them; or else that I should (as neare as I could) deliuer vnto them the contents of the same, supposing that my memory would not much faile me in a thing so studied, and aduisedly set downe in writing, as a translation must be.

49. Thomas Decker

1607

Thomas Decker (1570?–1641?), the dramatist and pamphleteer, supplies here in a very pleasant fashion, a tribute which neatly catches the tone of much later Elizabethan praise of Spenser.

From *A Knights Conjuring: Done in Earnest Discovered in Jest* (1607) sig. K4ᵛ:

Graue Spencer was no sooner entred into this *Chappell of Apollo*, but these elder *Fathers of the Diuine Furie*, gaue him a *Lawrer* & sung his *Welcome*: *Chaucer* call'de him his Sonne, and plac'de him at his right hand. All of them (at a signe giuen by the whole *Quire* of the *Muses* that brought him thither,) closing vp their lippes in silence, and tuning all their eares for attention, to heare him sing out the rest of his *Fayrie Queenes* praises.

50. Sir John Stradling

1607

Sir John Stradling (1563–1637) was educated at Brasenose and Magdalen Colleges, Oxford. He knew both Camden and Sir John Harington.

(a) From *Epigrammatum Libri Quatuor* (1607), p. 21:

To Edmund Spenser, the British Homer
If we are Trojans, we have a new Troy. You (as for the Greeks theirs is) shall be our Homer.[1]

(b) *Ibid.*, p. 165; repr. Chalmers, III. 13:

To Spenser and Daniel, famous poets
You divide the first and second places between you. Whoever comes third after you, has enough.[2]

---

[1] *Si nos Troiani, noua nobis Troia sit: Ipse*
   (*Vt Graecis suus est*) *noster Homerus eris.*

[2] *Diuiditis primas inter vos, atque secundas:*
   Tertius a vobis quisquis erit, sat habet.

51. Richard Niccols

1610

Richard Niccols (1584–1616) was educated at both Magdalen Hall and Magdalen College, Oxford. Apparently he spent his later time in London studying Spenser.

From *Englands Eliza: or The Victorious and Triumphant Reigne of* . . . *Elizabeth* . . . Part V of the *Mirrour for Magistrates* (1610), p. 779; repr. in edition of Joseph Haslewood (1815), pp. 823–4:

> (O) did that Fairie Queenes sweet singer liue,
> That to the dead eternitie could giue,
> Or if, that heauen by influence would infuse
> His heauenlie spirit on mine earth-borne Muse,
> Her name ere this a mirror should haue been
> Lim'd out in golden verse to th'eyes of men:
> But my sad Muse, though willing; yet too weak
> In her rude rymes *Elizaes* worth to speak,
> Must yeeld to those, whose Muse can mount on high,
> And with braue plumes can clime the loftie skie.

52. Henry Stanford

1610

Henry Stanford (*flor.* 1570–1610) was a Fellow of Trinity College, Oxford. The verses below are addressed to Lady Hunsdon, and dated 1610.

From Verses in Cambridge University Library MS. Dd.v. 75, fol. 19:

Hauing no other gift right noble dame
to testifie my mynde this booke I send
the autour when he liu'd did beare your name
& for to honour ladies this be penned
here may you reade in sugred verse set out
the praises of *Belphebe* worthie Quene
& faery landes adventures all about
with other exploites worthie to be seene
here Georges holines may vs direct
to conquer all the monstrous shapes of sin
& Guions temperance make vs suspect
the sugred baites of pleasures wanton ginnes
    Deign it to reade & reape such fruites it beares
    I still will wishe you long & happie years

53. Henry Peacham

1612

Henry Peacham the younger (1576?–1643?) was educated at Trinity College, Cambridge. As a schoolmaster he seems to have been free to develop an unusually wide range of interests. Spenser's influence on him as a poet is considerable. The extracts below indicate an early interest in Spenserian iconographies, of which incidentally his *Minerva Britanna* (1612) is full. A study of Spenser's influence on seventeenth-century emblem books might well prove fruitful. See Dorothy F. Atkinson, 'A Note on Spenser and Painting', *MLN*, LVII (1943), pp. 57–8; and Rosemary Freeman, *English Emblem Books* (1948), p. 71.

From *Graphice Or The Most Avncient and Excellent Art of Drawing and Limning* (1612), p. 27:

Feare is described [In his *Faery Queene*] by our excellent *Spencer* to ride in armour, at the clashing whereof he lookes deadly pale, as afeard of himselfe. [*Faerie Queene* III. xii. 12]

Ibid., p. 114:

Dissimulation
A lady wearing a vizard of two faces, in a long Robe of changeable colour, in her right hand a Magpie, the Poet *Spencer* described her looking through a lattice. [cf. *Faerie Queene* III. xii. 14–15]

Ibid., pp. 134–5:

August
August shall beare the forme of a young man of a fierce and cholericke aspect in a flame colored garment, vpon his head a garland of wheat and Rie, vpon his arme a basket of ripe fruites, as peares, plummes, apples, goodeberries: at his belt (as our *Spencer* describeth him) a sickle, bearing the signe *Virgo*. [cf. *Faerie Queene* VII. vii. 37]

54. Richard Zouche

1613

Richard Zouche (1590–1661) was a Fellow of New College, Oxford, and a practising lawyer.

From *The Dove: or Passages of Cosmography*, (1613) sig. E6ᵛ; repr. in edition of Richard Walker (Oxford, 1839), p. 51:

And truely, they who will be pleas'd to credit our owne tongue, and age, may finde our present, and later Poets, capable of that commendation, which was giuen the antien[ts] among the Greekes: That if their writings were preserued, no part of Learning should wholy perish. *Spencer*, hauing as well deliuered Morall, and Heroical matter for vse and action, as *Du Bartas* (now ours) Naturall and Diuine, for study and meditation.

55. Thomas Freeman

1614

Thomas Freeman (*flor.* 1614) was educated at Magdalen College, Oxford. His *Epigrams* include a number on literary figures, Shakespeare, Daniel, Donne, and Chapman among them.

From *Rubbe, and A great Cast. Epigrams* (1614), sig. 13 (*Epigram* 64):

> *Of Spencers Faiery Oueene*
> *Virgil* from *Homer*, th' *Italian* from him,
> *Spenser* from all, and all of these I weene,
> Were borne when *Helicon* was full to th'brim,
> Witnes *their* works, witnes our *Faiery Queene:*
>   That lasting monument of *Spensers* wit,
>   Was n'er come near to, much lesse equal'd yet.

56. E. Johnson

1614

The poet here must be identified with Edward Johnson (b. 1592), educated at Magdalen College, Oxford, and the Inner Temple. Browne would have met him at either place. Both sets of commendatory verses for the *Shepheards Pipe* are from members of the Inner Temple.

From *Of his Friend Maister William Browne*, prefatory to Browne' the *Shepheards Pipe* (1614), sig. A3; repr. *Poems of William Browne*, ed Gordon Goodwin (1893), II. 81–2:

> A Poets borne, not made: No wonder then
> Though *Spencer, Sidney*: (miracles of men,
> Sole English Makers; whose eu'n names so hie
> Expresse by implication Poesy)
> Were long vnparaleled: For nature bold
> In their creation, spent that precious mould,
> That Nobly better earth, that purer spirit
> Which Poets as their Birth-rights, claime t'inherite:
> And in their great production, Prodigall;
> Carelesse of futures well-nye spent her-all.

57. John Norden

1614

John Norden (1548–1625?) was apparently both a topographer and a religious writer. See A. W. Pollard, 'The Unity of John Norden, surveyor and religious writer', *The Library*, 4th Ser., VII (1927), 233–52. I take the remarks here to be more than specifically linguistic.

From *The Labyrinth of Mans Life. or Vertues Delight and Enuies Opposite* (1614), sig. A3ᵛ:

> *Chawcer, Gowre,* the *bishop of dunkell,*
> In ages farre remote were eloquent:
> Now *Sidney, Spencer,* others moe excell,
> And are in latter times more excellent,
>   To antique *Lauriats* paralell
>
> But matters of great admiration
> In Moderne *Poesies* are wordes estrang'd
> Inuention of hid speculation,
> The scope whereof hardly conceiu'd as it is rang'd
>   But by a *Comentation.*
>
> Who readeth Chaucer as a *moderne man,*
> Not looking back into the time he wrote,
> Will hardly his ambiguous *phrases* scan,
> Which in that time were vulgar, well I wote,
>   Yet we run back where he began.
>
> And all our praised *Poems* are beset,
> With *Chaucers* wordes and *Phrases* ancient:
> Which these our *moderne ages* quite forget
> Yet in their Poems, far more Eloquent,
>   Not yet from *Gowre* or *Chaucer* fett.

58. Tristram White

1614

Compare George de Malynes, No. 44, and Peter Heylyn, No. 73a.

From *The Martyrdom of Saint George of Cappadocia: Titular Patron of England* ... (1614), sigs. A2–A2ᵛ:

The Poet in his *Faerie Queene*, playing vpon the Etymologie of this Name, doth also allude to *Tilth*, though after a vaine, but very wittie manner, thus:*

> Thence shee thee brought into this lond. ...

Of S. *Georges* entitulation to the patronage of *England*, that Poet in the person of an holy propheticall Father, instructing the Champion of the crosse, after hee had grauely perswaded to the love of heauenly thins, hath these Verses:

> *For thou amongst those Saints whom thou dost see,*
> *Shalt be a Saint, and thine owne†* *Nations friend,*
> *And* PATRON: *thou S. George shalt called be,*
> *S. George of merry England, the signe of victorie.*

---

* Lib. 1. Cant. 10. Stanz. 60.

† *In S. Georges English birth the Poet followes the vulgar errour, of purpose, to fit his fabulous morall argument the rather.*

59. Thomas Collins

1615

The extract below is from an elegy on one Coravin, who remains unidentified. Nothing is known of Collins; his invocation of Spenser is conventional.

From *The Teares of Love: or Cupids Progresse* (1615), p. 47:

> *Sidney* and *Spencer*, be you aye renoun'd:
> No time hath pow'r your Pastorals to confound.
> *Drayton*, and all the rest that wrote of yore,
> Adorning time with your delicious store,
> Be euer honor'd, and (till th'end of time)
> On Fames peart tongue be praised for your Rimes.
> You worthy ones, oh, do not you disdaine
> My mournfull Muse, that in this humble vaine
> Dares for to sing, considering these are dayes,
> In which some Criticks will the best dispraise:
> But pardon me, should all be silent; then
> Who should praise Vertue, or check Vice in men?

60. William Browne

1616

William Browne (1591–1643?) left Exeter College, Oxford, without a degree and finished his education in the Inner Temple. The first part of *Britannia's Pastorals* is a youthful production, written before the poet was twenty. It was published along with commendatory pieces, mainly by his Exeter friends who announce him, to use the phrase of one of them (Heyward) as the 'second *Colin Clout*'. Browne is unquestionably the pleasantest of the new Spenserians.

(a) From *Britannia's Pastorals. The Seconde Booke* (1616), p. 24; repr. *Poems*, ed. Gordon Goodwin (1893–4), I. 221–2:

> Shew now faire *Muse* what afterward became
> Of great *Achilles Mother;* She whose name
> The *Mermaids* sing, and tell the weeping strand
> A brauer Lady neuer tript on land,
> Except the euer liuing *Fayerie Queene,*
> Whose vertues by her *Swaine* so written beene,
> That time shall call her high enchanced story
> In his rare song, *The Muses chiefest Glory.*

(b) *Ibid.*, pp. 26–7; repr. Goodwin, I. 225–6:

> And after reu'rence done, all being set
> Vpon their finny Coursers, round her throne,
> And shee prepar'd to cut the watry Zone
> Ingirting *Albion;* all their pipes were still,
> And *Colin Clout* began to tune his quill,
> With such deepe Art that euery one was giuen
> To thinke *Apollo* (newly slid from Heau'n)
> Had tane a humane shape to win his loue,

Or with the *Westerne Swaines* for glory stroue.
He sung th'heroicke Knights of *Faiery* land
In lines so elegant, of such command,
That had the * *Thracian* plaid but halfe so well
He had not left *Eurydice* in hell.
But e're he ended his melodious song
An host of *Angels* flew the clouds among,
And rapt this Swan from his attentiue mates,
To make him one of their associates
In heauens faire Quire: Where now he sings the praise
Of him that is the *first and last of dayes.*
Diuinest *Spencer* heau'n-bred, happy Muse!
Would any power into my braine infuse
Thy worth, or all that *Poets* had before
I could not praise till thou deseru'st no more.
A dampe of wonder and amazement strooke
Thatis attendants, many a heauy looke
Follow'd sweet *Spencer*, till the thickning ayre
Sights further passage stop'd. A passionate teare
Fell from each *Nymph*, no Shepheards cheeke was dry,
A doleful *Dirge*, and mournfull *Elegie*
Flew to the shore. When mighty *Nereus* Queene
(In memory of what was heard and seene)
Imploy'd a *Factor*, (fitted well with store)
Of richest Iemmes, refined *Indian Ore*)
To raise, in honour of his worthy name
A *Piramis*, whose head (like winged *Fame*)
Should pierce the clouds, yea seeme the stars to kisse,
And *Mausolus* great toombe might shrowd in *his*.
Her will had beene performance, had not *Fate*
(That neuer knew how to commiserate)
Suborn'd curs'd *Auarice* to lye in waite
For that rich prey: (*Gold is a taking baite*)
Who closely lurking like a subtile Snake
Vnder the couert of a thorny brake,
Seiz'd on the *Factor* by faire *Thetis* sent,
And rob'd our *Colin* of his Monument.

* Orpheus.

134

61. Ben Jonson

1616, 1619

Ben Jonson (1573?–1637) attended Westminster School under Camden, and probably did not proceed to either University. From Camden however he took his scholarly bent and was later reputed one of the best classicists of his age. In a different sense of the word, he is a severe classicist, and Spenser does not escape his censure. I have included in this section remarks made by Jonson and reported by Drummond. See also No. 148.

(a) From *The Golden Age Restored*, in *Workes* (1616), p. 1012; repr. *Works*, ed. Herford and Simpson (Oxford, 1925–1952), VII. 425:

> You farre-fam'd spirits of this happie Ile,
> That, for your sacred songs haue gain'd the stile
> Of *PHOEBVS* sons: whose notes they aire aspire
> Of th'old *AEgyptian*, or the *Thracian* lyre,
> That *Chaucer, Gower, Lidgate, Spencer* hight
> Put on your better flames, and larger light
> To waite vpon the age that shall your names new nourish
> Since vertue prest shall grow, and buried arts shall flourish.

(b) From *Conversations with William Drummond of Hawthornden* (written 1619) National Library of Scotland Adv. MS. 33.3.19 fol. 25^v; repr. in edition of G. B. Harrison (1923) p. 4:

Spenser's stanzaes pleased him not nor his matter the meaning of which Allegorie he had delivered in papers to Sir Walter Raughlie.

Ibid., fol. 26^v; repr. Harrison, p. 7:

He Jonson hath be heart some verses of Spensers Calender, about wyne, between Soline & percye.

Ibid., fols. 26^v-7; repr. Harrison, pp. 8–9:

That the Irish having robd Spensers goods, and burnt his house and a little child new born, he and his wyfe escaped, and after, he died for lake of bread in King Street, and refused 20 pieces sent to him by my Lord of Essex, and said, He was sorrie he had no time to spend them. That in that paper S. W. Raughly had of the Allegories of his Fayrie Queen, by the Blating Beast the Puritans were understood, by the false Duessa the Q. of Scots.

(c) From *Timber; or, Discoveries; Made vpon Men and Matter*, in *Workes . . . The second Volume* (1640), p. 97; repr. Herford and Simpson, VIII. 582:

If it were put to the question of the Water-rimers workes, against *Spencers*; I doubt not, but they would find more Suffrages; because the most favour common vices, out of a Prerogative the vulgar have, to lose their judgements; and like that which is naught.

62. The Author of *Apollo Christian*

1617

(a) From *Apollo Christian: or Helicon reformed* (1617), pp. 29–30 (Melos 7)

Come, let vs sing, that God may haue the glorie,
Some noble act; and let mine auditorie
Bee of the best: my Lyra now is strung,
And English, which I sing in, is a tongue.

The victory Saint *Michael* did obtaine
Against the Dragon in the open plaine,
And moouing champaine of the triple aër,
As braue a subject as high heauens are faire . . .
And whither Decasyllabons will you goe?
Great was the combat, great the ouerthrow
Which our Saint *George* did to this Dragon giue,
Whose fame in *Spensers* Red-crosse Knight doth liue:
Thither repair who loue descriptions life,
There hangs the table of the noble strife.
The spirit, and the sense of things our care is.
Wisdome is Queene, who fareth not with Faëries.

(b) *Ibid.*, p. 35 (Melos 12):

> *Greece* had her *Sappho*, and her spruce old wagg,
>   *Anacreon;*
> *Rome* her *Catullus*, and the like some bragg,
>   Of *Albion*.
> And would to God that heerein to seeme lagg,
> Were not a cause of absurd shame to many,
> Court who court list, bee not wits Ape to any.
> Without that noble Sidney heere I tax,
>   Or *Spensers* pomp:
> And gladly granting *Iohnson* nothing lacks
>   Of *Phoebus* stamp.
> For neuer wits were made of finer wax,
> Then *England* hath to vaunt of in these times,
> But them I tax whose reason's lost in rimes.

63. John Lane

1617, 1621

John Lane(*flor. c.* 1620) produced a great deal of doggerel, much of which is so bad as to be unintelligible. Though an intimate of Milton's father, he could not have taught Milton much. As a poet, he relies heavily on Spenser and the earlier English poets. To support the worthwhileness of his effort at a continuation of Chaucer's *Squire's Tale* (Bodleian MS. Douce 170), he cites Spenser on Chaucer as an authority. He also writes with considerable feeling on Spenser's death in *Tritons Trumphet*. The passages printed below must count as his most enlightening.

(a) From preface to revision of Lydgate's *History of Guy of Warwick*, B.M. MS. Harleian 5243, (written 1617) fol. 4; repr. in *Bishop Percy's Folio Manuscript, Ballads and Romances* (1868), p. 522ᵛ:

In which last, the heroical kind; Homer bestirred him selfe to lead the dawnce. Virgil blasoned the riches of his learninge in the same cloth of arras. The ancient English Poetes (meaning allwaies the sownd ones) have delivered them of heroical birthes in this kind; which doe survive of theire deceased parentes glorie, all of them adducinge a complete knight, in the personations of twoe in number; and maie as lawfullie bee instanced in one: and all as well in twoe, as pleaseth the ingenious. For so Mr Edm: Spencer in his allegorical declaratorie, faerely declameth.

Ibid.; repr. Hales and Furnivall, pp. 524–4ᵛ:

Thus Lidgat faierlie discharginge him selfe, leaveth it apparent, that the meere historien, is of all other infestus! the most malignant toward the Poet historical; whome hee vnderstandeth not: though him the Poet doth, at ann haier, is thearefore the most vnfitt to accuse, or censure the industrious, in the same case, that Prince Hector, and kings Artur maie also bee doubted of, because they likewise have binn poeticalie historified by poetes prosequutinge ideal veritie, as the historien pretendeth positive truith.

(b) From *Tritons Trumphet to the several moneths* . . . (written 1621), B.M. MS. Royal 17 B XV, fol. 82:

> From Faerie Lande I come quoth Danus now
> Ha that quoth June mee never chanced to knowe
> Ne could or noold high poet Spencer tell
> (so farr as mote my witt his riddle spell)
> Though none that breatheth livinge air doth knowe
> Wheare is that happie land of Faierie
> Wh' I so oft doe vaunt. Yet no wheare showe
> But vouch antiquities which nobodie maie knowe.

64. William Drummond

1619

William Drummond of Hawthornden (1585–1649) was educated at Edinburgh. As a practising poet, his tastes in modern literature were widely and deeply developed. He was a rather inferior Boswell to Ben Jonson, but the *Conversations* remain an important critical document – extracts from them can be found in the section devoted to Jonson. It is surprising, but I am assured privately by Mr R. MacDonald that it is so, that the commonplace books of Drummond contain no mention of Spenser.

From *Heads of a Conversation betwixt the Famous Poet Ben Johnson, and William Drummond of Hawthornden, January, 1619* in *Works* (1711), p. 226:

The Authors I have seen (saith he [Drummond]) on the subject of

Love, are the Earl of Surrey, Sir Thomas Wyat (whom, because of their Antiquity, I will not match with our better Times) *Sidney*, *Daniel*, *Drayton* and *Spencer*. . . . As to that which *Spencer* calleth his *Amorelli* [*sic*], I am not of their Opinion, who think them his; for they are so childish, that it were not well to give them so honourable a Father.

65. Robert Aylett

1621

Robert Aylett (1583?–1655?) was educated at Trinity Hall, Cambridge. As a poet Aylett has perhaps most in common with Herbert, but he makes a habit of plagiarizing lines, stanzas, and even longer stretches of verse from Spenser. The passages printed below are but an inadequate token of gratitude. See F. M. Padelford, 'Robert Aylett', *HLB*, X (1936), 1–48.

(a) From *The Song of Songs, Which Was Salomons, Metaphrased in English Heroiks by way of Dialogue. With Certayne of the Brides Orna-ments* (1621) repr. in *Divine, and Moral Speculations in Metrical Numbers* . . . (1654), sig. B8 (Proeme to *The Brides Ornaments*):

> Those sublime Wits that in high Court of Fame
> Do seek to rank themselves by Poesie,
> Eternizing the glory of their name
> By praise of Honour and of Chivalry,
> To some great Princes Court their youth applys
> Knights honourable actions to behold;
> Chaste Ladies loves, and Nobles courtesie.
> Of such have *Homer*, *Virgil*, *Spencer* told,
> And have thereby their names in Fames fair Court enrold.

(b) *Ibid.*, sig. H4 (*Of Truth*, stanza 32):

Divinest *Spencer*, thou didst shadow well
In *Legend* of true *Love* and *Chastity:*
By *girdle* fair of fairest *Florimell,*
This sacred *Belt* of *Truth* and *Verity,*
Which none on looser Ladies joints coud tie,
Yet their fair Limbs that had liv'd true and chaste,
It did adorn most rich and gloriously,
And was most fitting for their slender waste,
But they *Ungirt unblest*, were that had been *unchaste.*

(c) *Ibid.,* sig. Rr7ᵛ (from *Urania,* first published 1625):

And as the obiect of our Loue exceeds,
So strikes the *Muse* on high or lower strings;
Who lowly late did maske in Shepeards weeds,
In high Heroiques of *Armes*, and *Honour* sings.★

66. Robert Burton

1621, 1632

Robert Burton (1577–1640) migrated from Brasenose to a
Studentship at Christ Church where he spent the rest of his days
paucis notus. Paucioribus ignotus as the author of the *Anatomy of
Melancholy*, he hardly needs an introduction here. Burton treats
the *Faerie Queene* either as a source of finely phrased commonplaces,
or as a romance filled with examples of nicely illustrative types.

(a) The *Anatomy of Melancholy* (Oxford, 1621), pp. 519–20 (III. i. 3
(1)); repr. in edition of Floyd Dell and Paul Jordan-Smith (1927), p.
636:

★ Spencer.

Friendship is an holy name, and a sacred communion of friends. *As the Sunne is in the Firmament, so is friendship in the world*, a most diuine and heauenly band, take this away, and take all pleasure, all ioy, comfort, happinesse and true content out of the world, tis the greatest tye, and as the Poet decides [*1624 ed.*: as our modern *Maro* decides it], is much to be preferred before the rest.

> †Hard is the doubt, and difficult to deeme,
> When all three kindes of loue together meet;
> And doe dispart the heart with power extreme,
> Whether shall waigh the ballance downe, to wit,
> The deare affection vnto kindred sweet,
> Or raging fire of loue to women kind,
> Or zeale of friends combined by vertues meete.
> But of them all the band of vertuous minde,
> Me thinkes the gentle heart should most assured bind.

(b) *Ibid.*, p. 621 (III. ii. 3); repr. Dell and Jordan-Smith, pp. 759–60:

[Love is] the sole subiect almost of all Poetry, all our Inuention tends to it, all our songs, what euer those old *Anacrions*, *Greeke Epigrammatists*, Loue writers, *Anthony Diogenes* the most ancient, whose Epitome we finde in *Phocins Bibliotheca*, *Longus Sophista* . . . *Ovid*, *Catullus*, *Tibullus*, &c. Our new *Ariosto's*, *Boyardes*, autors of *Arcadia*, *Fairy Q.* &c. haue written in this kinde, are but as so many Symptomes of Loue.

(c) From *The Anatomy of Melancholy*, . . . *The Fourth Edition* (Oxford, 1632), p. 532 (III. ii. 3 (1)); repr. Dell and Jordan-Smith, pp. 746–7:
Our Knights errant, and the Sr *Lancelots* of these daies, I hope will adventure as much for ladies favours, as the *Squire of Dames*, *Knight of the Sunne*, Sr *Bevis of Southampton*, or that renowned peire,

> ‡*Orlando, who long time had loued deare*
> *Angelica the fayre, and for her sake*
> *About the world, in nations farre and neare,*
> *Did high attempts performe and vndertake,*

he is a very dastard, a Coward, a blocke and a beast, that will not doe

---

* *Lucianus Toxari. amicitia vt sol in mundo.*
† *Spencer Fairy Queene lib. 5 [4]. cant. 9. staffe. 1.2.*
‡ *Ariost. lib. 1. Cant. 1. staff. 5.*

as much, but they will sure, they will; For it is an ordinary thing for these enamorato's of our times to say and doe more, ... to make his corrivall doe as much. 'Tis frequent with them to challenge them the field for their lady and mistris sake, to runne a tilt,

> *That either beares (so furiously they meete)*
> *The other downe vnder the horses feet.*

And then up and to it againe,

> *And with their axes both so sorely power,*
> *That neither plate nor maile sustain the stour,*
> *But revelde wearke like rotten wood a sunder*
> *And fire did flash like lightning after thunder.*

(d) *Ibid.*, p. 537; repr. Dell and Jordan-Smith, pp. 752–3:

There is no man so pusillanimous, so very dastard, whom loue would not incense, make of a divine temper, and an herociall spirit. As hee said in like case, *Tota ruat coeli moles non terreor*, &c. Nothing can terrifie, nothing can dismay them, But as Sr *Blandamor* and *Paridell*, those two braue Fayrye K[n]ights, fought for the loue of faire *Florimel* in presence,

> †*And drawing both their swords with rage anew,*
> *Like two mad Mastiues each on other flew,*
> *And shields did share, and males did rash, and helmes did hew:*
> *So furiously each other did assaile,*
> *As if their soules at once they would haue rent,*
> *Out of their brests, that streames of blood did rayle*
> *Adowne, as if their springs of life were spent,*
> *That all the ground with purple blood was sprent,*
> *And all their armour stain'd with bloody gore,*
> *Yet scarcely once to breath would they relent.*
> *So mortall was their mallice and so sore,*
> *That both resolued (then yeeld) to dye before.*

... And for that cause‡ he would haue women follow the Camp, to be spectators and encouragers of noble actions: vpon such an occasion; the §*Squire of Dames* himselfe, S. *Lancelot*, or Sir *Tristram*, Caesar, or *Alexander* shall not be more resolute, or goe beyond them.

---

* *Fayry Queene cant. 1. lib. 4 & cant. 3. lib. 4.*
† Fayrie Qu. *Lib. 4. Cant. 2.*
‡ [Plato] *Lib. 5. de legibus.*
§ *Spencers Fairie Queene. 5. book. cant. 8.*

67. Alexander Gill

1621

Alexander Gill the elder (1565–1635) was Milton's Headmaster at St Paul's School. The *Logonomia Anglica*, first published in 1619, is a grammar of English, but its closing chapters deal specifically with poetics. See also No. 147.

From *Logonomia Anglica* (1621), pp. 124–5; repr. in edition of O. L. Jiriczek (Strasburg, 1903), pp. 129–30:

Now you will admit that nothing in the way of ornamented speech is beyond our poets, for our Homer is not alone in this kind. I have spoken triflingly – our Spenser, for he is more correct in beautifying his language, and as he is more fertile of neatly expressed general truths, so he is more serious, and as he is richer in the variety of his invention, so he is the more useful in his conception of any topic. This is obvious in as much as he has appropriately and fully described, by means of the loveliest poetical fictions, the moral virtues in all their circumstances.[1]

---

[1] *Iam fateris ad sermonis ornatum nihil a nostris praetermissum. Neque enim solus est in hoc genere Homerus noster; exiguum dixi, Spenserus noster: nam & sermonis cultu accuratior est; & sententiis vt crebrior, ita grauior; & inuentionis varietate locupletior; & materiae cognitione multo vtilior; vtpote qui morales virtutes, secundum omnes suas circumstantias, aptissime & copiosissime, iucundissimis figmentis poeticis descripsit.*

68. William Mason

1621

The passage below illustrates the early interest in Spenserian iconographies, first noted by Alastair Fowler, 'Oxford and London Marginalia to *The Faerie Queene*', *N&Q*, CCVI (1961), 416–19.

From *A Handfvl of Essaies. Or Imperfect Offers* (1621), sigs. F4ᵛ–F5:

When I behold Enuy (as the Poet describeth her) to haue a pale face without blood, a leane body without moysture (like one of Pharaohs leane kine) squint eyes, foule or blacke teeth, a heart ful of gall, a tongue tipt with poison, neuer laughing but when others weepe; neuer sleeping because she alwaies thinketh on mischiefe; I then abhorre this Monster.

[Compare *Faerie Queene* V. xii. 28–32]

69. Robert Salter

1626

See headnote to No. 11.

From *Wonderfull Prophecies* (1626), pp. 42–3:

And euen this very *Mysterie* is it, that a right learned and vertuous

Gentelman* hath so liuely decyphered, in his *Legend* of the *Patron of trew holinesse*, the *Knight of the Red-Crosse;* whereby, and by the rest of those his louely *Raptures*, hee hath iustly purchased the *Lawrel* of *honorable memory*, while the Pilgrimage of those his worthies are to indure.

Hee there hath brought forth our *Noble Saint George;* at the first onely in the state of a *Swayne*, before his *Glorious Queene* cast down on the ground (*Vncouth, vnkest*) *Vnacknowne, vncared off* as a dead trunke, and onely fit for the *fire* (as in our first *Period*).

But when hee had arrayed himselfe in the *Armor* of his Dying Lord, his presence is then become *Gracious*, and his person promising great things (*as one for sad incounters fit*). Which hee first *Passiuely* (as in our second *Period*), and after *Actiuely* (as in our third *Period*) doth so victoriously passe through and finish; that at the length (as in our fourth *Period*), hee is become altogether *Impassible*, whether of *Assalts* of the fraylety of *Nature* within, or *Affronts* of *Aduersaries* without, as being fully possessed of that Kingdome, against which there is none to stand vp.

70. William Lisle

1628

William Lisle (1569?–1637) was educated at Eton and King's College, Cambridge, of which he became a Fellow. Lisle was a keen Anglo-Saxonist and philologist. See also No. 138.

From the epistle *To the Worthy Reader*, prefatory to *Virgil's Eclogues Translated into English* (1628), sig. 5:

* *Mr. Edmund Spencer. The great contentment I sometimes enjoyed by his Sweete society, suffereth not this to passe me, without Respectiue mention of so trew a friend.*

... onely Master *Spencer* long since translated the Gnat, (a little fragment of *Virgils* excellence), giving the world peradventure to conceive, that hee would at one time or other have gone through the rest of this Poets workes: and it is not improbable, that this very cause was it, that made every man els very nice to meddle with any part of the Building which hee had begun, for feare to come short with disgrace, of the pattern which hee had set before them.

71. Sir Kenelm Digby

before 1628?, 1628

Sir Kenelm Digby (1603–65) left Gloucester Hall, Oxford, without a degree. He is the most exact and probably the best of Spenser's early critics, and his reputation as a Spenserian is undiminished by any later enterprise. Ben Jonson, in his *Epigram to my Muse, the Lady Digby, on her Husband* . . . hopes that Sir Kenelm will look on his verses '(next to Spenser's noble booke)/And praise them too.' The finest tribute to Digby's criticism comes, however, in Thomas May's lines on the *Observations* (B.M. MS. Add. 25303, fol. 187). The *Discourse* is addressed to May and must I think predate the *Observations*, dated 1628 and addressed to Sir Edward Stradling. The most elaborate commentary on the *Observations* is provided by Alastair Fowler, *Spenser and the Numbers of Time* (1964), pp. 266 ff. Digby's copy of the 1617 Folio is now in Wellesley College Library. Unfortunately, it contains no marginalia, but on the blank opposite the title-page Digby has transcribed Alabaster's obituary epigram.

(a) *A discourse concerning Edmund Spencer* in B.M. MS. Harleian 4153.

Whosoeuer will deliver a well grounded opinion and censure of any learned man, must at the least stand vpon the same leuell with him in matter of iudgement and ability: for otherwise, whiles remaining on the lower ground he looketh vp at him, he shall haue but a superficiall view of the most prominent parts, without being able to make any discouery into the large continent that lyeth behind those; wherein vsually is the richest soyle. This consideration maketh mee very vn-willing to say anything in this kind of our late admirable poet EDMUND SPENCER, who is seated soe high aboue the wreach of my weake eyes, as the more I looke to discerne and discry his perfections, the more faint and dazeled they grow through the distance and splendour of the obiect. Yet to comply with your desire, I will here briefly deliuer you (though with a hoar[s]e voyce and trembling hand) some of those rude and undigested conceptions that I haue of him; not daring to looke too farre into that sacrary of the MUSES and of learning, where to handle anything with boldness, were impiety. His learned workes confirme me in the beliefe that our NORTHEREN climate may give life to as well tempered a brain, and as rich a mind as where the sunne shineth fairest. When I read him methinks our country needth not enuy either GREECE, ROME or TUSCANY; for if affection deceiue me not very much, their POETS excell in nothing but he is admirable in the same: and in this he is the more admirable that what perfections they haue seuerally, you may find all in him alone; as though nature had striued to show in him that when she pleaseth to make a MASTER-PIECE, she can giue in one subject all those excellencies that to be in height would seeme to require euery one of them a different temper and complexion. And if at any time he plucketh a flower out their gardens, he transplanteth it soe happily into his owne, that it groweth there fairer and sweeter then it did where first it sprang vp. his works are such, as were their true worth knowne abroad, I am perswaded the best witts and most learned men of other parts, would study our long neglected language, to be capable of his rich conceptions and smooth delivery of them. For certainely, weight of matter was neuer better ioyned with propriety of language and with maiestey and sweetnes of verse, then by him. And if any should except his reuiuing some obsolete words, and vsing some ancient formes of speech, in my opinion he blameth that which deserueth much prayse: for SPENCER doth not that out of any affectation (although his assiduity in CHAUCER might make his language familier to him) but only then when they serue to expresse more liuely and more concisely what he would say:

and whensoeuer he vseth them, he doth so polish their natiue rudenes, as retaining the maiesty of antiquity the[y], want nothing of the elegancy of our freeshest speech. I hope that what he hath written will be a meanes that the english tongue will receiue no more alteration and changes, but will remaine & continue settled in that forme it now hath; for excellent authours doe draw vnto them the study of posterity, and whosoeuer is delighted with what he readeth in an other, feeleth in himselfe a desire to expresse like thinges in a like manner: and the more resemblance his elocutions haue to his authours the neerer he perswadeth himself he arriueth to perfection: and thus, much conversation [sic] and study in what he would imitate, begetteth a habite of doing the like. This is the cause that after the great lights of learning among the GRECIANS their language receiued no further alterations. and that the LATINE hath euer since remained in the same state whereovnto it was reduced by CICERO, VIRGILL, and the other great men of that time: and the TUSCANE tongue is at this day the same as it was left about 300 yeares agoe by DANTE PETRACHE and BOCCACE. If it is true that the vicissitudes of things (change being a necessary and inseperable condicion of all sublunary creatures) and the inundations of barbarous nations, may overgrow and ouerrune the vulgar practise of the perfectest languages, as we see of the forementioned GREEKE and LATINE; yet the vse of those tongues will flourish among learned men as long as those excellent authours remaine in the world. Which maketh me confident that noe fate nor length of time will bury SPENCERS workes and memory, nor ideed alter that language that out of his schoole we now vse vntill some general innouation happen that may shake as well the foundations of our nation as of our speech: from which hard law of stepmother Nature what Empire or kingdome hath euer yet bin free? And herein SPENCER hath bin very happy that he hath had one immediately succeeding him of partes and power to make what he planted, take deepe rootes; and to build vp that worke whose foundations he soe fairely layd; for it is beyond the compasse and reach of our short life and narrow power to haue the same man beginne and perfect any great thing. Noe Empire was euer settled to long continuance, but in the first beginnings of it there was an vninterrupted succession of heroick and braue men to defend and confirme it. A like necessity is in languages, and in cures we may promise our selues a long and flourishing age, when diuine SPENCERS sunne was noe sooner sett, but in JOHNSON a new one rose with as much glory and brightnes as euer shone withall; who being himself most excellent and admirable in the iudicious compositions that in seuerall kinds he hath made, thinketh no man more excellent or more admirable then this his late praedecessour in the Laurell crowne. To his wise and knowing iudgement faith may be giuen, whereas my weake one may be called in quaestion vpon any other occasion then this, where the conspicuity of truth beareth it out. SPENCER in what he saith hath a way of expression peculiar to him selfe; he bringeth downe the highest and deepest misteries that are contained in human learning, to an easy and gentle forme of deliuery: which sheweth he is Master of what he treateth of; he can wield it as he pleaseth: And this he hath done soe cunningly, that if one heed him not with great attention, rare and wonderful conceptions will vnperceived slide by him that readeth his works, & he will thinke he hath mett with nothing but familiar and easy discourses but let one dwell a while vpon them and he shall feele a straunge fulnesse and roundnesse in all he saith. The most generous wines tickle the palate least; but they are noe sooner in the stomach but by their warmth and strength there, they discouer what they are: And those streames that steale away with least noyse are vsually deepest, and most dangerous to pass ouer. His knowledge in profound learning both diuine and humane appeareth to me without controversie the greatest that any POET before him euer had, Excepting VIRGIL: Whom I dare not medle withall, otherwise then (as witty SCALIGER did) erecting an altar to him; And this his knowledge was not as many POETS are contented withall; which is but a meere sprinkling of seuerall superficiall notions to beautify their POEMS with; But he had a solide and deepe insight in THEOLOGIE, PHILOSOPHY (especially the PLATONIKE) and the MATHEMATICALL sciences, and in what others depend of these three, (as indeed all others doe). He was a Master of euery one of them: And where he maketh vse of any of them, it is not by gathering a posie out of others [sic] mens workes, but by spending of his owne stocke. And lastly where he treateth MORALL or POLITICAL learning, he giueth euidence of himself that he had a most excellently composed head to obserue and gouerne mens actions; & might haue bin eminent in the actiue part that way, if his owne choice or fortune had giuen him employment in the common wealth.

(b) *Observations on the 22. Stanza in the 9th Canto of the 2d. Book of Spencers Faery Queene* (1643, but written 1628):

My most honour'd Friend, I am too well acquainted with the weaknesses of mine abilities (far unfit to undergo such a Task as I have in hand) to flatter myself with the hope I may either inform your understanding, or do my self honour by what I am to write. But I am so desirous you should be possest with the true knowledge of what a bent will I have upon all occasions to do you service, that obedience to your command weigheth much more with me, then the lawfulnesse of any excuse can, to preserve me from giving you in writing such a testimonie of my ignorance and erring Phantasie as I fear this will prove. Therefore without any more circumstance, I will, as I can, deliver to you in this paper, what th'other day I discoursed to you upon the 22. Staffe of the ninth *Canto* in the second Book of that matchlesse Poem, *The Faery Queen*, written by our English *Virgil*; whose words are these:

[quotes stanza]

In this Staffe the Author seemes to me to proceed in a different manner from what he doth elsewhere generally though his whole Book. For in other places, although the beginning of his Allegory or mysticall sense, may be obscure, yet in the processe of it, he doth himself declare his own conceptions in such sort as they are obvious to any ordinary capacitie: But in this, he seems onely to glance at the profoundest notions that any Science can deliver us, and then on a sudden (as it were) recalling himself out of an Enthusiasme, he returns to the gentle Relation of the Allegoricall History he had begun, leaving his Readers to wander up and down in much obscuritie, & to come within much danger of erring at his Intention in these lines? Which I conceive to be dictated by such a learned Spirit, and so generally a knowing Soul, that were there nothing else extant of *Spencers* writing, yet these few words would make me esteeme him no whit inferiour to the most famous men that ever have been in any age: as giving evident testimonie herein, that he was thoroughly verst in the Mathematicall Sciences, in Philosophy, and in Divinity, to which this might serve for an ample Theme to make large Commentaries upon. In my praises upon this subject, I am confident that the worth of the Author will preserve me from this Censure, that my Ignorance onely begets this Admiration, since he hath written nothing that is not admirable. But that it may appear I am guided somewhat by my own Judgement (tho' it be a meane one) and not by implicite Faith, and that I may in the best manner I can, comply with what you expect from me, I will no longer hold you in suspense, but begin immediately, (tho' abruptly) with the declaration of what I conceive to be the true sense of this place, which

I shall not go about to adorne with any plausible examples drawne from other writings (since my want both of conveniency and learning would make me fall very short herein) but it shall be enough for me to intimate mine own conceptions, and offer them up to you in their own simple and naked form, leaving to your better Judgement the examination of the weight of them, and after perusall of them, beseeching you to reduce them and me if you perceive us erring.

Tis evident that the Authors intention in this *Canto* is to describe the bodie of a man inform'd with a rationall soul, and in prosecution of that designe he sets down particularly the severall parts of the one and of the other: But in this *Stanza* he comprehends the generall description of them both, as (being joyned together to frame a compleat Man) they make one perfect compound, which will the better appear by taking a survey of every severall clause thereof by it self.

> The Frame thereof seemed partly Circular,
> And part Triangular—

By these Figures, I conceive that he means the mind and body of Man; the first being by him compared to a Circle, and the latter to a Triangle. For as a Circle of all Figures is the most perfect, and includeth the greatest space, and is every way full and without Angles, made by the continuance of one onely line: so mans soul is the noblest and most beautifull Creature, that God hath created, and by it we are capable of the greatest gifts that God can bestow, which are Grace, Glory, and Hypostaticall Union of the Humane nature to the Divine, and she enjoyeth perfect freedome and libertie in all her Actions, and is made without composition, which no Figures are that have Angles (for they are caus'd by the coincidence of severall lines) but of one pure substance which was by God breath'd into a Body made of such compounded earth as in the preceding *Stanza* the Author describes. And this is the exact Image of him that breathed it, representing him as fully as tis possible for any creature which is infinitely distant from a Creator. For, as God hath neither beginning nor ending: so, neither of these can be found in a Circle, although that being made of the successive motion of a line, it must be supposed to have a beginning some where, but his circumference no where: But mans soul is a Circle, whose circumference is limited by the true center of it, which is onely God. For as a circumference doth in all parts alike respect that indivisible Point, and as all lines drawn from the inner side of it, do make right Angles within it, when they meet therein: so all the interiour actions of mans soul ought to have no other respective Point to direct themselves unto, but God; and as long as they make right Angles, which is, that they keep the exact middle of virtue, and decline not to either of the sides where the contrary vices dwell, they cannot fail, but meet in their Center. By the Triangular Figure he very aptly designes the body: for as the Circle is of all other Figures the most perfect and most capacious: so the Triangle is most imperfect, and includes least space. It is the first and lowest of all Figures; for fewer than 3 right Angles cannot comprehend and inclose a superficies, having but 3 angles they are all acute (if it be equilaterall) and but equall to 2 *right*; in which respect all other regular Figures consisting of more then 3 lines, do exceed it.

(May not these be resembled to the 3 great compounded Elements in mans bodie, to wit, Salt, Sulphur and Mercurie, which mingled together make the naturall heat and radicall moysture, the 2 qualities whereby man liveth?) For the more lines that go to comprehend the Figure, the more and the greater the Angles are, and the nearer it comes to the perfection and capacitie of a Circle. A Triangle is composed of severall lines, and they of Points, which yet do not make a quantitie by being contiguous to one another: but rather the motion of them doth describe the lines. In like manner the Body of man is compounded of the foure Elements which are made of the foure primarie qualities, not compounded of them (for they are but Accidents) but by their operation upon the first matter. And as a Triangle hath three lines, so a solid Body hath three dimensions, to wit, Longitude, Latitude and Profunditie. But of all bodies, Man is of the lowest rank, (as the Triangle is among Figures) being composed of the Elements which make it liable to alteration and corruption. In which consideration of the dignitie of bodies, I divide them by a generall division, into sublunarie (which are the elementated ones) and Aethereall, which are supposed to be of their own nature, incorruptible, and peradventure there are some other *species* of corporeall substances, which is not of this place to dispute.

O work divine!

Certainly of all Gods works, the noblest and perfectest is Man, and for whom indeed all others were done. For, if we consider his *soul*, it is the very Image of God. If his *bodie*, it is adornd with the greatest beautie and most excellent symmetry of parts, of any created thing: whereby it witnesseth the perfection of the Architect, that of so drossie mold is able to make so rare a fabrick: If his *operations*, they are free:

If his end, it is eternall glory. And if you take *all together*, Man is a little world, and of God himself. But in all this, me thinks, the admirablest work is the joyning together of the two *different* and indeed *opposite* substances in Man, to make one perfect compound; the *Soul* and the *Body*, which are of so contrary a nature, that their *uniting* seems to be a Miracle. For how can the one inform and work in the other, since there's no mean of operation (that we know of) between a spirituall substance and a corporeall? yet we see that it doth: as hard it is to find the true proportion betweene a Circle and a Triangle; yet, that there is a just proportion, and that they may be equall, *Archimedes* hath left us an ingenious demonstration; but in reducing it to a Probleme, it fails in this, that because the proportion between a crooked line and a straight one, is not known, one must make use of a Mechanick way of measuring the *peripherie* of the one, to convert it to the side of the other.

These two the first and last proportions are.

What I have already said concerning a Circle and a Triangle, doth sufficiently unfold what is meant in this verse. Yet twill not be amisse to speak one word more hereof in this place. All things that have existence, may be divided into three *Classes*; which are, either what is pure and simple in it self, or what hath a nature compounded of what is simple, or what hath a nature compounded of what is compounded. In continued quantitie this may be exemplified by a Point, a line, and a superficies in Bodies: and in numbers, by an unity, a Denary, and a Centenary. The first, which is onely pure & simple, like an indivisible point, or an unity, hath relation onely to the Divine nature: That point then moving in a sphericall manner (which serves to expresse the perfection of Gods actions) describes the Circles of our souls, and of Angels, and intellectual substances, which are of a pure and simple nature, but receiveth that from what is so, in a perfecter manner, and that hath his, from none else. Like lines that are made by the flowing of points; or Denaries that are composed of Unities: beyond both which there is nothing. In the last place, Bodies are to be rankt, which are composed of the Elements: and they likewise suffer composition, and may very well be compared to the lowest of the Figures which are composed of lines, that owe their being to Points (and such are Triangles) or to Centenaries that are composed of Denaries, and they of Unities. But if we will compare these together by proportion, God must be left out, since there is as infinite distance betweene the Simpli-

154

citie and Perfection of his nature, and the composition and imperfection of all created substances, as there is between an indivisible Point and a continuate quantitie, or between a simple Unitie and a compounded number. So that onely the other two kinds of substance do enter into this consideration: and of them I have already proved, that mans Soul is of the one the noblest, (being dignified by hypostaticall Union above all other intellectual substances) and his elementated Body, of the other the most low and corruptible. Whereby it is evident, that those two are the first and last Proportions, both in respect of their own Figure, and of what they expressed.

> The one imperfect, Mortall, Feminine:
> Th'other immortall, perfect, Masculine.

Mans Body hath all the proprieties of imperfect matter. It is but the Patient: of it self alone, it can do nothing: it is liable to corruption and dissolution if it once be deprived of the form which actuates it, and which is incorruptible and immortall. And as the feminine Sex is imperfect and receives perfection from the masculine: so doth the Body from the Soul, which to it is in lieu of a male. And as in corporall generations the female affords but grosse and passive matter, to which the Male gives active heat and prolificall vertue: so in spirituall generations (which are the operations of the minde) the body administers onely the Organs, which if they were not imployed by the Soul, would of themselves serve for nothing. And as there is a mutuall appetence between the Male and the Female, betweene matter and forme; So there is betweene the bodie and the soul of Man, but what ligament they have, our Author defineth not (and it may be Reason is not able to attaine to it) yet he tels us what is the foundation that this Machine rests on, and what keeps the parts together; in these words.

> And twixt them both, a Quadrate was the Base.

By which Quadrate, I conceive, that he meaneth the foure principall humors in mans Bodie, viz. *Choler, Blood, Phleme*, and *Melancholy*: which if they be distempered and unfitly mingled, dissolution of the whole doth immediately ensue: like to a building which falls to ruine, if the foundation and Base of it be unsound or disordered. And in some of these, the vitall spirits are contained and preserved, which the other keep in convenient temper; and as long as they do so, the soul and bodie dwell together like good friends: so that these foure are the Base of the conjunction of the other two, both which he saith, are

Proportion'd equally by seven and nine.

In which words, I understand he meanes the influences of the superior substances (which governe the inferiour) into the two differing parts of Man; to wit, of the *Starres* (the most powerfull of which, are the seven Planets, into his body: and of the Angels divided into nine Hierarchies or Orders into his soul: which in his *Astrophel*, he saith is

> By soveraigne choice from th'heavenly Quires select,
> And lineally deriv'd from Angels race.

And as much as the one governe the Body, so much the other do the Minde. Wherein is to be considered, that some are of opinion, how at the instant of a childs conception, or rather more effectually at the instant of his Birth, the conceived sperme or tender Body doth receive such influence of the Heavens as then raigne over that place, where the conception or birth is made: And all the Starres or virtuall places of the celestiall Orbes participating the qualities of the seven Planets (according to which they are distributed into so many Classes, or the compounds of them) it comes to passe, that according to the varitie of the severall Aspects of the one and of the other, there are various inclinations and qualities in mens bodies, but all reduced to seven generall heads and the compounds of them, which being to be varied innumerable wayes, cause as many different effects, yet the influence of some one Planet continually predominating. But when the matter in a womans wombe is capable of a soul to inform it, then God sendeth one from Heaven into it.

> Eternall God,
> In Paradise whilome did plant this Flower,
> Whence he it fetcht out of her native place,
> And did in Stock of earthly flesh inrace.
> [*Faerie Queene* III. v. 52].

And this opinion the Author more plainly expresses himself to be of, in another work, where he saith:

> There she beholds with high aspiring thought
> The cradle of her own Creation;
> Emongst the seats of Angels heavenly wrought.
> [*Colin Clout* 612-4].

Which whether it have been created ever since the beginning of the world, and reserv'd in some fit place till due time, or be created on

156

emergent occasion; no man can tell: but certain it is, that it is immortall, according to what I said before, when I spake of the Circle which hath no ending, and an uncertain beginning. The messengers to conveigh which soul into the bodie, are the Intelligences which move the Orbes of Heaven, who according to their severall natures communicate to it severall proprieties: and they most, who are Governours of those Starres at that instant, who have the superioritie in the planetary aspects. Whereby it comes to passe, that in all inclinations there's much affinitie betweene the Soul and the Body, being that the like is betweene the Intelligences and the Starres, both which communicate their vertues to each of them. And these Angels, being, as I said before, of nine severall Hierarchies, there are so many principle differences in humane souls, which participate most of their proprieties, with whom in their descent they made the longest stay, and that had most active power to work on them, and accompanied them with a peculiar *Genius* (which is according to their severall Governments) like the same kind of water that running through various conduits wherein severall aromatike and odoriferous things are laid, do acquire severall kinds of tastes and smels. For it is supposed, that in their first Creation, all Souls are alike, and that their differing proprieties arive to them afterwards when they passe through the spheres of the governing Intelligences. So that by such their influence, it may truly be said, that

> Nine was the Circle set in Heavens place.

Which verse, by assigning this office to the nine, and the proper place to the Circle, gives much light to what is said before. And for a further confirmation that this is the Authors opinion, read attentively the sixt *Canto* of the 3. Book, where most learnedly and at large he delivers the *Tenets* of this Philosophie; and for that, I commend to you to take particular notice of the 2d. and thirty two *Stanzaes*: as also the last of his *Epithalamion*: and survaying his works, you shall finde him a constant disciple of *Platoes* School.

> All which compacted, made a goodly Diapase.

In Nature there is not to be found a more compleat and more exact Concordance of all parts, then that which is betweene the compaction and conjunction of the Body and Soul of Man: Both which although they consist of many and most different faculties and parts, yet when they keepe due time with one another, they altogether make the most perfect Harmony that can be imagined. And as the nature of sounds,

that consist of friendly consonancies and accords, is to mingle themselves with one another, and to slide into the eare with much sweet-
nesse, where by their unity they last a long time and delight it: where
as contrarily, discords continually jarre, and fight together, and will
not mingle with one another: but all of them striving to have the
victory, their reluctation and disorder gives a speedie end to their
sounds, which strike the Eare in a harsh and offensive manner, and
there die in the very beginning of their Conflict: In like manner, when
a mans Actions are regular, and directed towards God, they become
like the lines of a Circle, which all meet in the Center, then his musick
is most excellent and compleat, and all together are the Authors of that
blessed harmony which maketh him happie in the glorious vision of
Gods perfections, wherein the minde is filled with high knowledges and
most pleasing contemplations; and the senses, as it were, drowned in
eternall delight; and nothing can interrupt this Joy, this Happinesse,
which is an everlasting Diapase: Whereas on the contrary, if a mans
actions be disorderly, and consisting of discords, (which is, when the
sensitive part rebels and wrastles with the Rationall, striving to oppresse
it) then this musick is spoiled, and instead of eternall life, pleasure and
joy, it causeth perpetuall death, horrour, paine, and misery. Which
infortunate estate the Poet describes elsewhere; as in the conclusion of
this Staffe he intimates: the other happy one, which is the never-
failing Reward of such an obedient bodie, and ethereall and vertuous
minde, as he makes to be the seat of the bright Virgin *Alma*, mans
worthiest inhabitant, *Reason. Her* I feele to speake within me, and chide
me for my bold Attempt, warning me to stray no further. For what I
have said (considering how weakly it is said) your Command is all the
excuse that I can pretend. But since my desire to obey that, may bee
seene as well in a few lines, as in a large Discourse, it were indiscretion
in me to trouble you with more, or to discover to you more of my
Ignorance. I will onely begge pardon of you for this blotted and
interlined paper, whose Contents are so meane that it cannot deserve
the paines of a Transcription, which if you make difficulty to grant it,
for my sake, let it obtain it for having been yours.

And now I return to you also the Book that contains my Text, which
yesterday you sent me, to fit this part of it with a Comment, which
peradventure I might have performed better, if either I had afforded
my selfe more time, or had had the conveniencie of some other books
apt to quicken my Invention, to whom I might have been beholding
for enlarging my understanding in some things that are treated here,

although the Application should still have been my own: With these helps perhaps I might have dived further into the Authors Intention (the depth of which cannot be sounded by any that is lesse learned than he was). But I perswade my self very strongly, that in what I have said there's nothing contradictory to it, and that an intelligent and well learned man proceeding on my grounds might compose a worthie and true Commentarie on this Theme: Upon which I wonder how I stumbled, considering how many learned men have failed in the Interpretation of it, and have all at the first hearing, approved my opinion.

But it was Fortune that made me fall upon it, when first this Stanza was read to me for an indissoluble Riddle. And the same Discourse I made upon it, the first halfe quarter of an houre that I saw it, I send you here, without having reduced it to any better form, or added any thing at all unto it.

72. Nicholas Ferrar

1630s

Nicholas Ferrar (1592–1637) was a Fellow of Clare Hall, Cambridge, but, like his friend George Herbert, withdrew from academic and public life to give himself to religion and letters. The two short passages below betray a mistrust of the whole tradition of heroic poetry – one shared perhaps, but overcome, by Milton. The *Story Books* date from after 1631.

(a) From *The Story Books of Little Gidding*, B.M. MS. Add. 34657, fols. 108ᵛ–9; repr. in edition of E. Cruwys Sharland (1899), p. 119:

. . . and now I see *the* reason, Why not onely Virgill & Homere, but Ariosto & Spencer & all other bookes of Chevalry, bring in their fayned worthies so defectiue in Patience. Mans witt can well enough, I perceiue, fitt all other weapons of Christian Religion to serue the worlds turnes even against religion; but onely Patience, thats too weighty to bee put on a Counterfeit. Hee must bee a Christian in earnest & not in appearance, that weares this peice of Armour. Which because these famous Deuices want, however compleat in the height of all other vertues they bee made, I cannot allow them to passe for good Examples of vertue amongst Christians.

73. Peter Heylyn

1631, 1652

Peter Heylyn (1600–62) was educated at Hart Hall and Magdalen College, Oxford, and became a Fellow of the second. At Oxford he lectured on historical geography, and successively over the years developed those lectures to yield the various editions of the *Microcosmus*. In the first edition (1621) he mentions Spenser along with Drayton and Daniel as 'chiefe in the matter of Poesie' in modern times, and already begins to use Spenser ornamentally in talking of Ptolemy's tower (p. 392). Predictably enough, mention of Spenser's treatment of the marriage of Thames and Medway finds its way into the second edition (1625). These incidental reference I have not recorded. Below can be found his remarks on St George, and his remarks on Fairy Land.

(a) From *The Historie of that most Famous Saint and Souldier of Christ Iesus St George of Cappadochia Asserted from the Fictions of the Middle Ages of the Church and opposition of the present* (1631), pp. 22–3:

(8) To this Relation, of his being borne of *English* Parentage, our admir'd *Spencer*, although poetically, doth seeme to give some countenance: where he brings in his *holy Hermite, heavenly Contemplation*, thus laying to St. *George*, the *Red-crosse Knight*, his Parentage and Country [quotes *Faerie Queene* I. x. 65–6].

Ibid., pp. 68–9:

Aeneas is not therefore to bee thought a Knight of *Faery Land*, the issue of an idle braine, a fiction or *Non ens*; because the Poets hath expres'd him, with some additions more than reall.

Ibid., p. 124:

The name of GEORGE, not to proceed in it more Grammatically, is originally Greeke: deriv'd Ἀπὸ τῶ Γεωργεῖν, which is; To till the Earth, or to play the Ploughman. It signifieth an Husband-man; and therefore Suidas doth expound the name by Γεωπόνος, a Tiller, or Labourer of the Earth. So *Camden*, in his *Remaines*, George, gr. *Husband-man*, the same with *Agricola*: and thereunto the famous *Spencer* thus alludeth in the wordes before recited [quotes *Faerie Queene* I. x. 66];

Ibid., p. 296:

From henceforth therefore, we must not looke upon *St.* GEORGE, as a Saint in generall; but as conceived, (such was the superstition of those times) the speciall Patron of the *English*: of which, the *Pilgrim* in the *Poet*, thus prophecieth unto his *Red-crosse Knight*, as hee there calls him [quotes *Faerie Queene* I. x. 61].

(b) From *Cosmographie in foure Bookes* (1652), p. 196 (Bk. IV):

4. FAERIE LAND, is another part of this *Terra Incognita*; the inhabitation of the *Faeries*, a pretty kind of *little fiends*, or *Pigmey devils*, but more inclined to sport then mishief; of which old Women, who remember the times of *Popery*, tell us many fine stories. A cleanlyer and more innocent cheat was never put opon poor ignorant people, by the *Monks* and *Friers*. Their habitation here or no where; though sent occasionally by *Oberon* and their other Kings, to our parts of the World. For not being reckoned amongst the *good Angels*, nor having malice enough to make them *Devils* (but such a kind of midling *Sprites*, as the *Latines* call *Lemures Larvae*) we must find out some place for them, neither *Heaven* or *Hell*, and most likely this. Their Country never more enobled, then by being made the Scene of that excellent Poem, called the *Faerie Queen*. Intended to the honour of Queen *Elizabeth*, and the greatest persons in her Court: but shadowed in such lively colours, framed so exactly by the Rules of *Poesie*, and represent-

ing such *Idaeas* of all moral goodness; that as there never was a *Poem* more *Artificial*; so can no *Ethical* discourse, more fashion and inflame the mind to a love of vertue. *Invisurum facilius aliquem quam imitaturum*, shall be *Spencers Motto*; and so I leave him to his rest.

74. John Milton

1631–49

John Milton (1608–74) was taught by Gill (*q.v.*) at St Paul's School, and from there proceeded to Christ's College, Cambridge. Humphrey Moseley in the prefatory epistle to the reader of the *Poems* (1645) writes that Milton's efforts have produced 'as true a Birth, as the Muses have brought forth since our famous *Spencer* wrote; whose poems in these English ones are as rarely imitated, as sweetly excell'd.' Rarely can publishers' promises be so sweetly fulfilled. In Milton's prose, the allusions to Spenser are disappointingly scrappy, and I have included here passages where a reference to Spenser might be disputed.

(a) From *Il Penseroso* II. 116–21 (written 1631?) in Poems (1645), pp. 41–2; repr. *Works*, gen. ed. F. A. Patterson (Columbia Univ. Press, 1931–40), I. 44:

> And if ought els, great *Bards* beside,
> In sage and solemn tunes have sung,
> Of Turney's and of Trophies hung;
> Of Forests, and inchantments drear,
> Where more is meant than meets the ear.

(b) From *Animadversions upon the Remonstrants Defence. Against Smectymnuus* (1641), pp. 58–9; repr. Columbia, III. 165–7:

Let the novice learne first to renounce the world, and so give himselfe to God, and not therefore give himselfe to God, that hee may close the better with the World, like that false Shepherd *Palinode* in the eclogue of *May*, under whom the Poet lively personates our Prelates, whose whole life is a recantation of their pastorall vow, and whose profession to forsake the World, as they use the matter, boggs them deeper into the world: those our admired *Spencer* inveighs against, not without some presage of these reforming times.

(c) From *The Reason of Church-government Urg'd against prelaty* (1641), p. 63; repr. Columbia, III. 275:

Him our old patron St. George by his matchlesse valour slew, as the Prelat of the Garter that reads his Collect can tell. And if our Princes and Knights will imitate the fame of that old champion, as by their order of Knighthood solemnly taken, they vow, farre be it that they should uphold and side with this English Dragon; but rather to doe as indeed their oath binds them, they should make it their Knightly adventure to pursue & vanquish this mighty sailewing'd monster that menaces to swallow up the Land, unlesse her bottomlesse gorge may be satisfi'd with the blood of the Kings daughter the Church.

(d) From *An Apology against a Pamphlet call'd A Modest Confutation of the Animadversations* (1642), pp. 16–17; repr. Columbia, III. 304:

I betook me among those lofty Fables and Romances, which recount in solemne canto's the deeds of Knighthood founded by our victorious Kings; & from hence had in renowne over all Christendome. There I read it in the oath of every Knight, that he should defend to the expence of his best blood, or of his life, if it so befell him, the honour and chastity of Virgin or Matron. From whence even then I learnt what a noble vertue chastity sure must be, to the defence of which so many worthies by such a deare adventure of themselves had sworne.

(e) From *Areopagitica* (1644), sigs. B3ᵛ–B4; repr. Columbia, IV. 311:

That vertue therefore which is but a youngling in the contemplation of evill, and knows not the utmost that vice promises to her followers, and rejects it, is but a blank vertue, not a pure; her whitenesse is but an excrementall whitenesse; Which was the reason why our sage and serious Poet *Spencer*, whom I dare be known to think a better teacher then *Scotus* or *Aquinas*, describing true temperance under the person of *Guion*, brings him in with his palmer through the cave of Mammon, and the bowr of earthly blisse that he might see and know, and yet abstain.

[The error here (the palmer does not enter the cave of Mammon) is in itself enlightening.]

(f) From *Eikonoklastes* (1649), p. 34; repr. Columbia, V. 110:

If there were a man of iron, such as *Talus*, by our Poet *Spencer*, is fain'd to be, the page of Justice, who with his iron flaile could doe all this, and expeditiously, without those deceitfull formes and circumstances of law, worse then ceremonies in religion; I say God send it don, whether by one *Talus*, or by a thousand.

75. Henry Reynolds

1632

Henry Reynolds (*flor. c.* 1630) was the friend to whom Drayton addressed his Epistle *Of Poets and Poesie*. He was a poet and a translator of Tasso.

From *Mythomystes Wherein a Short Survey Is Taken of the Nature and Value of True Poesy* (1632), p. 8; repr. J. E. Spingarn, *Critical Essays of the Seventeenth Century* (Oxford, 1908–9), I. 147:

I must approue the learned *Spencer*, in the rest of his Poëms, no lesse then his *Fairy Queene*, an exact body of the Ethicke doctrine: though some good iudgments haue wisht (and perhaps not without cause) that he had therein beene a little freer of his fiction, and not so close riuetted to his Morall.

76. E.C.

1632

It is possible that E.C. is Ezekiel Clarke, the friend of Phineas Fletcher; but this identification is no more than a guess. The poem from which these lines are taken is written against one John Vicars, and must immediately postdate his *XII Aeneids of Virgil* (1632).

From *Vindiciae Virgilianae*, Bodleian MS. Ashmole 38, fol. 130:
Virgil awake . . .

Spencer a wake thee from thy clayeie bed
Let tyme throw of deathes dusty coverlid;
Knocke up they Tytirus too, that bard of yore
Who sleeps close by thee, at next marble dore
Chaucer now scower thy rustye gat, and fyer
Stricke from his Flinty pate, who first did mare
The muses garden *with* his common shere
And stencht thes flowers, *with* Nessus poysnous gore,
That Garden wheare thy choysest flowers grew
Those flowers from whence thy bees ther honye drew
Spencer a wake thee see heer's one hos spoyld
Those Mantuan gemms, and their true Luster soyld
Those gemms, where *with* a round embellisht been
Th'embroydred robes of thy blest Fayrie Queen
Lett hym bee Counted as the mad dog starve
In thy everlasting sheppardes Callendar,
Spencer a wake the lett this scribler knowe
he doth a scorne to all the muses owe.
Thy tunes heroick for a scourg exchange
And whip from Phoebus hostes this made doges Mange.
Johnson a wake . . .

77. Phineas Fletcher

1633

Phineas Fletcher (1582–1650) was brother of Giles, and a Fellow of King's College. The two brothers together are the leaders of the neo-Spenserian school. The influence of Spenser on Phineas is dealt with in tabular form by A. B. Langdale in *Phineas Fletcher Man of Letters, Science and Divinity* (New York, 1937), Appendix B. The passages below reflect at once the pervasiveness of Spenser's influence, and the atmosphere of sentimental adulation created around Spenser by members of the school. Quarles overstates when he calls Phineas Fletcher 'the Spencer of this age'.

(a) From *The Purple Island, or the Isle of Man: together with Piscatorie Eclogs and other Poeticall Miscellanies* (1633), p. 6 (i. 19–21); repr. in *The Poetical Works of Giles Fletcher and Phineas Fletcher*, ed. F. S. Boas (Cambridge, 1908–9), II. 16:

> Witnesse our *Colin*;* whom though all the Graces,
> And all the Muses nurst; whose well taught song
> *Parnassus* self, and *Glorian* embraces,
> And all the learn'd and all the shepherds throng;
>   Yet all his hopes were crost, all suits deni'd;
>   Discourag'd, scorn'd, his writing vilifi'd:
> Poorly (poore man) he liv'd; poorly (poore man) he di'd.
>
> And had not that great *Hart*, (whose honour'd head
> Ah lies full low) piti'd thy wofull plight;
> There hadst thou lien unwept, unburied,
> Unblest, nor grac't with any common rite:
>   Yet shalt thou live, when thy great foe shall sink
>   Beneath his mountain tombe, whose fame shall stink;
> And time his blacker name shall blurre with blackest ink.

* Spencer.

O let th'Iambick Muse revenge that wrong,
Which cannot slumber in thy sheets of lead:
Let thy abused honour crie as long
As there be quills to write, or eyes to reade:
  On his rank name let thine own votes be turn'd,
  Oh may that man that hath the Muses scorn'd,
Alive, nor dead, be ever of a Muse adorn'd!

(b) *Ibid.*, p. 66 (vi. 5); repr. Boas, II. 70:

Two shepherds most I love with just adoring;
That *Mantuan* swain, who chang'd his slender reed
To trumpets martiall voice, and warres loud roaring,
From *Corydon* to *Turnus* derring-deed:
  And next our home-bred *Colins* sweetest firing;
  Their steps not following close, bur farre admiring:
To lackey one of these is all my prides aspiring.

(c) *Ibid.*, p. 77 (vi. 51–2); repr. Boas, II. 80:

But let my song passe from these worthy Sages
Unto this Islands highest Soveraigne,★
And those hard warres which all the yeare he wages:
For these three late a gentle shepherd-swain
  Most sweetly sung, as he before had seen
  In *Alma's* house: his memorie yet green
Lives in his well-tun'd songs, whose leaves immortal been.

Nor can I guesse, whether his Muse divine
Or gives to those, or takes from them his grace;
Therefore *Eumnestes* in his lasting shrine
Hath justly him enroll'd in second place:
  Next to our *Mantuan* poet doth he rest;
  There shall our *Colin* live for ever blest,
Spite of those thousand spites, which living him opprest.

(d) *Ibid.*, new pagination pp. 65–6 (*To my beloved Thenot*, Stanzas 2–3,
in *Piscatorie Eclogs* . . .); repr. Boas, II. 231–2:

★ The understanding.

But if my Thenot love my humble vein,
(Too lowly vein) ne're let him *Colin* call me;
He, while he was, was (ah!) the choicest swain,
That ever grac'd a reed: what e're befall me,
Or *Myrtil*, (so'fore *Fusca* fair did thrall me,
Most was I know'n) or now poore *Thirsil* name me,
Thirsil, for so my *Fusca* pleases frame me:
But never mounting *Colin*; *Colin's* high stile will shame me.

Two shepherds I adore with humble love;
Th'high-towring swain, that by slow *Mincius* waves
His well-grown wings at first did lowly prove,
Where *Corydon's* sick love full sweetly raves;
But after sung bold *Turnus* daring braves:
And next our nearer *Colin's* sweetest strain;
Most, where he most his *Rosalind* doth plain.
Well may I after look, but follow all in vain.

78. Robert Jegon

c. 1633

Robert Jegon is the son of John Jegon, Bishop of Norwich.
Ralph Knevett's *Supplement* (*q.v.*) was for a long time attributed
to him. See C. Bowie Millican, 'Ralph Knevett, Author of the
Supplement to Spenser's *Faerie Queene*', *RES*, XIV (1938), 45.

Spencero Posthumo prefatory to *A Supplement to the Faery Queene*,
Cambridge University Library MS. Ee. 3. 53:

You strive, O Spenser, to complete Herculean labours; alas, fates
hostile to things begun deny the completion, but the Pierian sisters

prevent you from perishing; behold, Posthumous will set sail to your fame: and just as the bird nourished on the Pharian shore rejoices to have restored the heavens by his own funeral pile, even so do the ages exult that our poet by his own pen has brought Spencer to life. You are writing poetry, O Renewed One, worthy of yourself and of the Muses: nor is your courage less; your fame will be everlasting.

> *Perficere Herculeos perges (Spencere) labores;*
> *Heu finem caeptis invida fata negant,*
> *At te Pierides prohibent periisse sorores;*
> *Vela dabit famae Posthumus tuae:*
> *Et veluti Pharia Volucris nutritus in ora,*
> *Gaudet axem proprio restituisse rogo:*
> *Haud aliter nostrum laetantur saecula Vatem,*
> *Spencerum calamo viuificesse suc.*
> *Dignam te, Musisque refers (rediuiue) poesin,*
> *Nec minor est virtus, fama perennis erit.*

79. Ralph Knevett

c. 1633

Ralph Knevett (1600–61) was Rector of Lyng in Norfolk. His shorter poems are very much in the manner of Herbert, but his longest and most ambitious piece, the *Supplement*, is pastiche of Spenser. Knevett suppressed the work for political reasons (see Sheppard) and it has never been published, though edited in 1955 by Andrew Lavender (New York University Ph.D. Dissertation). The *Supplement* remains in any case incomplete. Knevett finished the first three Books of his continuation in 1635 but, as far as is known, did not write the other three planned 'to make this Zodiacke perfect' (p. xv).

From *A Supplement of the Faery Queene, in three Bookes. Wherein are allegorically described Affaires both military and ciuill of these times*, Cambridge University Library MS. Ee. 3. 53, fols. vii–ix, xv:

The end of writeing Bookes, should be rather to informe the vnderstanding, then please the fancy: I haue knowne many great witts, as ambitious as Ixion, committ adultery with the clouds, and begett Monsters, either as deformed, as that absurd picture which Horace speaketh of in his Booke de Arte Poet. or like the Thebane Sphinx, vttering vnnecessary aenigmaes. Such volumes, or (like the Ghost of Euridice) vanish as soone as they are view'd, or stand as trophyes, of their Authors vanityes to posterity: But if the sayeing of the Poet stands for an infallible truth:

> Omne tulit punctum, qui miscuit vtile dulci
> [Horace, *Ars Poetica* 343]

Then our learned Spencer through whose whole Booke, a Grace seemes to walke arme in arme with a Muse, did merit best an honorarye garlande, from that Tree which Petrarch calleth

Arbor vittoriosa, triumphale,
Honor d'Imperadori, e di Poeti.
[Petrarch, *Rime* CCLXIII]

The worke being such

Quod nec Cecropia damnent Pandionis arces.
[Martial, *Epigrammata* I. xxvi. 3]

Homer the fountaine of the arts, yea from whom graue Philosophy
deriues her pedigree, did first deuise that kind of heroicke poesy,
which is of force, not onely to temper the affections, but also to rectifye
the will, and direct the vnderstanding. Wee reade of Agamemnon,
that hee beinge ingaged in the Troiane expedition, left a Doricke
Musicion to attend vpon his Wife Clytemnestra, who with his graue
spondaicke numbers, maintained in her such a coniugall chastity, that
Ageisthus the Adulterer, could no way tempt her to lightnes, vntill he
had cruelly destroyed this harmonious Guardian of her vertue. Euen
so doth diuine Poesye, excite the ingenious, such an ardent affection of
goodnes, and detestation of fice, that precepts taken either from Platos
Academye, or Aristotles Lycaeum, produce not the like effects:
Therefore did Horace write thus to his friend:

Troiani belli scriptorem, (Maxime Lolli)
Dum tu declamas Romae, Praenesti velegi,
Qui quid sit pulchrum, quid turpe, quid vtile, quid non,
Plenius, ac melius Chrysippo, et Crantore dicet.
[Horace, *Epistolae* I. ii. 1]

Homer in his Ilias, hath made Agamemnon . . . the patteren of a wise
Gouernour, and Vlysses in his Odysseis . . . the example of a Wise Man.
Virgill after him, in the Person of his Pius Aeneas, described a good
Gouernour, and an honest Man: Ariosto did the like in his Orlando.
But Tasso hath deduced these two regiments of vertues, politicall, and
morall, from two seuerall Persons, makeing Godfredo the fountaine of
Politickes, or those qualityes, which ought to bee inherent in a Gouernour, and Rinaldo the subiect of Ethickes; vertues pertaineing to a
priuate Man. But our late Spencer building his fabricke vpon the like
foundation, hath contriu'd his worke so symmetrically, that his
methode appeareth farre more exquisite, then theirs, hee haueing
designed twelue Bookes, for the tractation of twelue seuerall vertues:
which with their branches, allyes, and opposites, are so exactly by him
handled, in those sixe Bookes which he hath written, that I haue seene

many treatises fraught with more sophistry, but few with more sapience.

[quotes Letter to Ralegh]

Thus farre hath Mr Spencer declared his intention, from which auiso (doubtles) the ingenious Reader may without much labour investigate the Authors meaning, and rightly understand this Poeme, which is onely an exact treatise of Morall Philosophy, enveloped in an Allegorical Romance.

80. William Austin

before 1634

William Austin (1587–1634), professionally a barrister, was writer of a number of religious works. His literary activity in this field won him a place on the list of members of the projected Royal Society of Literature in 1620. On the pieces below see E. A. Strathmann, 'William Austin's "Notes" on *The Faerie Queene*', *Huntington Library Bulletin*, XI (1937), 155–60, and on the second piece see Carroll Camden, 'The Architecture of Spenser's "House of Alma"', *MLN*, LVIII (1943), 262–5, and Alastair Fowler, *Spenser and the Numbers of Time* (1964), 260 ff. See also Digby, in No. 71b.

(a) From *Deuotionis Augustinianae Flamma, or Certaine Deuout, Godly and Learned Meditations* (1635), p. 249:

Wherefore, since *Man* is (here) made a *Spectacle* to *Men and Angels*, fighting against the *World*, the *Flesh*, and the *Devill*, (*strong Enemies, and weake warriours*) therefore hee hath *charged these heavenly Soldiers* to ayde us *militant*, against *their*, and our *common-Enemies*: and, to *pitch their Tents round about us*: like *Fellow-Soldiers*, fighting *one*, and the *same Quarrell*.

[Cf. *Faerie Queene* II. viii. 1–2, quoted later, p. 255]

(b) From *Haec Homo, Wherein the Excellency of the Creation is described, By way of an Essay* (1637), pp. 75–80:

But, whether this *building* (for the *Form*) were *square*; like a *castle*, or *cornerd* like a *triangle*: or *round*; like a *tower*: or, like a *Roman* H. according to *most* of our *modern aedifices*, is partly questionable.

To this, must be answered; that it is made in *all the Geometricall* proportions, that are, or can be imagined: For, as all *Numbers* and *proportions*, for measure, (both of *inches, spannes, digits, cubits, feet,* &c.) are derived from the *members*, and dimensions of the *humane body*: so is the *body* answerable to *all proportions, buildings,* and *figures,* that are. Not onely answerable (I say) to the *whole world,* (of which it is an *epitome*) but, for the most part, to every particular *figure, character, building* and *fabrick,* in the World.

As for example (to give a *light* of *some,* instead of the *rest*): if the *armes* be stretched *forth-right,* from each *side,* in manner of a *Crucifix*; the *body* standing upright; and the *feet together*; it makes a *perfect Square.* For, it is just so much *in length,* from the *one midle fingers end,* crosse over the body, to the *other,* as it is in *length,* from the *head,* to the *heele*: Which is a *just square,* in *Geometricall* proportion. Which was the form of the *Temple,* and of the *mysticall Church,* in the *Revelation.*

Likewise, when the *body* stands in *that* form, draw a *line* from *each hand,* to the feet, and it makes a just *Triangle*: which is a *figure* of the *Trinitie.* Againe, let the hands fall *somewhat stradling a little* with the *legges*; and then, the *extreames* of the *fingers, head,* and *toes,* make a just *circle*; the *navell* or *bottome* of the belly being *center,* which is a *true figure* of the *Earth.* Moreover, elevate the *hands* againe, so that the *feet* (stradling) may imitate a Saint *Andrews Crosse*; and you may draw from this figure a true form of the *twelve houses* of the *seven Planets* in Heaven; All which *discourse* concerning the *severall proportions* of the body, are very elegantly and briefly contracted, by the *late dead Spencer,* * in his *everliving Fairy Queen*; where, coming to describe the *house of Alma,* (which, indeed, is no *other* but the *body*; the *habitation* of the Soule), he saith.

[quotes *Faerie Queene* II. ix. 22]

* *Mr. Spencer dyed above 30 yeares agon.*

81. George Wither

1641

George Wither (1588–1667) left Magdalen College, Oxford, without a degree, and studied law in London. The piece below, without mentioning Spenser's name, leaves little doubt about the identity of its subject. Wither was himself a poet of the Spenserian School, and was associated with William Browne.

From *Halelviah* . . . (1641), sigs. A8^{v}–A9:

Another sort of *Poesie*, is the Delivery of necessary Truths, and wholesome Documents, couched in so significant *Parables*; and illustrated by such flowres of Rhetorick, as are helpfull to work upon the Affections, and to insinuate into Apprehensive Readers, a liking of those Truths, and Instructions, which they expresse.

These *Inventions*, are most acceptable to those who have ascended the middle Region of *Knowledge*; For, though the wisest men make use of them in their writings; yet, they are not the wisest men for whose sake they are used. This *Poesie* is frequently varyed, according to the severall Growths, Ages, and Alterations of that *Language*, wherein it is worded: and, that, which this day is approved of as an elegancy, may seeme lesse facetious in another Age. For which cause, such *Compositions*, may be resembled to *Garments* of whole Silke, adorned with gold lace: For while the Stuffe, shape and trimming, are in fashion, they are a fit wearing for *Princes*; and (the *Materials* being unmangled) may continue useful to some purposes, for some other persons.

82. Henry More

1642–64

Henry More (1614–87) was educated at Christ's College (too late to have known Milton) and remained there as a Fellow. He is best known for his association with the group known as Cambridge Platonists. His Platonism may have predisposed him to an appreciation of Spenser, in whom at any rate he took great interest and to whom as a poet he is both generally and locally indebted. Thomas Vaughan in *The Man Mouse Taken in a Trap* (1650) calls him 'a *Poet* in the *Loll* & *Trot* of *Spencer*' (sig. A2ᵛ) and seems to enjoy making other insulting reference to More's particular predilection for the poet.

(a) From Ψυχωδία *Platonica or a Platonicall Song of the Soul* (1642) in *Philosophical Poems* (1647), sig. A2ᵛ (*Psychzoia, To his dear Father* . . .) repr. *Philosophical Poems*, ed. G. Bullough (Manchester, 1931), p. 1:

You deserve the Patronage of better Poems then these, though you may lay a more proper claim to these then any. You having from my childhood tuned mine ears to Spencers rhymes, entertaining us on winter nights, with that incomparable Peice of his, *The Fairy Queen*, a Poem richly fraught with divine Morality as Phansy.

Ibid., sig. B7ᵛ (*To the Reader* . . .); repr. Bullough, p. 8:

. . . Why may it not be free for me to break out into an higher strain, and under it to touch upon some points of Christianity; as well as all-approved *Spencer*, sings of Christ under the name of *Pan*?

(b) From *Conjectura Cabbalistica* (1653), p. 226:

It is much that *Philo* should take no notice of that which is so particularly set down in the Text, *the subtilty of the Serpent*, which methinks is notorious in *Pleasure*, it looking so smoothly and innocently on't, and insinuating it self very easily into the minds of men upon that consideration, and so deceiving them; whenas other Passions cannot so slily surprise us, they bidding more open warre to the quiet and happiness of mans life, as that judicious Poet *Spenser* has well observed in his Legend of Sir *Guyon* or *Temperance*.

(c) From *An Explanation of The grand Mystery of Godliness* (1660), pp. 169–70 (chap. 14):

Methinks *Spencer's** description of *Una*'s Entertainment by Satyrs in the Desart, does lively set out the condition of Christianity since the time that the Church of a Garden becam a *Wilderness*. They danc'd and frisk'd and play'd about her, abounding with externall homages and observances; but she could not inculcate any thing of that *Divine law of life* that she was to impart to them. The Representation is so lively, and the Verses so musical, that it will not be tedious to recite some of the chief of them; as Stanza 11, where he makes the Satyrs to lay aside their rudeness and roughness as much as they could to revive the dismayed Virgin after her great Distress.

(d) From *Philosophical Writings of Dr Henry More* (1662), p. 148:

Whereas therefore it is said that these *Flaming Cherubims* keep the way to the Tree of Life, being placed before the Garden of *Eden*, it is but such a sense as when Hesiod sayes, *That God has made Labour the porter of the Gate of Vertue*; and in such as *Virgil* places *Grief*, and *Care*, and *Sickness*, and *Old Age* at the entrance of *Orcus*. . . . Of which certainly there is no other sense in either place, then that by being *laborious* a man shall attain unto Vertue, and no otherwaies; and that by being overcharged with *Care*, *Grief*, *Sickness*, or *Old Age*, a man shall be sent packing into the state of the dead. So *Spencer*, to omit several other instances in him, in making those two grave personages, *Humilita* and *Ignaro*, the one the Porter of the House of Holiness, the other of the Castle of *Duessa*, can understand nothing else thereby but this, That he that would enter into the House of Holiness must be like *Humilita*, an humble man; and he that can conscientiously passe into the communialty of the imposturous *Duessa*, must be a very *Ignaro*.

* In his *Fairy Queen*, Book 1 Cant 6.

(e) From *The Apology of Dr Henry More* in *A Modest Inquiry into the Mystery of Iniquity* (1664), pp. 514–15:

My observation of Passages in the late great change of affairs in this Nation has given me too great occasion to surmise so, and made me look upon *Spencer* as a *Prophet* as well as *Poet*, in his second Eclogue, he has so lively set down the effects of the extirpation of *Episcopacy* upon the *Presbyters* themselves, when once that great shelter of Church-Government was removed. For when the Lord of the Field had cut down the aged and sacred *Oak*, having been complained to by the busie *Briar* that had a minde to domineer alone, pretending forsooth that the spreading *Oak* hundered his tender growth, keeping off the light of the Sun, and spoiling his beautiful Flowers with dropping of his hoary moss upon them; the *Briar* wanting this shelter against greater storms was utterly born down by the next Winterly weather, and troden into the dirt by Beasts. His condition is so lively described in the Poet, that I have thought it worth transcribing. After he has set out the dismal fall of the Oak.

The *Apodosis* is easie, though it were demanded in rhyme. But no semblance of mirth can well suit with so sad a consideration. Nothing were more desirable than that all men would lay aside any sense they have of their popular faculties, and make use of their talents to the common Interest of the Reformed Christianity, and not seek a victory over those who are their most impregnable shelter against their greatest enemies. This intimation is enough for them that are willing to see, and all that I can say will be nothing to as many as are wilfully blind.

[*Cf.* John Worthington, *Diary and Correspondence*, ed. J. Crossley (1847–86), II. 344–5.]

83. George Daniel

1646

George Daniel of Beswick (1616–57), studious and reserved, lived on private means. As a poet, he writes most under the influence of Daniel and Drayton.

(a) From the *Vindication of Poesie* in *Poems written upon Severall Occasions, Apud Biswicke: Anno Domini MDCXLVI*, B.M. MS. Add. 19255, fol. 12ᵛ; repr. *Poems* ed. A. B. Grosart (1878), I. 28:

> The Shepherds Boy; best knowen by that name
> Colin; vpon his homely oaten Reed.
> With Roman Titirus may share in Fame;
> But when a higher path hee seem's to tread,
> Hee is my wonder; for who yet has seene
> Soe Cleare a Poeme, as his Faierie Queene?

(b) From *Time and Honour, ibid.*, fol. 14; repr. Grosart, I. 33–4:

> The proud Italian
> And iustly proud in Poesie, will allow
> The English (though not Equall) next him now;
> The noble Sidney crown'd with liveing Bayes;
> And Spencer chief, (if a peculiar praise
> May pass, and from the rest not derogate)
> The learned Jonson, whose Dramaticke State
> Shall stand admir'd Example, to reduce
> Things proper, to the light, or buskind Muse.

(c) From *An Essay; Endevouring to ennoble our English Poesie, ibid.*, fol. 31; repr. Grosart, I. 82:

> And take the Radix, or our Poesie
> To honour more, in this last Centurie;

The noble Sidney; Spencer liveing Still
In an abundant fancie; Ionsons Qvill
Ever admir'd; these iustly wee may call
Father; high placed, in Apolloes Hall.

(d) From *The Author, ibid.*, fol. III^v; repr. Grosart, II. 130–1:

Next see in-imitable Colin, moves
Our Admiration; Hee: poore Swaine; in bare
And thin-set Shades, did sing; whil'st (ah) noe care
Was had of all his Numbers; numbers which,
Had they bene sung of old, who knowes, how rich
A Fame, had Crown'd him? had he lived, when
Phillips Great Son (that prodigie of men)
Spread, like Aurora, in the Easterne light;
Hee had not wish'd a Homer for to write
His Storie, but ev'n Peleus Son, had sate
A step below, in Fame, as well as Fate;
But Hee, poor man, in an vngratefull Age
Neglected lived; still borne downe, by the Rage
Of Ignorance: for tis an Easier Thing
To make Trees Leape, and Stones selfe-burthens Bring
(As once Amphion to the Walls of Thaebes',)
Then Stop the giddie Clamouring of Pleb's;
He poorlie dyed; (but vertue cannot dye)
And scarce had got a Bed, in Death to lye
Had not a noble Heroe, made a Roome,
Heed beene an Epitaph, without a Tombe;
For that Hee could not want; whilst verse or witt
Could move a wing: they'd bene obliged to it;
Or say, the bankrupt Age could none Afford;
Hee left a Stocke, sufficient; on Record.

84. Samuel Sheppard

1646–55

Samuel Sheppard (*flor. c.* 1646) began his literary career early in the century as amanuensis to Ben Jonson. It is to Ben Jonson, in however inferior a fashion, that he owes most as a poet, and not to Spenser with whom he persistently aligns himself. On *The Fairie King*, see R. B. Brinckley, *Arthurian Legend in the Seventeenth Century*, Johns Hopkin's Monographs in Literary History, III (1932), 111–13.

(a) From *The Sixth Sestyad* (stanza 7) in *The times displayed in Six Sestyads* (1646), p. 21; repr. Sir Egerton Brydges, *British Bibliographer* (1810), I. 528:

> Although the *Bard*, whose lines unequalled,
> To my Eternal grief, be long since dead,
> His lines for ever shal preserve his Fame.
> So his★ who did so neer his foot paths tread
> Whose lines as neer as *Virgils Homers* came,
> Do equal *Spencers*, who the soul of verse
> In his admired Poems doth rehearse.

(b) *On Mr Spencers inimitable Poem, the Faerie Queen* in *Epigrams Theological, Philosophical, and Romantick* (1651), pp. 95–7 (*Epigram* 28):

> *Collin* my Master, O Muse sound his praise
> Extoll his never to be equal'd Layes,
> Whom thou dost Imitate with all thy might,
> As he did once in *Chawcers* veine delight
> And thy new *Faerie* King, shall with Queen
> When thou art dead, still flourish ever green.
> Cease wealthy *Italy* to brag and boast,

★ *Samuel Daniel*

That thou for Poesie art famed most
Of any Nation, *Ariostos* veine,
Though rare, came short of our great *Spencers* streine:
His great *Orlando* hath receiv'd great losse
By *Spencers Faerie* Knight of the Red Cross:
Warrelike *Rogeros* honour clouded is
By his *Arthegall*, and much fame doth misse,
His sweet Angellica describ'd with Art,
Is wan withered, to his *Brittomart*,
His admirable Poems darkned quite,
As if he onely had known how to write,
Nor may that wonder of your Nation claime
Supremacie, before our *Spencers* Fame:
Admired *Tasso*, (pardon) I must do
That right the Muses all perswade me to,
Although to *Godfrey* by thy worthy Layes,
Thou dost a *Mausolean* Trophey raise,
Yet *Spencer* to *Eliza* hath done more,
And by his fullnesse lesseneth thy store:
He like the grand *Meonian* sits on high,
Making all Verse stoope to his Poesie;
Like to some mighty River *Nile* or *Po*,
All that obstruct him, hee'l soon overthrow:
And shallow Brooks, if any list to strive,
From forth his Ocean soon they may derive.
Hee next unto *Apollo* sits above
With *Homer*, and sweet *Maro*, who approve
Of his society, and joy to see
Him that did equall their fam'd Poesie.
Niggardly Nation be ashamed of this,
A Tombe for they great Poet wanting is,
While fooles, not worth the naming, seated high
On Sepulchers of Marble God-like lie:
The learned in obscurity are thrust,
But yet their Names shall long out-live their dust:
Although Great *Spencer* they did thee interre,
Not Rearing to thy name a Sepulcher,
Yet thou hast one shall last to the last day,
Thy *Faerie* Queen, which never shall decay:
This is a Poets Priviledge, although

His person among sordid dolts do goe
Unto the Grave, his Name shall ever live,
And spite of Time, or Malice shall survive.

(c) From *The Faerie King Fashioning Love and Honovr. In an Heroicall Heliconian Dresse* (written *c.* 1655), Bodleian MS. Rawlinson Poet. 28, fol. 25 (III. i. 1):

CLIO thou first of the Caelestiall Nine
APOLLO'S DARLING, Sacred QUEENE of STORIES
unto whose famous everlasting SHRINE
(to their admired never-dying glories)
great HOMER, VIRGILL, TASSO the Divine
SPENSER (who Rules the two faire Promontories)
offerd their Charming Volumes, & from thee
were crowned with fulgent IM-MORTALLITIE

(d) *Ibid.*, fols. 65ᵛ–66 (V. vi. 44–5):

SPENSER the next, whom I doe thinke't no shame
to Immitate; if now his worke affords
so vast a Glory o how faire a Fame
had hee not doated on Exploded words
had waited on him; let his honourd name
find veneration 'bove the Earths great Lords,
great PRINCE OF POETS, thou canst never die
lodg'd in thy rare Immortal History.

Immortal Mirrour of all Poesie
SPIRRIT OF ORPHEUS; bring your pretious Balms,
GOD OF INUENTION, to thy memory
we'l offer Incense, singing Hymns and Psalms,
joy to our Laurell, JOVES deare MERCURY
ingyrt his grave with Myrtle and with palms,
whose rare Desert first kindled my Desire
& gave me confidence, thus to Aspire.

85. Joseph Beaumont

1648

Joseph Beaumont (1616–99) rounded off a brilliant career at Cambridge as Master of Peterhouse and Professor of Divinity. The whole conception of his chief poetic enterprise, *Psyche*, is pervasively influenced by the *Faerie Queene*. The distaste he records for that poem in the lines below mark more the anxiety of the practising poet not to be overwhelmed by his model, than any genuine neo-classical spirit. See also No. 122.

From *Psyche, or Loves Mysterie* (1648), p. 48; repr. in *Works*, ed. A. B. Grosart, Chertsey Worthies' Library (1880), I. 68:

(Not far from whom [Homer, Pindar, Tasso], though in a lower clime,
Yet with a goodly Train doth *Colin* sweep:
Though manacled in thick and peevish Rhyme,
A decent pace his painful Verse doth keep
Well limm'd and featur'd is his mystick *Queen*,
Yet, being mask'd, her beauties less are seen.)

86. Mathias Prideaux

1648

Mathias Prideaux (1622–46) was educated at Exeter College, Oxford. The book from which the extract below is taken was published posthumously, probably edited by his father John Prideaux, Bishop of Worcester.

From *An easy and Compendious Introduction for Reading all sorts of Histories* (1648), sig. Xxv:

The *wandering Knights, Spencers Fairy Queene, Sir Philip Sidnies Arcadia*, with other pieces of like straine, may passe with singular Commendations for morall *Romances*, being nothing else but Poeticall Ethicks, that with apt contrivanse, and winning Language, informe *Morality*.

87. Abraham Cowley

1650, 1668

Abraham Cowley (1618–67) was educated at Westminster School and Trinity College, Cambridge. His own efforts in heroic poetry and his praise of D'Avenant's stand out against what may be partly a sentimental enthusiasm for Spenser, though the portrait of Envy in the *Davideis* borrows from the *Faerie Queene*. I quote from Thomas Sprat's *Account of the Life of Mr Abraham Cowley* (1668), sig. A2:

The occasion of this first inclination to Poetry, was his casual lighting on *Spencer*'s *Fairy Queen*, when he was but just able to read. That indeed is a Poem fitter for the examination of men, than the consideration of a Child. But in him it met with a Fancy, whose strength was not to be judged by the number of his years.

Sprat also thinks it worth mentioning that Cowley was buried near Chaucer and Spenser, 'the two most Famous *English* poets of former times'.

(a) From the epistle *To Sir William D'Avenant* . . . prefatory to D'Avenant's *Discourse upon Gondibert* (Paris 1650) sig. A3; repr. in *Poems*, ed. A. R. Waller (Cambridge, 1905), p. 42:

> Methinks Heroick Poesie, till now
> Like some fantastick Fairy land did show;
> Gods, Devils, Nymphs, Witches, & Giants race,
> And all but man, in mans best work had place.
> Thou like some worthy Knight, with sacred Arms
> Dost drive the *Monsters* thence, and end the Charms.

(b) From *Of Myself* in *The Works* (1668), p. 144; repr. in *Essays and Other Prose Writings*, ed. A. R. Waller (Cambridge, 1906), pp. 457–8:

I believe I can tell the particular little chance that filled my head first with such Chimes of Verse, as have never since left ringing there: For I remember when I began to read, and to take some pleasure in it, there was wont to lie in my Mothers Parlour (I know not by what accident, for she her self never in her life read any Book but of Devotion) but there was wont to lie *Spencers* Works; this I happened to fall upon, and was infinitely delighted with the Stories of the Knights, and Giants, and Monsters, and brave Houses, which I found every where there: (Though my understanding had little to do with all this) and by degrees with the tinckling of the Rhyme and Dance of the Numbers, so that I think I had read him all over before I was twelve years old, and was thus made a Poet as irremediably as a Child is made an Eunuch. With these affections of mind, and my heart set upon Letters, I went to the University.

88. William D'Avenant

1650

Sir William D'Avenant (1606–68) briefly attended Lincoln College, Oxford, and attached himself for a short while to the ageing Fulke Greville, in whose service he learned the court manners that stood him well for the remainder of his life. He evidently liked to imagine himself the natural son of Shakespeare. Richard Flecknoe, in *Sir William D'avenant's Voyage to the Other World* . . . (1668), represents him arriving in Elysium, and being amazed

to find never a Poet there, Antient nor Modern, whom in some sort or other he had not disoblig'd by his discommendations, as Homer, Virgil, Tasso, Spencer, and especially Ben. Johnson . . . Nay, even Shakespear, whom he thought to have found his greatest Friend . . .

His 'discommendation' of Spenser is not remarkable for special insight, but H. E. Cory [in *The Critics of Edmund Spenser*, Univ. of California Publications in Modern Philology, II (1911), 104], rather untypically, forgives D'Avenant his reservations.

From *A Discourse upon Gondibert* . . . (1650), pp. 11–13; repr. J. E. Spingarn, *Critical Essays of the Seventeenth Century* (Oxford, 1908–9), II. 5–6:

Spencer may stand here as the last of this short File of Heroick Poets; Men, whose intellectuals were of so great a making, (though some have thought them lyable to those few censures we have mention'd) as perhaps they will in worthy memory out-last even Makers of Laws, and Founders of Empire, and all but such as must therefore live equally with them, because they have recorded their Names; and consequently with their own hands led them to the Temple of Fame. And since we have dar'd to remember those exceptions which the Curious have against them; it will not be expected I should forget what is objected against *Spencer*; whose obsolete language we are constrain'd to mention, though it be grown the most vulgar accusation that is lay'd to his charge.

Language (which is the onely Creature of Man's creation) hath, like a Plant, seasons of flourishing, and decay; like Plants, it remov'd from one Soil to another, and by being so transplanted, doth often gather vigour and increase. But as it is false Husbandry to graft old Branches upon young Stocks: so we may wonder that our Language (not long before his time created out of a confusion of others, and then beginning to flourish like a new Plant) should (as helps to its increase) receive from his hand new Grafts of old wither'd Words. But this vulgar exception shall onely have the vulgar excuse; which is, That the unlucky choise of his *Stanza*, hath by repitition of Rime brought him to the necessity of many exploded words.

If we proceed from his Language to his Argument, we must observe with others, that his noble and most artfull hands deserv'd to be employ'd upon matter of a more naturall, and therefore of a more usefull kind. His Allegoricall Story (by many held defective in the Connexion) resembling (me thinks) a continuance of extraordinary Dreams; such as excellent Poets, and Painters, by being over-studious may have in the beginning of Feavers: And those morall visions are just of so much use to Humane application, as painted History, when with the cousenage of lights it is represented in Scenes, by which we are much lesse inform'd then by actions on the Stage.

89. R.C.

1651

The following two passages are taken from the prefatory material to William Bosworth's *The Chast and Lost Lovers* (1651). Bosworth probably died in 1650 and R.C. took care of the publication.

(a) From *The Epistle Dedicatory* in *The Chast and Lost Lovers* (1651), sig. A2:

If *Poetry* be truly conceived to carry some *Divinity* with it, and *Poets*, on what Subjects soever their Fancies have discoursed, have bin intituled *Divine*, as the *Divine Mr Spencer*, the *Divine Ronsard*, the *Divine Ariosto*; how much more properly may they be esteemed to be *Divine*, who have made chast Love their Argument.

(b) From the epistle *To the Reader, ibid.,* sigs. A3ᵛ–A4:

The high, the fluent, and the pathetick discourse of his lovers, and the transformation of them after their death . . . you shall finde hath allusion to *Ovids Metamorphosis* . . . The strength of his fancy, and the shadowing of it in words he taketh from Mr *Marlow* in his *Hero and Leander* . . . The weaving of one story into another and the significant flourish that doth attend it is the peculiar Grace of Sir *Philip Sidney*, whom our Author doth so h[a]ppily imitate . . . His making the end of one Verse to be the frequent beginning of the other (besides the Art of the Trope) was the labour and delight of Mr *Edmund Spe[n]cer*, whom Sir *Walt. Raleigh* and S. *Kenelm Digby* were used to call the *English Virgill*.

90. William Basse

1653

See headnote to No. 40.

From *The Pastorals And Other Works* (written 1653), repr. R. W. Bond *Poetical Works* (1893), p. 170:

> The famous Shepheard Collin, whom we looke
> Never to match, (though follow him we may
> That follow sheep, and carry scrip and hooke)
> By iust aduantage of his time and way
> Has plac'd the moneths in his eternall booke,
> All in their owne due order and aray;
> (A Kalendar to last, we cannot say
> For one yeare, but as long as yeares shal bee);
> Yet of the weeke has left me euery day
> Vertues to sing, though in more low degree.
> And could they reach, my Lord, a higher key,
> Yours as the Shepheard is the songes should be.
> Great merit may claime grace in Noble breast;
> Favour is greatest where desart is least.

91. Sir Robert Southwell

c. 1654

Sir Robert Southwell (1635–1702), was educated at Queen's College, Oxford, and Lincoln's Inn before entering on a diplomatic career.

From the *Commonplace Book* 1654–7. Bodleian MS. Eng. poet. f. 6, fol. 24ᵛ:

> In *the* prayse of *the* Poet Spen[s]er
> Spenser can *the* Encomium of thy skill,
> Flow through *the* slender channel of a Quill.
> Can Mortalls speake thy verses goodn*ess*, when
> They strike *the* praise of silence into men.
> Fountaine of Fancy, whose mellifluous streame
> Flotes in applause the dresse of every theme.
> Purgeth obscurely, and does impart
> To every line *the* Harmony of Art.
> It makes (since murmers be with musick meete)
> Thy Muse to dance on her Poetick feete
> She leads the rest and when their strength is past
> She can cut capers in a verse at last
> 'Tis not im*m*odest, lest he sprightly rise
> She'l reach the Lawrel from the lofty skies.

92. Sir Richard Fanshawe

1655

Sir Richard Fanshawe (1608–66) was educated at Jesus College, Cambridge, and passed through the Inner Temple, before developing his considerable linguistic accomplishments in travel. His translation of *Aeneid* IV (1648) is in Spenserian stanzas, and his verse in general displays the sort of mellifluousness made possible by Spenser. The sentence below takes to an extreme the neo-classical insistence on the historicity of heroic poetry.

From *The Translator's Postscript* to *The Lusiad, or Portugals Historicall Poem* ... (1655), sig. b2ᵛ:

For (to name no more) the *Greek* HOMER, the *Latin* VIRGIL, *our* SPENCER, and even the *Italian* TASSO (who had a *true*, a *great*, and *no obsolete story*, to work upon) are in effect wholly *fabulous*.

93. Samuel Holland

1656

For a notice of this work, see Sir Egerton Brydges, *Restituta* (1816), IV. 196–9. *Don Zara del Fogo* was republished in 1660 under the title *Romancio-Mastix*. Holland may have contributed commendatory verses to Samuel Sheppard's *Epigrams*.

From *Don Zara del Fogo. A Mock-Romance* (1656), pp. 101–2:

The fire of Emulation burnt fiercely in every angle of this Paradise; the British Bards (forsooth) were also ingaged in quarrel for Superiority; and who think you, threw the Apple of Discord amongst them, but *Ben Johnson*, who had openly vaunted himself the first and best of English Poets; this Brave was resented by all with the highest indignation, for *Chawcer* (by most there) was esteemed the Father of English Poesie, whose onely unhappiness it was, that he was made for the time he lived in, but the time not for him: *Chapman* was wondrously exasperated at *Bens* boldness, and scarce refrained to tell (his own *Tale of a Tub*) that his *Isabel* and *Mortimer* was now compleated by a Knighted Poet, whose soul remained in Flesh; hereupon *Spencer* (who was very busie in finishing his *Fairy Queen*) thrust himself amid the throng, and was received with a showt by *Chapman, Harrington, Owen, Constable, Daniel*, and *Drayton*, so that some thought the matter already decided; but behold *Shakespear* and *Fletcher* (bringing with them a strong party) appeared, as if they meant to water their Bayes with blood, rather then part with their proper Right, which indeed *Apollo* and the Muses (had with much justice) conferr'd upon them, so that now there is like to be trouble in Triplex: *Skelton, Gower* and the Monk of *Bury* were at Daggers-drawing for *Chawcer: Spencer* waited upon by a numerous Troop of the best Book-men in the World: *Shakespear* and *Fletcher* surrounded with their Life-Guard, viz. *Goffe, Massinger, Decker, Webster, Suckling, Cartwright, Carew*, &c.

94. Sir Aston Cockayne

1658

Sir Aston Cockayne (1608–84) was educated at Trinity Hall, Cambridge, and the Inns of Court. Of antiquarian leanings, he was a friend of Dugdale. The praise of Spenser in the pieces below can be only conventional: the appearance of Mr Humphrey C.'s *Loves Hawking Bag* moved Sir Aston to dismiss to oblivion all the luminaries of earlier English poetry, including Spenser.

(a) From *A Remedy for Love* in *Small Poems of Divers Sorts* (1658), p. 8 (reissued with the same pagination as *A Chain of Golden Poems*); repr. Sir Egerton Brydges, *Restituta* (1815), II. 138–9:

> There thou upon the Sepulchre maist look
> Of *Chaucer*, our true *Ennius*, whose old book
> Hath taught our Nation so to Poetize,
> That English rythmes now any equalize;
> That we no more need envy at the straine
> Of *Tiber*, *Tagus*, or our neighbor *Seine*.
> There *Spencers* Tomb thou likewise maist behold,
> Which he deserved, were it made of gold:
> If honour'd *Colin*, thou hadst liv'd so long,
> As to have finished thy Faery Song,
> Not onely mine, but all tongues would confess,
> Thou hadst exceeded old *Maeonides*.

(b) *Ibid.*, p. 11; repr. Brydges, II. 139–40:

> For *Colins* sake (who hath so well exprest
> The vertues of our Faery Elves, and drest
> Our Poesie in such a gallant guise)
> On happy *Pembroke-Hall* employ thine eyes.

(c) *Ibid.*, p. 16; repr. Brydges, II. 139:

> Though the *Arcadia* be a book approv'd,
> *Arcadia* must not be by thee belov'd.
> The Lady *Wrothes Vrania* is repleat
> With elegancies, but too full of heat.
> *Spencers* and *Daniels* Sonets do not view,
> Though they are good, they are not so for you.
> From feigned Histories refrain thy sight,
> Scarce one is there but is an amorous Knight.
> *Musaeus* English'd by two Poets shun;
> It may undo you though it be well done.
> *Harrington*'s *Ariosto* do not touch,
> For wanton lines scarce any book hath such.
> And my old friend *Drayton*'s Epistles you
> (Being too soft and languishing) eschew.

(d) Of *Edmond Spencer*, *Epigrams The first Book*, 37, *ibid.*, p. 155; repr. Brydges, II. 140:

> Our *Spencer* was a Prodigie of wit,
> Who hath the Faery Queen so stately writ:
> Yield *Grecian* Poets to his Nobler Style;
> And ancient *Rome* submit unto our I'le.
> You modern wits of all the four-fold earth
> (Whom Princes have made Laureates for your worth)
> Give our great *Spencer* place, who hath out-song
> *Phoebus* himself with all his Learned Throng.

THE PERIOD 1660–1715

(See Introduction pp. 18–21)

95. John Worthington

1660

John Worthington (1618–71) was Master of Jesus College, Cambridge, and associated with the Cambridge Platonists. Samuel Hartlib is the friend of Milton. A second letter to him on a similar subject can be found in Crossley, II. 76.

Letter to Samuel Hartlib, 11 January 1660 in *Diary and Correspondence of Dr Worthington*, ed. James Crossley, Chetham Society Publication (1847–86) I. 261–3:

Sir,

Yours I receiv'd last week; which exprest a great desire of the catalogue of those pieces of the renowned Spenser, which are only mentioned, but were never yet printed. This I now give you, as it was collected out of several scatter'd intimations of them in his printed works.

1. A Translation of Ecclesiastes
2. A Translation of Canticum Cantorum
3. The Dying Pelican
4. The Hours of the Lord
5. The Sacrifice of a Sinner
6. The 7 Psalms
7. His Dreams★
8. His English Poet★

★ These two [7 and 8] were promised by E.K. to be set forth with his Comment. Which E.K. was he that did comment upon Spenser's Kalendar.

These are the smaller poems of his, besides many others in the hands of noble persons, and his friends. He had for his friends Sir Philip Sidney, (whom, as also the Countess of Pembroke, he highly honoured,) Sir Walter Raleigh, Mr Gabriel Harvey, besides E.K. who wrote the Comment upon the Shepherd's Calendar; and others whose initial letters of their names only are set down, as R.S., H.B., W.L., G.W., senior, which need some Oedipus to discover them. But the greatest want is of the other six books of that incomparable poem, the Faery Queen; of which only 2 canto's and 2 stanza's of another canto are printed in the folio.

And this is an account of all that I have seen of his printed, except a short Discourse of Ireland in prose.

The printer in one place intimates. that divers of his poems were disperst abroad in sundry hands; and some were purloyn'd from him since his going into Ireland. These (if not quite lost) may perhaps lie hid in some libraries or closets. He lived heretofore in the north of England, and in the south, viz., Kent, as is intimated by the Kentish Downs, so often mentioned by him.

Next to his Faery Queen, I should most desire to see the English Poet, and the Divine Poems: for that in his latter years he most relish'd the more divine strain of poesie, appears by several passages in his printed poems.

96. Sir John Denham

1668

Sir John Denham (1615–69) attended Trinity College, Oxford, where he apparently spent more time gambling than in study. Like Cowley he was himself buried near Chaucer and Spenser. As a poet he was until the end of the eighteenth century quite extraordinarily fashionable; at the moment his reputation is unjustly low.

From *On Mr Abraham Cowley His Death and Burial amongst the Ancient Poets* in *Poems and Translations, with the Sophy* (1668), pp. 89–90; repr. in *Poetical Works*, ed. T. H. Banks (New Haven, 1928), pp. 149–50:

> Old Chaucer, like the morning Star,
> To us discovers day from far,
> His light those Mists and Clouds dissolv'd,
> Which our dark Nation long involv'd;
> But he descending to the shades,
> Darkness again the Age invades.
> Next (like *Aurora*) *Spencer* rose,
> Whose purple blush the day foreshows. . . .
>
> Time, which made them their Fame outlive,
> To *Cowly* scarce did ripeness give.
> Old Mother Wit, and Nature gave
> *Shakespeare* and *Fletcher* all they have;
> In *Spencer*, and in *Johnson*, Art,
> Of slower Nature got the start.

97. Edward Phillips

1669

Edward Phillips (1630–96) was a nephew of Milton, privately educated by his uncle before passing on to Magdalen College, Oxford, which he left without a degree. See also Nos. 153, 173.

From *Tractulus de Carmine Dramatico* . . ., in John Buchler's *Sacrarum Profanarumque Phrasium poeticarum Thesaurus* (1669), pp. 396–7:

Edmund Spenser is a man worthy immortal memory, one who described in heroic song the sum of Christian and moral virtues, most of them at any rate, for a wretched death preventing him (he is supposed to have died of starvation) he left his work unfinished. This is the more surprising since he was well known to the Queen, who had received the highest praise in his poem. The verses or stanzas of this poem accord with what is, after the Italian sonnet, the very finest arrangement of lines; as everyone knows in the ninth and last line a disyllabic foot longer than the others for the sake of grandeur. How the lines rhyme in this stanza is best seen from an example:

[quotes *Faerie Queene* II. xii. 71, omitting line 5]

There are also additional works which survive, such as the *Shepheardes Calender* and certain others, but many are lost.[1]

---

[1] *Edmundus Spenserus vir immortali memoria dignus, qui carmine Heroico descripsit Encyclopaediam Christianarum & moralium virtutum, saltem maxima ex parte, siquidem misera morte praeveniente (nam vertur inedia periise) Opus imperfectum reliquit, hocque magis est mirum cum Reginae, quam in poemate summis laudibus in coelum evexerat, minime ignotus esset. Stichi seu Stanzae hujus poematis constant versuum Congerie post Italicum sonettum pulcherrima, nempe novenaria, & postremo versu caeteris dissyllabam longiore, Majestatis gratia; in hos Sticho quomodo versus inter se respondeant hoc exemplum decebit. . . . Sunt etiam praeterea ex operibus ejus quae extant, ut Calendarium pastorale atq; alia quaedam, at multa desiderantur.*

98. John Hacket

c. 1670

John Hacket (1592–1670) was educated at Trinity College, Cambridge. He had some reputation as a Latin poet (not to be judged on the piece here), and with Ben Jonson translated Bacon's *Essays* into Latin.

From the flyleaf of Cambridge University Library Syn. 4.60.2., a copy of the 1609 Folio repr. *N&Q*, ser. 2, VII (1859), 235:

> Homers the Captain of Apollo's race:
> Renowned Virgil claims the second place:
> Spenser, our glorie tis' thy golden pen
> Admitts thee third before all other men.
> Sage Homer, Virgil, Spenser Laureat
> Make a poetical Triumvirat.
> Greece, Rome, and England chaleng to your merits
> T'haue nurst the brauest Heliconian spirits.
> Only King Dauid's muse, Jehoua's birth,
> Excells, as much as Heau'n excells the earth.

[Hacket's Latin, on the same page, reads:]

> *Apollinaris dux Homerus est chori,*
> *Teneas secundum Virgili! merito locum:*
> *Capesse sortem tertiam, nostrum decus.*
> *Spensere lauriger, Maro, Maeonides sacer*
> *Vos fama celebret Tresviros Phoebi sacros.*
> *Pelasga terra, Roma, dulcis Anglia,*
> *Tres nutricastis optimos vates gregis.*
> *Solum Dauidis musa de caelo sata*
> *Superat O, caelum ut superat has terrae plagas.*

99. Richard Graham, Viscount Preston

1670

Richard Graham, Viscount Preston (1648–95) was educated at Westminster School and Christ Church, Oxford. The criticism offered here has much in common with Dryden's.

From *The Poet*, in *Angliae Speculum Morale* . . . (1670), pp. 66–8; repr. in *Works of Spenser*, ed. H. J. Todd (1805), II. cxli:

The Bards and Chroniclers in the Isles of *Britain* and *Ireland* have been in former times even ador'd for the Ballads in which they extoll'd the Deeds of their forefathers; and since the ages have been refined, doubtless, *England* hath produced those, who in this way have equalled most of the Antients: and exceeded all the Moderns. *Chaucer* rose like the morning Starr of Wit, out of those black mists of ignorance; since him, *Spencer* may deservedly challenge the Crown; for though he may seem blameable in not observing *decorum* in some places enough, and in too much, in the whole, countenancing Knight-errantry; yet the easie similitudes, the natural Pourtraicts, the so refined and sublimated fancies, with which he hath so bestudded every Canto of his subject will easily reach him the Guerdon; and though some may object to him that his Language is harsh and antiquated; yet his design was noble; to shew us that our Language was expressive enough of our own sentiments; and to upbraid those who have indenizon'd such numbers of forreign words.

100. John Dryden

1672–1700

John Dryden (1631–1700) was educated at Westminster School and Trinity College, Cambridge. Dryden is a powerfully original critic of Spenser (as he is in general), and, with Digby, the profoundest of all the early critics. See also No. 155.

(a) From *Of Heroique Players. An Essay*, prefatory to *The Conquest of Granada by the Spaniards* (1672), sig. A4; repr. In *Works*, ed. Walter Scott (1808) rev. George Saintsbury (Edinburgh, 1882–93), IV. 23:

For my part, I am of opinion, that neither *Homer*, *Virgil*, *Statius*, *Ariosto*, *Tasso*, nor our *English Spencer*, could have form'd their Poems half so beautiful, without those Gods and Spirits, and those Enthusiastick parts of Poetry, which compose the most noble parts of all their writings and I will ask any man who loves Heroick Poetry, (for I will not dispute their tastes who do not) if the Ghost of *Polydorus* in *Virgil*, the Enchanted wood in *Tasso*, and the Bower of bliss, in Spencer (which he borrows from that admirable *Italian*) could have been omitted without taking from their works some of the greatest beauties in them.

(b) From the epistle *To the Right Honourable John Lord Haughton* prefatory to *The Spanish Fryar* ... (1681), sig. A3; repr. Scott-Saintsbury, VI. 407:

Thus an injudicious Poet who aims at Loftiness runs easily into the swelling puffie style, because it looks like Greatness. I remember, when I was a Boy, I thought inimitable *Spencer* a mean Poet, in comparison of *Sylvester's Dubartas*.

(c) From the *Dedication To the Right Honourable Charles Earl of Dorset and Middlesex* in *The Satires of Decimus Junius Juvenalis. Translated into English Verse* (1693), pp. viii–ix; repr. Scott-Saintsbury, XIII. 17–19:

The *English* have only to boast of *Spencer* and *Milton* who neither of them wanted either Genius, or Learning, to have been perfect Poets; and yet both of them are liable to many Censures. For there is no Uniformity in the Design of *Spencer*: He aims at the Accomplishment of no one Action: He raises up a Hero for every one of his Adventures; and endows each of them with some particular Moral Virtue, which renders them all equal, without Subordination of Preference. Every one is most Valiant in his own Legend; only we must do him that Justice to observe, that Magnanimity, which is the Character of Prince *Arthur*, shines throughout the whole Poem; and Succours the rest, when they are in Distress. The Original of every Knight, was then living in the Court of Queen *Elizabeth*: And he attributed to each of them that Virtue, which he thought was most conspicuous in them: An Ingenious piece of Flattery, tho' it turned not much to his Account. Had he liv'd to finish his Poem, in the six remaining Legends, it had certainly been more of a piece; but cou'd not have been perfect, because the Model was not true. But Prince *Arthur*, or his chief Patron, Sir *Philip Sidney*, whom he intended to make happy, by the Marriage of his *Gloriana*, dying before him, depriv'd the Poet, both of Means and Spirit, to accomplish his Design: For the rest, his Obsolete Language, and the ill choice of his Stanza, are faults but of the Second Magnitude: For notwithstanding the first he is still Intelligible, at least, after a little practice; and for the last, he is the more to be admir'd; that labouring under such a difficulty, his Verses are so Numerous, so Various, and so Harmonious, that only *Virgil*, whom he profestly imitated, has surpass'd him, among the *Romans*; and only Mr *Waller* among the *English*. . . .

[Milton's] Antiquated words were his Choice, not his Necessity; for therein he imitated *Spencer*, as Spencer did *Chawcer*.

Ibid., p. xxviii; repr. Scott-Saintsbury, XIII. 67:

In the English I remember none, which are mix'd with Prose, as *Varro*'s were: But of the same kind is Mother *Hubbard*'s Tale in *Spencer*. [That is, no satires.]

(d) From *Observations on the Art of Painting* in *De Arte Graphica. The Art of Painting, by C. A. Du Fresnoy with Remarks. Translated into English* (1695), pp. 108–9; repr. Scott-Saintsbury, XVII. 418–19:

And other Books of the like Nature, the reading of which are profitable

to warm the Imagination [of the painter]: such as in *English*, are
Spencer's Fairy Queen; The *Paradise Lost* of *Milton; Tasso* translated by
Fairfax; and the History of *Polybius*, by Sir *Henry Shere.*

(e) From the Dedication of the Pastorals *To the Right Honourable Hugh
Lord Clifford* in *The Works of Virgil. . . . Translated into English Verse*
(1697), p. 3; repr. Scott-Saintsbury, XIII. 324–5:

Our own Nation has produc'd a third Poet in this kind, not inferiour
to the two former. For the Shepherd's Kalender of *Spencer*, is not to be
match'd in any Modern Language. Not even by *Tasso's Amynta*, which
infinitely transcends *Guarini's Pastor-Fido*, as having more of Nature
in it, and being almost wholly clear from the wretched affectation of
Learning. I will say nothing of the *Piscatory Eclogues* [of Sannazaro],
because no modern *Latin* can bear Criticism. 'Tis no wonder that
rolling down through so many barbarous Ages, from the Spring of
Virgil, it bears along with it the filth and ordures of the *Goths* and
Vandals. Neither will I mention Monsieur *Fontenelle*, the living Glory
of the *French*. 'Tis enough for him to have excell'd his Master *Lucian*,
without attempting to compare our miserable Age with that of *Virgil*
or *Theocritus*. . . . But *Spencer* being Master of our Northern Dialect;
and skill'd in *Chaucer's* English, has so exactly imitated the *Doric* of
Theocritus, that his Love is a perfect Image of that Passion which God
infus'd into both Sexes, before it was corrupted with the Knowledge of
Arts, and the Ceremonies of what we call good Manners.

(f) From the Dedication of the *Aeneid, To the Right Honourable John,
Lord Marquess of Normandy, Earl of Mulgrave, Ibid*, p. 208; repr. Scott-
Saintsbury, XIV. 144:

Spencer has a better plea for his Fairy-Queen, had his action been
finish'd, or had been one.

Ibid., p. 213; repr. Scott-Saintsbury, XIV. 157:

Spencer favours this Opinion, what he can. His Prince*Arthur*, or whoever
he intends by him, is a *Trojan*. Thus the Heroe of *Homer* was a *Grecian*,
of *Virgil* [a] *Roman*, of *Tasso* an *Italian*.

Ibid., p. 217; repr. Scott-Saintsbury, XIV. 166:

Ariosto, the two *Tasso*'s, *Bernardo* and *Torquato*, even our own *Spencer*; in a word, all Modern Poets have Copied *Homer* as well as *Virgil*.

Ibid., p. 238; repr. Scott-Saintsbury, XIV. 210:

Spencer wanted only to have read the Rules of *Bossu*; for no Man was ever Born with a greater Genius, or had more Knowledge to support it.

Ibid., p. 240; repr. Scott-Saintsbury, XIV. 214–15:

⌈*Spencer* and *Milton* are the nearest in English to *Virgil* and *Horace* in the Latin.⌋

(g) From the *Preface to Fables Ancient and Modern* . . . (1700), sig. A; repr. Scott-Saintsbury, XI. 209–10:

For *Spencer* and *Fairfax* both flourish'd in the Reign of Queen *Elizabeth*: Great Masters in our Language; and who saw much farther into the Beauties of our Numbers, than those who immediately followed them. *Milton* was the Poetical Son of *Spencer*. . . . *Spencer* more than once insinuates, that the Soul of *Chaucer* was transfus'd into his Body; and that he was begotten by him Two hundred years after his Decease. *Milton* has acknowledged to me, that *Spencer* was his Original.

Ibid., sig. B2ᵛ; repr. Scott-Saintsbury, XI. 226:

We must be Children before we grow Men. There was an *Ennius*, and in the process of Time a *Lucilius*, and a *Lucretius*, before *Virgil* and *Horace*; even after *Chaucer* there was a *Spencer*, a *Harrington*, a *Fairfax*, before *Waller* and *Denham* were in being.

(h) From *The Art of Poetry, written in French by The Sieur de Boileau*, translated with Sir William Soame (1683), pp. 7–8:

> Our ancient Verse, (as homely as the Times,)
> Was rude, unmeasur'd, only Tagg'd with Rhymes:
> Number and Cadence, that have Since been Shown,
> To those unpolish'd Writers were unknown.
> *Fairfax** was He, who, in that Darker Age,

* Fairfax in his Translation of *Godfrey* of Bullen.

By his just Rules restrain'd Poetic Rage;
Spencer did next in Pastorals excel,
And taught the Noble Art of Writing well:
To stricter Rules the Stanza did restrain,
And found for Poetry a richer Veine.
Then D'Avenant came.

101. Thomas Rymer

1674

Thomas Rymer (1641–1713) left Sidney Sussex College, Cambridge, without a degree, and entered Gray's Inn. He is notorious for his aggressive neo-classicism. But Spenser is such a name, he says, 'as will ever be sacred to me' (in *The Tragedies of the Last Age Consider'd...*) and fares considerably better than Shakespeare.

From *The Preface of the Translator* in Rapin's *Reflections on Aristotle's Treatise of Poesie* (1674), sig. A6ᵛ–A7; repr. J. E. Spingarn, II. 167–8:

Spencer, I think, may be reckon'd the first of our *Heroick Poets*; he had a large spirit, a sharp judgement, and a *Genius* for *Heroick Poesie*, perhaps above any that ever writ since *Virgil*. But our misfortune is, he wanted a true *Idea*, and lost himself, by following an unfaithful guide. Though besides *Homer* and *Virgil* he had read *Tasso*, yet he rather suffer'd himself to be misled by *Ariosto*; with whom blindly rambling on *marvellous* Adventures, he makes no Conscience of *Probability*. All is fanciful and chimerical, without any uniformity, without any foundation in truth; his Poem is perfect *Fairy-land*.

They who can love *Ariosto*, will be ravish'd with *Spencer*; whilst men of juster thoughts lament that such great Wits have miscarried in their Travels for want of direction to set them in the right way. But the truth is, in *Spencer*'s time, *Italy* it self was not well satisfied with *Tasso*; and few amongst them would then allow that he had excell'd their *divine Ariosto*. And it was the vice of those Times to affect superstitiously the *Allegory*; and nothing would then be current without a mystical meaning. We must blame the Italians for debauching great *Spencer*'s judgement; and they cast him on the unlucky choice of the *Stanza*, which in no wise is proper for our Language.

102. Peter Sterry

1675

Peter Sterry (d. 1672) was educated at Emmanuel College, Cambridge, of which he became a Fellow. Sterry's association with the Platonists did not prevent his appointment as Chaplain to Cromwell. He may have assisted Milton as Latin Secretary.

From *A Discourse of the Freedom of the Will* (1675), p. 179:

A poetical History, or work framed by an excellent Spirit, for a pattern of Wisdom, and Worth, and Happiness, hath this, as a chief rule, for the contrivance of it, upon which all its Graces and Beauties depend. That persons and things be carried to the *utmost extremity*, into a state where they seem altogether uncapable of any return to Beauty or Bliss: That then by just degrees of harmonious proportions, they be raised again to a state of highest Joy and Glory. You have examples of this in the Divine pieces of those Divine Spirits, (as they are esteemed and stiled) *Homer*, *Virgil*, *Tasso*, our English *Spencer*, with some few others like to these; the *Works* of these persons are called *Poems*. So is the Work of God in Creation, and contrivance from the beginning to the end, ποίημα τῷ θεῷ, God's Poem.

103. Samuel Woodford

1679

Samuel Woodford (1636–1700) was educated at Wadham College, Oxford and the Inner Temple. For an account of his use of Spenser, see A. C. Judson, 'Samuel Woodford and Edmund Spenser', *N&Q*, CLXXXIX (1945), 191–2.

(a) From *The Preface* to *A Paraphrase Upon the Canticles* . . . (1679), sig. b2:

Among the several other Papers that we have lost of the Excellent and Divine *Spenser*, one of the happiest Poets that this Nation ever bred, (and out of it the World, it may be (all things considered) had not his Fellow, excepting only such as were immediately Inspired) I bewail nothing me-thinks so much, as his Version of the *Canticles*. For doubtless, in my poor Judgement, never was Man better made for such a Work, and the Song it self so directly suited, with his Genius, and manner of Poetry (that I mean, wherein he best shews and even excels himself, His *Shepherds Kalendar*, and other occasional Poems, for I cannot yet say the same directly for his *Faery Queen* design'd for an Heroic Poem) that it could not but from him receive the last Perfection, whereof it was capable out of its Original.

(b) *Ibid.*, sig. c2ᵛ:

If therefore Our selves, or the *French* will use Blank Verse, either in an Heroick Poem, where they should be I think Couplets, as in Mr *Cowley's Davideis* (for the Quadrains of Sir *William Davenant*, and the Stanza of Nine in *Spensers Faery Queen*, which are but an Improvement of the Ottava Rima, to instance in no more, seem not to me so proper) or in an Ode or Sonnet, (which remains yet to be attempted). . . . let us give it the Character, as to its Form, which it anciently had.

(c) *Ibid.*, sigs. c4–c4ᵛ:

The Legend forther of Love I have stiled it, for honours sake to the great *Spenser*, whose Stanza of Nine I have used, and who has Intituled the six Books which we have compleat of his *Faery Queen*, by the several Legends of *Holiness, Temperance, Chastity, Friendship, Justice* and *Courtesy*, and to any who knows what the word Legend there, or in its true and first notion signifies, it will neither seem strange, ridiculous, or improper.

104. John Chatwin

c. 1680

John Chatwin (*flor. c.* 1680–90) was educated at Emmanuel College, Cambridge. His poetry is preserved only in manuscript.

A Pastoral Elegy on the Death of that Great Master of Poesie Mr Edmond Spenser, from *Poems* in Bodleian MS. Rawl. poet. 94, fols. 273–5:

Corydon and Thyrsis
  Corydon: Look Thyrsis, See the Sun withdraws his Light,
           Muffled in darkness & the Shades of Night,
           The drooping Birds hang down their flagging Wing,
           No more the Woods will with their Sonnets ring,
           All the inspir'd Musicians of the Sky
           Husht in deep Silence & in Sorrow lye,
           For Colin's dead who Sung Soft Strains of Love,
           In ev'ry flow'ry Vale & ev'ry blooming Grove.
  Thyrsis: Careless of food the Sheep their Lambs forsake,
           And o'er the Hills unwonted paths do take,
           Thro' all the fields they unregarded Stray,

No more their Master on his Pipe can play,
No more can handle his Sweet oaten Reed,
Whilst all around his Flocks were wont to feed,
Dear Colin's dead! the Wonder of the Plain,
Belov'd by Pan, and ev'ry jolly Swain.

Corydon: When Colin Sung pleas'd Eccho would repeat
His melting Strains, beyond Expression sweet,
Soft Philomel her Self attentive Stood,   ⎫
And awful Silence dwelt in ev'ry Wood,   ⎬
The list'ning Beasts forgot to eat their food.   ⎭
The River Nymphs forsook their watry Beds,
Above the Streams they Shew'd their Radiant heads.
Each Fawn and Satyr left his private Shade,
To hear the Musick which the Shepherds made.
The haughty Maid who Scorn'd to hear of Love,
His softning Tunes could to Complyance move,
Her tender Breast Soon felt an Am'rous Fire,
And Strait She languished in a kind Desire.
But, ah! this dear-lov'd Shepherd now is dead,
Gastly & Pale, he in the Grave is laid.

Thyrsis: The faded flow'rs have all their glory lost,
Roses no more can of Vermilion boast.
The wither'd Lillyes hang their drooping heads,
Ready to fall into their Native Beds.
No Daizies now do paint th'enamell'd Green,
Mildews & Blasts in all the Meads are Seen;
The murm'ring Winds as thro' the Groves they fly,
Tell all their Woes in an unwonted Sigh;
Each aged Tree bows down its Rev'rent head,   ⎫
The fields & flow'rs do mourn the Shepherd dead, ⎬
And Grief & Sorrow all around do Spread.   ⎭

Corydon: Well may we mourn for Colin dead and gone, ⎫
For Dear-lov'd Colin all the Muses moan,   ⎬
The Glory of the Woods, the Shepherds Crown.   ⎭
The Nymphs Delight, the Love of ev'ry Swain,
The Grief & Wonder of th' Astonisht Plain.
With Sweetest Garlands we'll adorn his Hearse,
And Sing his Triumphs in immortal Verse;
In Such Soft Strains as he himself did frame,
We'll yearly celebrate his deathless Name,

And mourning Shepherdesses to his Tomb
With richest Spices & perfumes Shall come.
Thyrsis: But See, the Sun is hasting to the Deep,
In briny Waves his golden Locks to Steep;
Soft Dews are now descending from the Skies,
And Smoke from tops of Villages does rise,
Which mind us that We homeward Should return,
And there abide till the Approach of Morn.

105. Thomas D'Urfey

1681

Thomas D'Urfey (1653–1723) was poet, dramatist, and friend of
Dryden.

From the epistle *To The Right Honourable George Earl of Berkeley*
prefatory to *Sir Barnaby Whigg* . . . (1681), sigs. A2ᵛ–A3:

My Lord, 'tis not only a nice, but a very difficult thing to write a good
Comedy, and therefore a tolerable one should be the more excusable;
for there is not only Wit, but Plot, Invention, and a quick and ingenious
fancy requir'd: Fancy! the brightest Jewel of Poetry, of which the
Famous *English Spencer* was the great and only Master, as we may see
in all his Descriptions, but more particularly in his Legend of Temperance, when he speaks of *Mammon* or Covetousness.

[quotes *Faerie Queene* II. iii. 3, 5]

But this is a sort of Poetry of a different nature from *Dramaticks*; and
therefore the fancy must of necessity vary, because in one it is digested
into Characters, that are to speak before a carping Audience: and in the
other, perhaps, only to be read or spoken of before one or two persons.

106. Henry Keepe

1682

Henry Keepe (1652–88) was educated at New Inn, Oxford, and the Inner Temple. An antiquary, he raises the common academic objection to Spenser.

From *Monumenta Westmonasteriensa* (1682), p. 46:

On the South side of this Cross, hard by the little East door, is a decayed Tomb of grey Marble, very much defaced, and nothing of the antient Inscription remaining, which was in Latine, but of late there is another in English to inform you that *Edmund Spencer*, a most excellent *Poet*, lies there intombed, who indeed had a sweet and luxuriant fancy, and expressed his thoughts with admirable success, as his FAIRY-QUEEN, and other Works of his sufficiently declare; and pity it was such true Poetry should not have been imployed in as true a subject; he died in the year 1596.

107. A Pastoral

1683

From *A Pastoral, Written at Dublin, in May 1683* in *Poems by Several Hands. . . . Collected by N. Tate* (1685), pp. 45–7:

Thyrsis
O Coridon! Who shall presume to sing?
Who to these Groves shall foreign Numbers bring?
Where once great *Spencer* did triumphant reign,
The best, the sweetest, of the inspir'd Train;
Scarce from the God of Wit such Verse did flow,
When he vouchsaf'd to follow Sheep below;
Here sigh'd the love-sick Swain, here fed his Sheep
Near *Mullas* Stream, whose Waves he taught to weep:
While hungry'st Herds forgot the flowry Meads,
And the unshorn Hills inclin'd their list'ning Shades;
Oft as I've heard the Muses hither came,
The Muses slighted the inspiring Stream,
Charm'd with the merit of their *Colins* fame:
While hoarser Goatherds in some wretched strain
Invok'd the absent Deities in vain.
Ah! liv'd he now, what Subjects might he chuse,
The deathless Theams of his immortal Muse,
Of God-like *Ossory* his Song would tell,
How much belov'd he liv'd, how much bewail'd he fell.
In War unconquer'd, but betray'd in Peace
By fraud of Death, and snares of a Disease. . . .

Say happy Bard! immortal *Spencer* say!
What numbers would'st thou choose, what Praise display,
When of *Armagh* thy mighty Song should be,
Of *Armagh's* Justice and his Piety?

108. Knightly Chetwood

1684

Knightly Chetwood (1650–1720) was educated at Eton and King's College, Cambridge. He was a friend of both Roscommon and Dryden.

From the epistle *To the Earl of Roscommon, on his Excellent Poem* prefatory to *An Essay on Translated Verse* (1684), sig. A4ᵛ:

> As when by *labouring* Stars new Kingdoms rise
> The mighty *Mass* in *rude* confusion lies,
> A Court *unform'd*, *disorder* at the Bar,
> And even in *Peace* and *rugged Meen* of War,
> Till some wise States-man into *Method* draws
> The parts, and Animates the frame with *Laws*;
> Such was the case when *Chaucer's early* toyl
> *Founded* the *Muses* Empire in *our* Soyl.
> *Spencer* improv'd it with his painful hand
> But *lost* a *Noble* Muse in *Fairy-land*.
> *Shakespear* say'd all that Nature cou'd impart,
> And *Johnson* added *Industry* and *Art*.

109. Anonymous Comment following Rymer

1685

From *Preface to the Translation*, in *Mixt Essays Upon Tragedies, Comedies, Italian Comedies English Comedies and Operas. Written Originally in French By the Sieur de Saint Euremont* (1685), sig. A4:

The *Dutch* and *Germans* (as though frozen up) have produced little in this kind; yet we must confess that *Grotius, Heinsius, Scaliger,* and *Vossius* were Learned *Criticks*. Some of the *English* have indeed rais'd their Pens, and soar'd as high as any of the *Italians,* or *French*; yet *Criticism* came but very lately in fashion amongst us; without doubt *Ben. Johnston* had a large stock of Critical Learning; *Spencer* had studied *Homer,* and *Virgil,* and *Tasso,* yet he was misled, and debauched by *Ariosto,* as Mr *Rymer* judiciously observes.

110. The Author of *Spenserus Redivivus*

1687

The Preface to *Spenserus Redivivus* (1687), sigs. A3–A7^v:

There are few of our Nation that have heard of the Name of *Spencer*, but have granted him the repute of a famous Poet.

But I must take leave to affirm, that the esteem which is generally allow'd to his Poetical Abilities, has rather been from an implicite or receiv'd Concession, than a knowing Discernment paid to the Value of his Author: Whose Design, in his Books of the *Fairy Queen*, howsoever admirable, is so far from being familiarly perceptible in the Language he deliver'd it in, that his Stile seems no less unintelligible at this Day, than the obsoletest of our *English* or *Saxon* Dialect.

On which ground I believe it ought to have been long ago wish'd, as well as readily embrac'd, by all politely judicious, that something of this Eminent Poet had been genuinely and succinctly convey'd by the Purity of our Tongue.

An Endeavour undertaken by me, supposing it could not be less acceptable to others than my self. By which I have not only discharg'd his antiquated Verse and tedious Stanza, but have likewise deliver'd his Sense in Heroick Numbers: much more sutable to an *Epick Poem*, the deserv'd Denomination of his, than can possibly be accomplish'd by any sort of Measures in Stanza's, both in respect of their Freedom & Pleasure above any other Form that can be us'd in a Poem of this Nature.

For as the Writing in Stanza's must render Verse sententious and constrain'd, the most weighty part of their meaning still being to be expected at the Period of the Stanza; so, in that consideration, their Composure must needs be less difficult than where the force of each single Line is to be weigh'd apart. As who can judge, had *Virgil* writ or been render'd by any alternate Meeter, that either his design or expressions had appear'd so unconfin'dly elevate, as he is to be acknowledg'd in his own, or in such measures as should most resemble the unlimited nature and freedom proper to the greatness of his Subject.

As for the essential Story of *Spencer*, contain'd in this one Book of his *Fairy Queen*: I have entirely preserv'd his Matter and Design, except where both are abreviated, and, as I conceive, improv'd by my Thoughts.

Nor do I doubt but every impartial Reader will find, that in the way I have undertaken to delineate and express him by, he is render'd what he ought to have been instead of what is to be found in himself.

Not that I believe, his Language being wav'd, any *Poetical Genius*, since the incomparable *Virgil*, has exceeded the wonderful Variety, Beauty, and Strength of Conception that is to be found in our famous *Spencer*.

If we consider him as an extraordinary *Inventer* or *Tale teller*, the main Engine and Fabrick of Poesie, we shall find him more fruitfully new and delicate than any that have preceded him to the Age in which *Virgil* liv'd.

The most esteem'd of whose Successors, in the Heroick way, *Statius* and *Tasso*, have borrow'd so much from their great Poetical Predecessor, that it may be said of them, as *Scaliger* does of *Statius*, that they had very probably been greater in themselves, had they not endeavour'd to be like *Virgil*, whose Excellency was above all subsequent Imitation.

Whereas the Compositions of our wonderful *Spencer* are not only purely created throughout his Works by his unally'd Invention, but vary'd in every *Canto* with such a singular Method, that he is granted, at this day, abating his Expressions and manner of Verse, to compleat a distinct Original of Heroick Poesie.

The late ingenious Sir *William Dav'nant* taking occasion in his Preface before his *Gondibert* to commend this Author, compares his Poem of the *Fairy Queen* to an admir'd Course of Poetical Dreams and Extasies, or an Allegory of Things and Persons deliver'd from extraordinary Result of Imagination. And I conceive him so far in the right in his judicious esteem of this Poet, that, in his kind, perhaps he may remain perpetually unparallel'd.

Having thus far explain'd the Value and Form of this Author's Work, I will take leave to present my Reader with a Taste of what I judge the Essential Parts of Heroick Poesie.

And this must consist either in Action or in Allegory, or rather in a mixture of both. As for Action as it relates to an Heroick Poem, or is exemplary from thence; its greatness chiefly consists in Military Deeds, Stratagems, and Counsels, or in Political or Moral Reflections occasionally intervening. And these particulars, tho great Embellishments of *Epike Poetry*, are seldom so numerously various as can alone form so vast a Composition.

Besides all which, they cannot by any Art or Expression of the Poet be render'd much above the ordinary level of human Discussion and Imitation; by reason that the Prudence or Morality of any Actions, howsoever great they tend to Instruction, will concenter, in some degree, with common Thought and Observance. But in that part of such a Poem that includes an Allegory of Things and Persons, the Notions are more sublimely fitted to that purpose, as they have Reference to the unlimited Productions and Conduct of the Mind.

Thus in Magical Transformations, Visions, Apparitions, Extasies, Dreams, extraordinary Adventures, and the like; there is an unconfin'd Nature of Representation, or such as will not be found to accompany our passions and Affections in any ordinary Act or Contemplation: wherefore, of such, the most spiritual and wonderful part of an Epike Composition must consist, that it may be deliver'd thereby more remote and surprizing.

To which effect *Ulysses* in *Homer*, and the Hero of the *Aeneads* are not so much Objects of Admiration and extraordinary note, as they were great in Fortitude or prudence, Things, as I have already express'd, that most men presume in some measure to understand and imitate: but as they had encounter'd Monsters, convers'd with Apparitions and Ghosts in their Infernal Visits, whereby Admiration is rais'd, and their Characters convey'd more superlative and perfect, because exalted above usual Thought or Example.

And who does not more erect his Imagination in reading of the Descent of *Aeneas* into the *Elysian Fields*, and the extraordinary Notions and Descriptions arising from thence, than in taking notice of his more familiar Actions of Magnanimity and Conduct.

I had almost forgot a very pertinent passage in reference to what I now assert in behalf of this kind of Poesy.

And that shall be taken from the appearing of *Hector* after Death unto *Aeneas*, and his speech represented by way of Dream or Vision.

By which, whosoever considers the superlative Impression of passion that was character'd by this Hero, reviv'd by the poetical Summons of *Virgil*, shall find, if the Circumstances of his appearance are duely consider'd, that all the glorious Atchievements of *Hector* joyn'd to his Heroick Fall by the Sword of *Achilles*, could not so Emphatically consummate the Story of his past Life, as in being thus briefly describ'd by the Poet, tho but in an imaginary Method.

I could instance likewise as much in the Case of *Polydorus*, where *Virgil*, to express the covetous Guilt of a King of *Thrace*, who had murder'd that young Prince for his Treasure, has in the Miracle of his speaking from under Ground, divinely fix'd a due Detestation of so horrid a Crime, as also excited the most pathetick Sorrow that can be imagin'd for the cruelty of his end.

All which, if according to ordinary Fact they had been describ'd, would have fallen far short of their Efficacy, on all accounts, as wanting their preternatural force and esteem, or the Reputation of Wonder reveal'd by permission from above.

And thus it appears, that things marvellous, and of highest admiration, or such as cannot be personated by Deeds and Words of the living, must be the supream Ornaments of an *Epike Poem*.

Whereas in the Dramatick way it is far otherwise, because similitude to genuine Converse and action is chiefly there to be resembled; tho not always unaccompanyd with things preternatural and prodigious, as may be gather'd from the use of Magical Enchantments, and the Apparitions of Ghosts and Spirits in divers of our old and best Playes.

Some there are that would so far unsoul Poesy, as to allow nothing represented by it other than what familiarly resembles the ordinary Results of our Actions and Converse, and this they term likening of Truth; not considering that there is a similitude allowable for Contemplation and Opinion receiv'd by Men.

As the Doctrine of separated Forms and Spirits, the total practices of Conjurations and Magick. By which means incorporeal Apparitions have been conceded to appear: and he that denies their Credibility, must likewise disallow the Revelations of holy Writ, which gives authority, more than enough, to Poesy to take that for Truth which is there affirmed to be such.

On which ground I do not conceive why a Heroick Poem, which some undertake to deny, should not be as extraordinarily written in consonance to Christian Belief, as any was perform'd by the Ancients in their fictitious introducing of Hobgoblins, imaginary Deities and Visions: since we may have poetical Recourse to spiritual Existencies and Apparitions, if properly apply'd, as aptly to our purpose as they could invent to assist their Designs. In like manner, instead of their Designs. In like manner, instead of their *Centaurs*, *Harpy's*, *Cyclops's*, and the like, we have our Prodigies, and Monsters of Men and Creatures: so that I do not see why our Fictions may not be as duely supplied and grounded on any such account, as the ancient Poets could pretend to. Besides all which, there is no useful Poetical Nominal, or Ornament relating to things above or below, but may be as pertinently appropriated by us, as by whatsoever former Writer.

As who can doubt but Concupiscence may be signify'd by *Venus*, the Winds by *Aeolus*, the Sea by *Neptune*, and so of other fictitious Attributes usefully common to us and them.

And we ought rather to blame the narrowness of our Invention, than to conceive that there is not Furniture enough in Poetry to embellish the Grandeur of an Epick Contrivance.

True it is, that according to holy Religion, we must not presume to transform our Hero's into Demi-gods, which I confess was some advantage to the Ancients in magnifying their Heroicks above the ordinary Exaltation and Endowments of Men: However I believe that the sublime Piety and Fortitude incident to a Christian Hero duely convey'd by the Poet in reference to Exploits of highest Admiration and Glory, may well compare with what could be feign'd of the best of theirs.

And this I suppose is sufficient for their Conviction, who affirm that an *Epike Poem* is not to be produc'd within the bounds of Christianity. Not but I grant that it is a Work of highest difficulty, and no less to be admir'd, if perfect, than some wondrous Architecture hardly to be equall'd in point of Design, Magnitude, and Beauty.

But not impossible to be effected since there needs not be urged a surer Refutation of all Opposers, than the marvellous esteem of this Author, notwithstanding the Obsoleteness of his *English* and Verse, who liv'd within a hundred years of our time. But how to excuse the choice of the Language he writ in, that he could not but know, was of too antiquate a Date, if not generally exploded by all Writers in the time he liv'd; or why he should not conceive himself oblig'd to impart the Tongue of that season as currant as he found it, I cannot apprehend.

Unless he was resolv'd, as is reported of him, to imitate his ancient Predecessor *Chaucer*, or affected it out of design to restore our *Saxon English*. However it was, the Reader may peruse him here, as far as I have gone, in more fashionable *English* and Verse; and I hope without Diminution to his Fame in any regard.

III. Edward Howard

1689

Edward Howard (*flor.* 1669) met with failure and contempt both as poet and dramatist. Rochester saw fit to ridicule especially *The Brittish Princes*. See also No. 151.

From *The Preface* to *Caroloiades, or, The Rebellion of Forty One* (1689), sigs. A4–A4ᵛ:

In the mean time, to come closer to my purpose by alledging such Authorities as have the most undoubted Modern reception: I need but mention the Great *Tasso*, and our famous *Spencer*, by whose Poems, tho' the Productions of Latter Times, and agreeable to Evangelical persuasion, it is very clear that neither as to Fiction or Allegory, they wanted any necessary Ingredients or supplements, if compar'd with such Poets who had been precedent to Christian Belief. I shall not present my Reader with any Inspections into the Poem of *Spencer*, it being upon the matter wholly Allegory, and therefore not so proper to the Application I intend.

112. Sir William Temple

1690

Sir William Temple (1628–99) was educated at Emmanuel College, Cambridge, where he was a student of Cudworth, but left without a degree. Temple was with the Ancients in the controversy with Bentley, and since he secured the services of his amanuensis, Swift, for *The Battle of the Books*, he can be said, at one level, to have won.

From *Upon Poetry* in *Miscellanea. The Second Part* (1690) pp. 46–7:

Petrarch, Ronsard, Spencer, met with much Applause upon the Subjects of Love, Praise, Grief, Reproach. *Ariosto* and *Tasso* entered boldly upon the Scene of *Heroick* Poems, but having not Wings for so high Flights, began to Learn of the old Ones, fell upon their Imitations, and chiefly of *Virgil,* as far as the Force of their Genius or Disadvantage of New Languages and Customs would allow. The Religion of the Gentiles had been woven into the Contexture of all the antient Poetry, with a very agreeable mixture, which made the Moderns affect to give that of Christianity, a place also in their Poems. But the true Religion, was not found to become Fiction so well, as a false had done, and all their Attempts of this kind seemed rather to debase Religion than to heighten Poetry. *Spencer* endeavoured to Supply this, with Morality, and to make Instruction, instead of Story, the Subject of an *Epick* Poem. His Execution was Excellent, and his Flights of Fancy very Noble and High, but his Design was Poor, and his Moral lay so bare, that it lost the Effect; 'tis true, the Pill was Gilded, but so thin, that the Colour and the Taste were too easily discovered.

113. The *Athenian Mercury*

1691

From the *Athenian Mercury*, vol. II, no. 14, Saturday, 11 July 1691:

Quest. 3. Which is the best Poem *that ever was made and who in your Opinion, deserves the* Title *of the best* Poet *that ever was?*

Answ. . . . Plautus wrote *wittily, Terence* neatly – and *Seneca* has very fine thoughts. But since we can't go through all the world, let's look home a little. *Grandsire Chaucer,* in spite of the Age, was a Man of as much wit, sence and honesty as any that have writ after him. Father *Ben* was excellent at *Humour, Shakespeare* deserves the Name of *sweetest,* which *Milton* gave him. – Spenser was a noble poet, his *Fairy-Queen* an excellent piece of Morality, Policy, History. *Davenant* had a great genius. – Too much can't be said of *Mr Coley. Milton's Paradise Lost,* and some other Poems of his will never be equal'd. *Waller* is the most *correct* Poet we have.

114. Joseph Addison

1694–1712

Joseph Addison (1672–1719) was educated at Charterhouse, where he met Steele, and then at Queen's College, and Magdalen College, Oxford. He became a Fellow of the latter, but his reputation quickly spread to London, where he came to dominate literary society. *An Account* is little more than a summary of current opinion: Addison had not read Spenser when he wrote it (see Spenser's *Observations, Anecdotes...*, ed. J. M. Osborn [Oxford, 1966], I. 74). Addison's interest in Spenser's allegory is attested also in the *Guardian* No. 152.

(a) From *An Account of the Greatest English Poets. To Mr H.S. Apr., 1694* in *The Annual Miscellany: for the Year 1694. Being the Fourth Part of Miscellany Poems*, pp. 318–19; repr. *The Miscellaneous works of Joseph Addison*, ed. A. C. Guthkelch (1914), I. 31–2:

> Old *Spencer* next, warm'd with Poetick Rage,
> In Antick Tales amus'd a Barb'rous Age;
> An Age that yet uncultivate and Rude,
> Where-e're the Poet's Fancy led, pursu'd
> Through pathless Fields, and unfrequented Floods,
> To Dens of Dragons, and Enchanted Woods.
> But now the Mystick Tale, that pleas'd of Yore,
> Can Charm an understanding Age no more;
> The long-spun Allegories fulsom grow,
> While the dull Moral lyes too plain below.
> We view well-pleas'd at distance all the sights ⎫
> Of *arms* and *Palfries*, Cattel's, Fields and Fights, ⎬
> And Damsels in Distress, and Courteous Knights. ⎭
> But when we look too near, the Shades decay,
> And all the pleasing Lan-skip fades away.

(b) From *The Spectator* No. 62 (11 May 1711); repr. *The Spectator*, ed. R. W. Bond (Oxford, 1965), I. 265:

... there is another kind of Wit, which consists partly in the Resemblance of Ideas, and partly in the Resemblance of Words; which for Distinction Sake I shall call *mixt wit*. This kind of Wit is that which abounds in *Cowley*, more than in any Author that ever wrote. ... *Milton* had a Genius much above it. *Spencer* is in the same class with *Milton*. The *Italians*, even in their Epic Poetry are full of it.

(c) From *The Spectator* No. 183 (29 September 1711); repr. Bond, II. 221:

But besides this kind of Fable there is another in which the Actors are Passions, Virtues, Vices and other imaginary Persons of the like Nature ... The greatest Italian Wits have applied themselves to the Writing of this latter kind of Fables; as *Spencer's Fairy Queen* is one continued Series of them from the beginning to the end of that admirable Work.

(d) From *The Spectator* No. 297 (9 February 1712); repr. Bond, III. 60:

I must in the next Place observe, that *Milton* has interwoven in the Texture of his Fable some Particulars which do not seem to have Probability enough for an Epic Poem, particularly in the Actions which he ascribes to *Sin* and *Death*, and the Picture which he draws of the *Lymbo* of *Vanity*, with other Passages in the second book. Such allegories rather savour of the Spirit of *Spencer* and *Ariosto*, than of *Homer* and *Virgil*.

(e) From *The Spectator* No. 419 (1 July 1712); repr. Bond, III. 573:

There is another sort of Imaginary Beings, that we sometimes meet with among the Poets, when the Author represents any Passion, Appetite, Virtue, or Vice, under a visible Shape, and makes it a Person or an Actor in his Poem. Of this Nature are the Descriptions of Hunger and Envy in *Ovid*, of Fame in *Virgil*, and of Sin and Death in *Milton*. We find a whole Creation of the like shadowy Persons in *Spencer*, who had an admirable Talent in Representations of this kind.

115. Sir Richard Blackmore

1695, 1716

Sir Richard Blackmore (1660?–1729) was educated at Westminster School, St Edmund Hall, Oxford, and Padua. Spenser appears, though in distinctly Miltonic guise, in Blackmore's epic *Eliza* (1705).

(a) From *The Preface* to *Prince Arthur. An Heroick Poem. In Ten Books* (1695), sig. b2; repr. J. E. Spingarm, *Critical Essays of the Seventeenth Century* (Oxford 1908–9), III. 238:

But *Ariosto* and Spencer, however *great Wits*, not observing this judicious Conduct of *Virgil*, nor attending to any sober Rules, are hurried on with a *boundless, impetuous* Fancy over Hill and Dale, till they are both lost in a Wood of Allegories. Allegories so *wild, unnatural,* and *extravagant,* as greatly displease the Reader. This way of writing mightily offends in this Age; and 'tis a wonder how it came to please in any.

(b) From *Essays upon Several Subjects* (1716), pp. 41–2:

But an allegory is sometimes taken in another Sense, that is, when Vertues and Vices are represented as Persons either Humane or Divine, and proper Passions and Manners are ascrib'd to their respective Characters: Of this are several examples in *Homer's Ulysses,* and too many in the modern Epick Writers, and there is one Instance of this sort in the sixth Book of King *Arthur.* . . . In the second Sense, the modern Epick Poets, especially *Ariosto* and *Spencer,* have ran too far into Allegory. This sort of allegorical Imaging resembles the emblematic Draughts of great Painters, where Vertues are represented as Goddesses, and Vices as Furies; and where Liberty, Peace, Plenty, Pleasure, and various Qualities of the Mind are exhibited in Humane Forms, with peculiar Properties and Marks of Distinction. An elegant

Instance of this kind of Writing is the Representation of Sin and Death in the appearance of two odious and terrible Monsters, by our celebrated *Milton* in his *Paradise Lost*; of which, I imagine, he took the Hint from the famous *Spencer*. This sort of Allegories, tho not strictly Epick, us'd with Temperance and Judgement, affect the Mind with Wonder and Delight, and enliven and beautify the Poem.

116. Patrick Hume

1695

Patrick Hume (*flor.* 1695) was a London schoolmaster. His commentary on Milton is generally acknowledged to be remarkable both for its learning and for its method.

From *Notes on Milton's Paradise Lost*, with sixth ed. of *Paradise Lost* (1695) p. 134 [on *PL* IV 151 ff.]

But to make a Comparison more obvious to most Understandings, read the Description of the *Bower of Bliss*, by a Poet of our own Nation, and famous in his time; but 'tis *impar congressus!* and Rhyme fetter'd his Fancy.

[quotes *Faerie Queene* II. xii. 42]

Ibid., p. 157 [on *PL* IV. 703]:

Now if we compare the foregoing Description of this blissful Bower, with one of a Poet our Country-man, and deservedly famous in his time, we shall find the difference of their Genius to be great as that of their Language.

[quotes *Faerie Queene* II. v. 29] as far short of ours, as his Garden of *Adonis*, Bo. 3. C. 6. Stan. 30. is of inimitable *Eden*, V. 210.

SPENSER

Ibid., p. 232 [note on *P.L.* VIII.152]:

Of the Probability of a Plurality of Worlds, hear what another of our Country-men, and a Poet excellent in his time, said:

[quotes *Faerie Queene* II, proem 3]

Ibid., p. 314 [note on *P.L.* XI.180]:

IMBOSS – A Word used by our *Spencer*.

[quotes *Faerie Queene* I. ix. 29]

117. Luke Milbourne

1698

Luke Milbourne (1649–1720), educated at Pembroke Hall, Cambridge, was himself a translator of Virgil. Dryden himself and later Pope both answered Milbourne's objections. See also No. 160.

(a) From *Notes on Dryden's Virgil* (1698), p. 26:

Spencer wanted only to have read the rules of *Bossu* It's well if *Virgil* and *Homer* did not want 'em too; for it seems, if our *French Criticks* may be believ'd, neither of 'em had the luck to write a *true Heroic Poem*.

(b) *Ibid.*, p. 29:

Spencer, and *Milton* are nearest in English to *Virgil*, and *Horace* in the Latine. But which of the them resembles *Horace*? *Spencer* aim'd at an *Heroic Poem*, and so did *Milton*, (tho neither of 'em with that *success* which might have been wish'd) . . .

118. John Dennis

1698–1717

John Dennis (1657–1737) was educated at Caius College and Trinity Hall, Cambridge. He combines neo-classical tastes with extraordinary open-mindedness, as his partiality for Milton, if not for Spenser, demonstrates.

(a) From *The Usefulness of the Stage* (1698), p. 40; repr. *Critical Works*, ed. E. N. Hooker (Baltimore, 1939), I. 160:

But immediately upon the Establishment of the Drama, Three Prodigies of Wit appeared all at once, as it were so many Suns, to amaze the learned World. The Reader will immediately comprehend that I speak of *Spencer*, *Bacon*, and *Raleigh*; Three mighty Genius's, so extraordinary in their different Ways, that not only *England* had never seen the like before, but they almost continue to this very Day, in spight of Emulation, in spight of Time, the greatest of our Poets, Philosophers, and Historians.

(b) From *The Grounds of Criticism in Poetry* (1704) sigs. ab–ab^v; repr. Hooker, I. 331:

When by doing this we have laid down the Rules, we come briefly to examine, Whether those Rules are always to be kept inviolable; and if they are not, in what parts, and by whom, they may be alter'd. Then we shew how *Spencer*, by not following those Rules, fell so very far short of the Ancients: and afterwards we endeavour to make it appear, how *Milton*, by daring to break a little loose from them in some particulars, kept up in several others to the Nature of the Greater Poetry in general, and of Epick Poetry in particular, better than the best of the Ancients.

(c) *Ibid.*, pp. 113–14; repr. Hooker, I. 369:

The Rules for employing Religion in Poetry, are Principally these which follow.

1. The First is, That the Religion ought to be one, that the Poet may be mov'd by it, and that he may appear to be in earnest. And the not observing this Rule, was one Reason why *Spencer* miscarried as we shall shew anon. . . .

2. The Third is, that it may run thro' and be incorporated with the Action of the Poem, and consequently that it may always be a part of Action, and Productive of Action; for from the Neglect of this third Rule, strange inequalities would follow in a Poem, as shall be shewn more at large, when we treat of *Spencer* and *Cowley*.

(d) From *Remarks upon Mr Pope's Translation of Homer* . . . (1717), p. 8; repr. Hooker, II. 122:

. . . the Capacity and Profoundness of BACON, the fine Painting of SPENSER, the Force and Sublimity, and Elevation of MILTON. . . .

119. Samuel Wesley

1697

Samuel Wesley the elder (1662–1735) was educated at Exeter College, Oxford. See also No. 162.

From *The Essay on Heroic Poetry*, prefatory to *The Life of our Blessed Lord* (1697), p. 22:

To begin with Spencer, who I think comes the nearest Ariosto of any other; he's almost as Irregular, but much more Natural and Lovely: But he's not only Irregular but Imperfect too, I mean, as to what he intended; and therefore we can't well imagine what it wou'd have been, had he liv'd to complete it. If Fable be the Essence of Epic, his Fairy Queen had certainly enough of that to give it that Name. He seems, by the account he gives of it to Sir Walter Rawleigh, to have design'd one Principal Hero King Arthur, and one main important Action bringing him to his Throne; but neither of these appear sufficiently distinct, or well defin'd, being both lost in the vast Seas of Matter which compose those Books which are finish'd. This however must be granted, the Design was Noble, and required such a comprehensive Genius as his, but to draw the first Sketch of it: And as to the Design, so the Thoughts are also very great, the Expressions flowing natural and easie, with such a prodigious Poetical Copia as never any other must expect to enjoy.

120. Samuel Cobb

c. 1700

Samuel Cobb (1675–1713) was educated at Christ's Hospital and Trinity College, Cambridge, from which he returned to his former school as a master.

From *Poetae Britannici. A Poem* (*c.* 1700), p. 10:

> Sunk in a Sea of Ignorance we lay,
> Till *Chaucer* rose, and pointed out the Day,
> A Joking Bard, whose Antiquated Muse,
> In mouldy Words could solid Sense produce.
> Our *English Ennius He*, who claim'd his part
> In wealthy Nature, tho' unskilled in Art.
> The sparkling Diamond on his Dunghill shines,
> And Golden Fragments glitter in his Lines.
> Which *Spencer* gather'd for his Learning known,

And by successful Gleanings made his own.
So careful bees, on a fair Summers Day,
Hum o'er the Flowers, and suck the Sweets away.
Of *Gloriana*, and her Knights he sung,
Of Beasts, which from his pregnant Fancy sprung.
O had thy Poet, *Britany*, rely'd
On Native Strength, and Foreign Aid deny'd;
Had not wild Fairies blasted his design,
Moeonides and *Virgil* had been Thine!
Their finish'd Poems he exactly view'd,
But *Chaucer's* Steps Religiously pursued.
He cull'd and pick'd, and thought it greater praise
T'adore his Master, than improve his Phrase.
'Twas counted Sin to deviate from his Page;
So sacred was th'Authority of Age!

121. Henry Hall

1700

Henry Hall the younger (d. 1713) succeeded his father as organist
of Hereford Cathedral. He contrived however to compose more
verse than music.

From *Luctus Britannici: of The Tears of the British Muses; for the Death
of John Dryden, Esq.* (1700), p. 10:

Let us look back, and Noble Numbers trace
Directly up from Ours, to *Chaucer's* days;
Chaucer, the first of Bards in Tune that Sung,
And to a better bent reduc'd the stubborn Tongue.

Spencer upon his Master much Refin'd,
He Colour'd sweetly, tho he ill Design'd;
Too mean the Model for so vast a Mind.
Thus while he try'd to make his stanza's Chime,
Good *Christian* Thoughts Turn *Renegade* to Rhime.

122. A note on Spenser's influence

1702

From a review of the second edition of Joseph Beaumont's *Psyche*, in *History of the Works of the Learned* (March 1702), p. 100:

If this Divine poet is not so smooth and exact in his Numbers, as our Modern Poets are, 'tis to be attributed to his strict following the measures and stanza of the Great *Spenser*, who was ever accounted an excellent Master of Poetry in his Time, and who has ever since been look'd upon as a Model fit to be imitated by all the succeeding Pretenders to that Art.

123. N.N.

1704

I am unable to identify N.N. While the translation *Advertisements from Parnassus* is certainly by him, it is not even clear if the same man is responsible for the *Secretaria di Apollo*. Since, however, both works appear in the same year, and since the title page of the first promises but does not print the second, it is safe to assume that N.N. is the translator of both Works of Boccalini.

From *Secretaria di Apollo or, Letters from Apollo* (1704), I. 230–1 (Letter addressed 'To Spencer', originally to Petrarch):

The Advertisements which we daily receive in *Parnassus*, concerning the miserable condition of our beloved Poetry, encrease our desire to provide some Remedy against the Disorders it labours under; and for this end we formerly sent *Homer* and *Virgil* our faithful Servants, Embassadors to most of the Princes in the World, to perswade 'em to take Care in this Matter; but since those Endeavours have proved vain, we command you as the Prince of English Poetry, to declare our Intention; which is, that all those foolish Bards, who have never drunk the Waters of *Aganippe*, amongst our Muses, but only Muddy Ale in the Cellars amongst the drunken Rabble, may be made to understand that they merit the Punishment of perpetual Infamy, if they hereafter presume to defile Paper with Ink and filthy *Grubstreet* Rhimes. . . . You know, in former times the Subjects of Poetry, were only Heroical and glorious, great, virtuous and conspicuous Persons, whose Actions were renown'd all the World over; whereas the necessitous Bards of the present Age choose worthless and obscure Subjects; and what is still more ridiculous, whereas one Poet was formerly to celebrate many Heroes, now many Poets are not able to satisfie one ambitous Upstart who deserves a Satyr, not an Epick Poem in his Commendation. . . .

124. Alexander Pope

1704?, 1713

Alexander Pope (1688–1744) takes Spenser primarily as a pastoralist. His own *Pastorals* he no doubt considered as being at least on a par with the *Shepheardes Calender* (and compare Walsh, in Pope's *Correspondence*, ed. G. Sherburn [Oxford, 1956], p. 21), but his criticisms here are not to be taken seriously. Pope was after all an admirer of Hughes, and incidental remarks betray the seriousness of his admiration for Spenser (for example those reported in Spence's *Observations, Anecdotes...*, ed. J. M. Osborn [Oxford, 1966], I. 171, 178). See also No. 167.

(a) From *A Discourse on Pastoral Poetry* in *Works* (1717), pp. 8–10 (written 1704); repr. *The Poems of Alexander Pope* (Twickenham Edition) I (1961), 31–3:

Spenser's Calendar, in Mr Dryden's opinion, is the most complete work of this kind which any Nation has produc'd ever since the time of *Virgil*. Not but that he may be thought imperfect in some few points. His Eclogues are somewhat too long, if we compare them with the ancients. He is sometimes too allegorical, and treats of matters of religion in a pastoral style as *Mantuan* had done before him. He has employ'd the Lyric measure, which is contrary to the practice of the old Poets. His Stanza is not still the same, nor always well chosen. This last may be the reason his expression is sometimes not concise enough: for the Tetrastic has oblig'd him to extend his sense to the length of four lines, which would have been more closely confin'd in the couplet.

In the manners, thoughts, and characters, he comes near to *Theocritus* himself; tho' notwithstanding all the care he has taken, he is certainly inferior in his Dialect. For the *Doric* had its beauty and propriety in the time of *Theocritus*; it was used in part of *Greece*, and frequent in the mouths of many of the greatest persons; whereas the old *English* and country phrases of *Spenser* were entirely obsolete, or spoken only by people of the lowest condition. As there is a difference between simplicity and rusticity, so the expression of simple thoughts should be plain, but not clownish. The addition he has made of a Calendar to his Eclogues is very beautiful: since by this, besides the general moral of innocence and simplicity, which is common to other authors of pastoral, he has one peculiar to himself; he compares human Life to the several Seasons, and at once exposes to his readers a view of the great and little worlds, in their various changes and aspects. Yet the scrupulous division of his Pastorals into Months, has oblig'd him either to repeat the same description, in other words, for three months together; or when it was exhausted before, entirely to omit it: whence it comes to pass that some of his Eclogues (as the sixth, eighth, and tenth for example) have nothing but their Titles to distinguish them. The reason is evident, because the year has not that variety in it to furnish every month with a particular description, as it may every season.

(b) From *The Guardian* No. 40 (27 April 1713):

Nor would I have a Poet slavishly confine himself (as Mr *Pope* has done) to one particular Season of the Year, one certain time of the Day, and one unbroken Scene in each Eclogue. 'Tis plain *Spencer* neglected this Pedantry, who in his Pastoral of *November* mentions the mournful song of the nightingale: *Sad Philomel her song in tears doth steep*. And Mr *Philips*, by a Poetical Creation hath raised up finer Beds of Flowers than the most industrious Gardiner; his Roses, Lillies, and Daffodils blow in the same Season.

125. Matthew Prior

1706, c. 1708

Matthew Prior (1664–1721) was educated at Westminster School, and with the help of the Earl of Dorset, proceeded to St John's College, Cambridge. He combined his poetical career with a diplomatic one, and, as was apparently his wish, was buried at the feet of Spenser. See W. L. Godshalk, 'Prior's Copy of Spenser's *Works*, 1679', *Papers of the Bibliographical Society of America*, LXI (1967), 52–5, for an account of his marginalia.

(a) From *The Preface* to *An Ode, Humbly Inscrib'd to the Queen* ... *Written in Imitation of Spenser's Stile* (1706), sig. A^v; repr. *The Literary Works*, ed. H. B. Wright, and M. K. Spears (Oxford, 1959), I. 231–2:

My Two Great Examples, HORACE and SPENSER, in many Things resemble each other: Both have a Height of Imagination, and a Majesty of Expression in describing the *Sublime*; and both know to temper those Talents, and sweeten the Description, so as to make it Lovely as well as Pompous: Both have equally That agreeable Manner of mixing Morality with their Story, and That *Curiosa Felicitas* in the Choice of their Diction, which every Writer aims at, and so very few have reach'd: Both are particularly Fine in their Images, and Knowing in their Numbers.

(b) From *The Preface* to *Solomon on the Vanity of the World* (1718, but written *c.* 1708), sigs. Ffff2–Ffff2^v; repr. Wright and Spears, I. 307–8:

In our Language SPENSER has not contented himself with this submissive Manner of Imitation: He launches out into very flowery Paths, which still seem to conduct him into one great Road. His *Fairy Queen* (had it been finished) must have ended in the Account, which every Knight was to give of his Adventures, and in the accumulated Praises of his Heroine GLORIANA. The Whole would have been an *Heroic* Poem, but

I

in another Cast and Figure, than any that had ever been written before. Yet it is observable, that every Hero (as far as we can judge by the Books still remaining) bears his distinguished Character, and represents some particular Virtue conducive to the whole Design.

126. Ambrose Philips

1710

Ambrose Philips (1675?–1749) was educated at St John's College, Cambridge, of which he became a Fellow. His famous quarrel with Pope was occasioned by the publication of *The Guardian* No. 40 (*q.v.*), where Pope ironically answers previous material on pastoral, and all at Philip's expense. His pastoral poetry is affectedly Spenserian, though Addison thought highly enough of him to hope that his *Pastorals*, like those of Virgil and Spenser, would be the prelude to something greater (see Addison's *Letters*, ed. W. Graham (Oxford, 1941), pp. 229–30).

From the *Preface* to *Pastorals* (1710), sig. [A1]ᵛ:

It is strange to think, in an Age so addicted to the *Muses*, how *Pastoral* Poetry came to be never so much as thought upon; considering especially, that it has always been accounted the most considerable of the smaller Poems. *Virgil* and *Spencer* made use of it as a Prelude to *Heroick Poetry*. But I fear the innocency of the Subject makes it so little inviting at present. . . . *Theocritus*, *Virgil*, and *Spencer* are the only Writers, that seem to have hit upon the true Nature of *Pastoral* Poems.

127. Sir Richard Steele

1710, 1712

Sir Richard Steele (1672–1729) was educated at Charterhouse, where he met Addison, and proceeded to Christ Church and Merton. The *Spectator* piece comes in response to a letter from one M.R., reprinted in Bond, IV. 432: 'I am now in the country, and reading in Spencer's fairy-queen. Pray what is the matter with me? When the poet is sublime my heart burns, when he is compassionate I faint, when he is sedate my soul is becalm'd.' The writer asks for a stanza [a canto?] to be treated each week, but the request was never met. The *Tatler* piece may be by Hughes (see G. A. Aitken, *The Tatler* (1899), IV. 7), but the possibility is not in my opinion at all strong.

(a) *The Tatler*, No. 194, 4–6 July 1710:

I was this Morning reading the Tenth Canto in the Fourth Book of *Spencer*, in which Sir *Scudamore* relates the Progress of his Courtship to *Amoret* under a very beautiful Allegory, which is one of the most natural and unmixed of any in that most excellent Author. I shall transpose it, to use Mr *Bays*'s Term, for the Benefit of many *English* Lovers, who have by frequent Letters desired me to lay down some Rules for the Conduct of their virtuous Amours; and shall only premise, That by the Shield of Love, is meant a generous constant Passion for the Person beloved.

When the Fame, says he, of this celebrated Beauty first flew Abroad, I went in Pursuit of her to the *Temple of Love*. This Temple, continues he, bore the Name of the Goddess *Venus*, and was seated in a most fruitful Island, walled by Nature against all Invaders. There was a single Bridge that led into the Island, and before it a Castle garrison'd by 20 Knights. Near the Castle was an open Plain, and in the midst of it a Pillar, on which was hung the Shield of Love; and underneath it, in Letters of Gold, was this Inscription:

Happy the Man who well can use his Bliss;
Whose ever be the Shield, Fair Amoret be his.
[IV. x. 8.]

My Heart panted upon reading the Inscription; I struck upon the Shield with my Spear. Immediately issued forth a Knight well mounted, and completely armed, who, without speaking, ran fiercely at me. I receiv'd him as well as I could, and by good Fortune threw him out of the Saddle. I encounter'd the whole Twenty successively, and leaving them all extended on the Plain, carried off the Shield in Token of Victory. Having thus vanquish'd my Rivals, I passed on without Impediment, till I came to the outermost Gate of the Bridge, which I found locked and barred. I knocked and called, but could get no Answer. At last I saw one on the other Side of the Gate, who stood peeping thro' a small Crevice. This was the Porter; he had a double Face resembling a *Janus*, and was continually looking about him, as if he mistrusted some sudden Danger. His Name, as I afterwards learned, was *Doubt*. Over-against him sat *Delay*, who entertain'd Passengers with some idle Story, while they lost such Opportunities as were never to be recovered. As soon as the Porter saw my Shield, he open'd the Gate; but upon my entring, *Delay* caught hold of me, and would fain have made me listen to her Fooleries. However, I shook her off, and pass'd forward, till I came to the Second Gate, *The Gate of good Desert*, which always stood wide open; but in the Porch was an hideous Giant that stopp'd the Entrance. His Name was *Danger*. Many Warriors of good Reputation, not able to bear the Sternness of his Look, went back again. Cowards fled at the first Sight of him, except some few, who watching their Opportunity, slipp'd by him unobserved. I prepared to assault him; but upon the first Sight of my Shield, he immediately gave Way. Looking back upon him, I found his hinder Parts much more deformed and terrible than his Face; *Hatred*, *Murther*, *Treason*, *Envy*, and *Detraction*, lying in Ambush behind him, to fall upon the Heedless and Unwary.

I now entered *The Island of Love*, which appeared in all the Beauties of Art and Nature, and feasted every Sense with the most agreeable Objects. Amidst a pleasing Variety of Walks and Allies, shady Seats, and flowry Banks, sunny Hills, and gloomy Vallies, were Thousands of Lovers sitting or walking together in Pairs, and singing Hymns to the Deity of the Place.

I could not forbear envying this happy People, who were already in

Possession of all they could desire. While I went forward to the Temple, the Structure was beautiful beyond Imagination; The Gate stood open. In the Entrance sat a most amiable Woman, whose Name was *Concord*.

On either Side of her stood Two young Men, both strongly armed, as if afraid of each other. As I afterwards learn'd, they were both her Sons, but begotten of her by Two different Fathers; their Names *Love* and *Hatred*.

The Lady so well tempered and reconciled them both, that she forced them to join Hands; tho' I could not but observe, that *Hatred* turned aside his Face, as not able to endure the Sight of his younger Brother.

I at length entered the Inmost Temple, the Roof of which was raised upon an Hundred Marble Pillars, decked with Crowns, Chains, and Garlands. The Ground was strow'd with Flowers. An Hundred Altars, at each of which stood a Virgin Priestess cloathed in White, blazed all at once with the Sacrifice of Lovers, who were perpetually sending up their Vows to Heaven in Clouds of Incense.

In the Midst stood the Goddess her self upon an Altar, whose Substance was neither Gold nor Stone, but infinitely more precious than either. About her Neck flew numberless Flocks of little *Loves*, *Joys*, and *Graces*; and all about her Altar lay scattered Heaps of *Lovers*, complaining of the Disdain, Pride, or Treachery, of their Mistresses. One among the rest, no longer able to contain his Griefs, broke out into the following Prayer:

'*Venus*, Queen of Grace and Beauty, Joy of Gods and Men, who with a smile becalmest the Seas, and renewest all Nature; Goddess, whom all the different Species in the Universe obey with Joy and Pleasure, grant I may at last obtain the Objects of my Vows.'

The impatient Lover pronounced this with great Vehemence; but I in a soft Murmur besought the Goddess to lend me her Assistance. While I was thus praying, I chanced to cast my Eye on a Company of Ladies, who were assembled together in a Corner of the Temple waiting for the Anthem.

The foremost seemed something elder, and of a more composed Countenance, than the rest, who all appeared to be under her Direction. Her Name was *Womanhood*. On one Side of her sat *Shamefacedness*, with Blushes rising in her Cheeks, and her Eyes fixed upon the Ground. On the other was *Chearfulness*, with a smiling Look, that infused a secret Pleasure into the Hearts of all that saw her. With these sat *Modesty*, holding her Hand on her Heart; *Courtesy*, with a graceful

Aspect, and obliging Behaviour; and the Two Sisters, who were always linked together, and resembled each other, *Silence* and *Obedience*.

> *Thus sat they all around in seemly Rate,*
> *And in the Midst of them a goodly Maid,*
> *Ev'n in the Lap of* Womanhood *there sat,*
> *The which was all in Lilly white array'd;*
> *Where Silver Streams among the Linen stray'd;*
> *Like to the Morn, when first her shining Face*
> *Hath to the Gloomy World it self bewray'd.*
> *That same was fairest* Amoret *in Place,*
> *Shining with Beauty's Light, and Heav'nly Virtue's Grace.*
>
> [IV. x. 52.]

As soon as I beheld the charming *Amoret*, my Heart throbbed with Hopes. I stepped to her, and seized her Hand; when *Womanhood* immediately rising up, sharply rebuked me for offering in so rude a Manner to lay hold on a Virgin. I excused myself as modestly as I could, and the same Time displayed my Shield; upon which, as soon as she beheld the God emblazoned with his Bow and Shafts, she was struck mute, and instantly retired.

I still held fast the fair *Amoret*, and turning my Eyes towards the Goddess of the Place, saw that she favoured my Pretensions with a Smile, which so emboldened me, that I carried off my Prize.

The Maid, sometimes with Tears, sometimes with Smiles, entreated me to let her go: But I led her through the Temple-Gate, where the Goddess *Concord*, who had favoured my Entrance, befriended my Retreat.

This Allegory is so natural, that it explains itself. The Persons in it are very artfully described, and disposed in proper Places. The Posts assigned to *Doubt*, *Delay*, and *Danger*, are admirable. The Gate of *Good Desert* has something noble and instructive in it. But above all, I am most pleased with the beautiful Grouppe of Figures in the Corner of the Temple. Among these, *Womanhood* is drawn like what the Philosophers call an Universal Nature, and is attended with beautiful Representatives of all those Virtues that are the Ornaments of the Female Sex, considered in its natural Perfection and Innocence.

(b) From *The Spectator* No. 540 (19 November 1712); repr. *The Spectator*, ed. R. W. Bond (Oxford, 1965), IV. 428–31:

There is no Part of your Writings which I have in more Esteem than your Criticism upon *Milton*. It is an honourable and candid Endeavour to set the Works of our Noble Writers in the graceful Light which they deserve. You will lose much of my kind Inclination towards you, if you do not attempt the Encomium of *Spencer* also, or at least indulge my Passion for that charming Author so far as to print the loose Hints I now give you on that Subject.

Spencer's general Plan is the Representation of six Virtues, Holiness, Temperance, Chastity, Friendship, Justice, and Courtesy, in six Legends by six Persons. The six Personages are supposed under proper Allegories suitable to their respective Characters, to do all that necessary for the full Manifestation of the respective Virtues which they are to exert.

These one might undertake to shew, under the several Heads, are admirably drawn; no Images improper, and most surprizingly beautiful. The Red-cross Knight runs thro' the whole Steps of the Christian Life; *Guyon* does all that Temperance can possibly require; *Britomartis* (a Woman) observes the true Rules of unaffected Chastity; *Arthegal* is in every Respect of Life strictly and wisely just; *Calidore* is rightly courteous.

In short, in *Fairy-Land*, where Knights-Errant have a full Scope to range, and to do even what *Ariosto*'s or *Orlando*'s could not do in the World without breaking into Credibility, *Spencer*'s Knights have, under those six Heads, given a full and a truly Poetical System of Christian, Publick, and Low Life.

His Legend of Friendship is more diffuse, and yet even there the Allegory is finely drawn, only the Heads various, one Knight could not there support all the Parts.

To do Honour to his Country, Prince *Arthur* is an Universal Hero; in Holiness, Temperance, Chastity, and Justice super-excellent. For the same Reason, and to compliment Queen *Elizabeth*, *Gloriana*, Queen of Fairies, whose Court was the Asylum of the Oppressed, represents that glorious Queen. At her Commands all these Knights set forth, and only at her's the Red-Cross Knight destroys the Dragon, *Guyon* overturns the Bower of Bliss, Arethegal (i.e. *Justice*) beats down *Geryoneo* (i.e. *Phil.* II. King of *Spain*) to rescue *Belge* (i.e. *Holland*) and he beats the *Grantorto* (the same *Philip* in another Light) to restore *Irena* (i.e. *Peace to* Europe).

Chastity being the first Female Virtue, *Britomartis* is a *Britain*; her Part is fine, tho' it requires Explication. His Stile is very Poetical; no

Puns, Affectations of Wit, forced Antitheses, or any of that low Tribe.

His old Words are all true *English*, the Numbers exquisite; and since of Words there is the *Multa Renascentur*, since they are all proper, such a Poem should not (any more than *Milton*'s) subsist all of it of common ordinary Words. See Instances of Descriptions.

[quotes *Faerie Queene* V. vi. 14; V. vi. 8, 9; IV. vi. 32, 34, 35]

Homer's Epithets were much admired by Antiquity: See what great Justness and Variety is in these Epithets of the Trees in the Forest where the Red-cross Knight lost *Truth*.

[quotes *Faerie Queene* I. i. 8, 9]

I shall trouble you no more, but desire you to let me conclude with these Verses, tho' I think they have already been quoted by you: They are Directions to young Ladies opprest with Calumny.

[quotes *Faerie Queene* VI. vi. 14]

128. Leonard Welsted

1712

Leonard Welsted (1688–1747) was educated at Westminster School and Trinity College, Cambridge. The translation of Longinus is his first and an early work. His later reputation rests on his achievement as a poet, and is in consequence slight.

From *Longinus on the Sublime* (1712), p. 149:

What can be more great and terrible than *Spencer*'s Dragon?

His blazing Eyes . . . [quotes *Faerie Queene* I. xi. 14]

And in another place

>   *An hideous Giant* . . . [quotes *Faerie Queene* I. vii. 8]

Longinus takes occasion from hence to censure *Hesoid*'s Description of
the *Goddess* of Darkness, very justly remarking that he does not
properly render her terrible, but nauseous and distasteful.

>   *A foetid Humour trickled from her Nose*

It must be confessed that our Countryman *Spencer*, however excellent
in other respects, is frequently faulty in this particular, as for Instance,
speaking of Duessa he says

>   *Her dried Dugs* . . . [quotes *Faerie Queene* I. viii. 47]

This observation is finely touch'd upon by my Lord *Roscommon*, in
his Essay on translated Verse.

Ibid., p. 154:

Spencer's Description of his Dragon's Flight, tho' not directly applicable to this Point [that Longinus makes about Homer's description of
Neptune], seems to be conceiv'd with great Strength of Thought.

Ibid., pp. 168–9.

[Longinus has compared some lines of Homer with those of an
anonymous author.] This sort of Writing, he tells us, is perhaps pretty
and fanciful, but not great. If I forget not, some gawdy strokes of this
glittering Tinsel-Vein may be found sometimes in Mr *Waller*; and the
Italian Poets, as far as the little Knowledge I have of that Tongue will
permit me to judge, seem to abound with ornaments of a mixed kind,
as our own *Spencer*, who, if I may use the Expression, copies from
Homer, *Virgil*, and *Ovid* in the same Breath.

129. Henry Felton

1713

Henry Felton (1679–1740) was educated at St Edmund Hall, Oxford. The *Dissertation* was first published in 1713 and quickly ran through several editions.

From *A Dissertation on Reading the Classics* (1713), pp. 222–3:

... For though I think *Spencer* and *Shakespeare* as great Genius's as ever were produced in *Rome* or *Athens*, they will not bear a strict Comparison upon all the Beauties of Writing. Milton, alone, in *Epic* Writing hath transcended the Greek and the Latin Poet: He hath excelled the *First* in the Force and Richness of Imagination; and hath rivalled the *Last* in Justness of Thought, and Exactness of the Work. *Spencer* may, perhaps, dispute the *Pastoral*, even with *Theocritus*, for I dare prefer him to *Virgil*, and in him alone the Sweetness and Rusticity of the *Doric* Muse was to be found, till of late Years some happy Genius's among our selves have assembled all the Beauties of Arcadian Poetry, and restored their Simplicity, Language, and Manners, to the Swains.

130. Thomas Parnell

1713

Thomas Parnell (1679–1718) was educated at Trinity College, Dublin. He took orders, but was evidently committed to a literary career. In his own time, as now, he enjoyed most fame as a poet, but he also contributed papers to the *Spectator* and the *Guardian*.

From the *Preface* to the *Essay on the Different Styles of Poetry* (1713), sigs. A4–A4ᵛ; repr. Alexander Chalmers, *The Works of the English Poets* (1810), IX. 413:

We are much beholden to *Antiquity* for those excellent Compositions by which Writers at present form their Minds; but it is not so much required of us to adhere merely to their Fables, as to observe their Manner. For if we preclude our own Invention, Poetry will consist only in Expression, or Simile, or the Application of old Stories; and the utmost Character to which a Genius will arrive will depend on Imitation, or a borrowing from others, which we must agree together not to call Stealing, because we take only from the Ancients. There have been Poets amongst ourselves, such as *Spencer* and *Milton*, who have successfully ventured further. These Instances may let us see that Invention is not bounded by what has been done before, they may open our Imaginations, and be one Method of preserving us from Writing without Schemes.

131. John Hughes

1715

John Hughes (1677–1720) had an eccentric education and began his literary career early. He contributed a number of papers to the *Tatler*, the *Guardian*, and the *Spectator* but is most famous for his edition of Spenser in 1715 – a publication of quite astonishing originality. See also Nos. 159, 178.

(a) *An Essay on Allegorical Poetry*, in his edition of Spenser's *Works* (1715), I. xxv–lvii:

It is a Misfortune, as Mr *Waller* observes, which attends the Writers of *English* Poetry, that they can hardly expect their Works shou'd last long in a Tongue which is daily changing; that whilst they are new, Envy is apt to prevail against them; and as that wears off, our Language it self fails. Our Poets therefore, he says, shou'd imitate judicious Statuaries, that chuse the most durable Materials, and shou'd carve in *Latin* or *Greek*, if they wou'd have their Labours preserv'd for ever.

Notwithstanding the Disadvantage he has mention'd, we have two Antient *English* Poets, *Chaucer* and *Spenser*, who may perhaps be reckon'd as Exceptions to this Remark. These seem to have taken deep Root, like old *British* Oaks, and to flourish in defiance of all the Injuries of Time and Weather. The former is indeed much more obsolete in his Stile than the latter; but it is owing to an extraordinary native Strength in both, that they have been able thus far to survive amidst the Changes of our Tongue, and seem rather likely, among the Curious at least, to preserve the Knowledg of our Antient Language, than to be in danger of being destroy'd with it, and bury'd under its Ruins.

Tho *Spenser*'s Affection to his Master *Chaucer* led him in many things to copy after him, yet those who have read both will easily observe that these two Genius's were of a very different kind. *Chaucer* excell'd in his Characters; *Spenser* in his Descriptions. The first study'd Humour, was an excellent Satirist, and a lively but rough Painter of the Manners of that rude Age in which he liv'd: The latter was of the serious Turn, had an exalted and elegant Mind, a warm and boundless Fancy, and was an admirable Imager of Vertues and Vices, which was his particular Talent. The Embellishments of Description are rich and lavish in him beyond Comparison: and as this is the most striking part of Poetry, especially to young Readers, I take it to be the Reason that he has been the Father of more Poets among us, than any other of our Writers; Poetry being first kindled in the Imagination, which *Spenser* writes to, more than any one, and the Season of Youth being the most susceptible of the Impression. It will not seem strange therefore that *Cowley*, as himself tells us, first caught his Flame by reading *Spenser*; that our great *Milton* own'd him for his Original, as Mr *Dryden* assures us; and that *Dryden* study'd him, and has bestow'd more frequent Commendations on him, than on any other *English* Poet.

The most known and celebrated of his Works, tho I will not say the most perfect, is the *Fairy Queen*. It is conceiv'd, wrought up, and colour'd with a stronger Fancy, and discovers more the particular Genius of *Spenser*, than any of his other Writings. The author, in a Letter to Sir *Walter Raleigh*, having call'd this Poem, *a continu'd Allegory, or dark Conceit*, it may not be improper to offer some Remarks on Allegorical Poetry in general; by which the Beauties of this Work may more easily be discover'd by ordinary Readers. I must at the same time beg the Indulgence of those who are conversant with Critical Discourses, to what I shall here propose; this being a Subject something out of the way, and not expresly treated upon by those who have laid down Rules for the Art of Poetry.

An Allegory is a Fable or Story, in which, under imaginary Persons or Things, is shadow'd some real Action or instructive Moral; or, as I think it is somewhere very shortly defin'd by *Plutarch*, it is that *in which one thing is related, and another thing is understood*. It is a kind of Poetical Picture, or Hieroglyphick, which by its apt Resemblance conveys Instruction to the Mind by an Analogy to the Senses; and so amuses the Fancy, whilst it informs the Understanding. Every Allegory has therefore two Senses, the Literal and the Mystical; the literal Sense is like a Dream or Vision, of which the mystical Sense is the true Meaning or Interpretation.

This will be more clearly apprehended, by considering, that as a Simile is but a more extended Metaphor, so an Allegory is a kind of continu'd Simile, or an Assemblage of Similitudes drawn out at full length. Thus, when it is said, That *Death is the Offspring of Sin*, this is a Metaphor, to signify that the former is produc'd by the latter, as a Child is brought into the World by its Parent. Again, to compare Death to a meager and ghastly Apparition, starting out of the Ground, moving towards the Spectator with a menacing Air, and shaking in his Hand a bloody Dart, is a Representation of the Terrors which attend that great Eenemy to Human Nature. But let the Reader observe, in *Milton*'s *Paradise Lost*, with what exquisite Fancy and Skill this common Metaphor and Simile, and the Moral contain'd in them, are extended and wrought up into one of the most beautiful Allegories in our Language.

The Resemblance which has been so often observ'd in general between Poetry and Painting, is yet more particular in Allegory; which, as I said before, is a kind of Picture in Poetry. *Horace* has in one of his Odes pathetically describ'd the ruinous Condition of his Country after the Civil Wars, and the Hazard of its being involv'd in new Dissensions, by the Emblem of a Ship shatter'd with Storms, and driven into Port with broken Masts, torn Sails, and disabled Rigging; and in danger of being forc'd by new Storms out to Sea again. There is nothing said in the whole Ode but what is literally applicable to a Ship; but it is generally agreed, that the Thing signify'd is the *Roman* States.[1] Thus *Rubens*, who had a good Allegorical Genius in Painting, has, in his famous Work of the *Luxemburg* Gallery, figur'd the Government of *France*, on *Lewis* the Thirteenth's arriving at Age, by a Galley. The King stands at the Helm; *Mary* of *Medicis*, the Queen Mother and Regent, puts the Rudder in his Hand; Justice, Fortitude, Religion, and Publick Faith are seated at the Oars; and other Vertues have their proper Employments in manging the Sails and Tackle.

By this general Description of Allegory, it may easily be conceiv'd that in Works of this kind there is a large Field open to Invention, which among the Antients was universally look'd upon to be the principal Part of Poetry. The Power of raising Images or Resemblances of things, giving them Life and Action, and presenting them as it were before the Eyes, was thought to have something in it like Creation: And it was probably for this fabling Part, that the first Authors of such Works were call'd *Poets* or *Makers*, as the Word signifies, and as it is literally translated and used by *Spenser*; tho the learned *Gerard*

[1] *Odes* I. xiv. The allegorical character of the ode was in fact disputed, for example, by Mme Dacier.

*Vossius** is of opinion, that it was rather for the framing their Verses. However, by this Art of Fiction or Allegory, more than by the Structure of their Numbers, or what we now call *Versification*, the Poets were distinguish'd from Historians and Philosophers; tho the latter sometimes invaded the Province of the Poet, and deliver'd their Doctrines likewise in Allegories or Parables. And this, when they did not purposely make them obscure, in order to conceal them from the common People, was a plain Indication that they thought there was an Advantage in such Methods of conveying Instruction to the Mind; and that they serv'd for the more effectual engaging the Attention of the Hearers, and for leaving deeper Impressions on their Memories.

Plutarch, in one of his Discourses, gives a very good Reason for the use of Fiction in Poetry, because *Truth of it self is rigid and austere, and cannot be moulded into such agreeable Forms as Fiction can.* 'For neither the Numbers, says he, nor the ranging of the Words, nor the Elevation and Elegance of the Stile, have so many Graces as the artful Contrivance and Disposition of the Fable.' For this Reason, as he relates it after *Plato*, when the Wise *Socrates* himself was prompted by a particular Impulse to the writing of Verses, being by his constant Employment in the Study of Truth, a Stranger to the Art of inventing, he chose for his Subject the Fables of *Aesop*; not thinking, says *Plutarch, That any thing cou'd be Poetry which was void of Fiction.* The same Author makes use of a Comparison in another place, which I think may be most properly apply'd to Allegorical Poetry in particular: That *as Grapes on a Vine are cover'd by the Leaves which grow about them, so under the pleasant Narrations and Fictions of the Poets, there are couch'd many useful Morals and Doctrines.*

It is for this reason, that is to say, in regard to the moral Sense, that Allegory has a liberty indulg'd to it beyond any other sort of Writing whatsoever; that it often assembles things of the most contrary kinds in Nature, and supposes even Impossibilities; as that a Golden Bough shou'd grow among the common Branches of a Tree, as *Virgil* has describ'd it in the Sixth Book of his *Aeneis*. Allegory is indeed the *Fairy Land* of Poetry, peopled by Imagination; its Inhabitants are so many Apparitions; its Woods, Caves, wild Beasts, Rivers, Mountains and Palaces, are produc'd by a kind of magical Power, and are all visionary and typical; and it abounds in such Licences as wou'd be shocking and monstrous, if the Mind did not attend to the mystick Sense contain'd under them. Thus in the Fables of *Aesop*, which are some of the most

* De Arte Poetica, *Cap.* 3. §. 16.

antient Allegories extant, the Author gives Reason and Speech to Beasts, Insects and Plants; and by that means covertly instructs Mankind in the most important Incidents and Concerns of their Lives.

I am not insensible that the word *Allegory* has been sometimes us'd in a larger Sense than that to which I may seem here to have restrain'd it, and has been apply'd indifferently to any Poem which contains a cover'd Moral, tho the Story or Fable carries nothing in it that appears visionary or romantick. It may be necessary therefore to distinguish Allegory into the two following kinds.

The first is that in which the Story is fram'd of real or historical Persons, and probable or possible Actions; by which however some other Persons and Actions are typify'd or represented. In this sense the whole *Aeneis* of *Virgil* may be said to be an Allegory, if we consider *Aeneas* as representing *Augustus Caesar*, and his conducting the Remains of his Countrymen from the Ruins of *Troy*, to a new Settlement in *Italy*, as emblematical of *Augustus*'s modelling a new Government out of the Ruins of the Aristocracy, and establishing the *Romans* after the Confusion of the Civil War, in a peaceable and flourishing Condition. It does not, I think, appear that *Homer* had any such Design in his Poems, or that he meant to delineate his Co[n]temporaries or their Actions under the chief Characters and Adventures of the *Trojan* War. And tho the Allusion I have mention'd in *Virgil* is a Circumstance, which the Author has finely contriv'd to be co-incident to the general Frame of his Story, yet he has avoided the making it plain and particular, and has thrown it off in so many Instances from a direct Application, that his Poem is perfect without it. This then, for distinction, should, I think, rather be call'd a Parallel than an Allegory; at least in Allegories, fram'd after this manner, the literal Sense is sufficient to satisfy the Reader, tho he should look no further; and without being consider'd as emblematical of some other Persons or Action, may of itself exhibit very useful Morals and Instructions. Thus the Morals which may be drawn from the *Aeneis* are equally noble and instructive, whether we suppose the real Hero to be *Aeneas* or *Augustus Caesar*.

The second kind of Allegory, and which, I think, may more properly challenge the Name, is that in which the Fable or Story consists for the most part of fictitious Persons or Beings, Creatures of the Poet's Brain, and Actions surprizing, and without the Bounds of Probability or Nature. In Works of this kind, it is impossible for the Reader to rest in the literal Sense, but he is of necessity driven to seek for another Meaning under these wild Types and Shadows. This Grotesque Invention claims, as I have observ'd, a Licence peculiar to it self, and is what I wou'd be understood in this Discourse more particularly to mean by the word Allegory. Thus *Milton* has describ'd it in his Poem call'd *Il Penseroso*, where he alludes to the Squire's Tale in *Chaucer*:

[quotes ll. 110–120.]

It may be proper to give an Instance or two, by which the Distinction of this last kind of Allegory may more plainly appear.

The Story of *Circe* in the *Odysses* is an Allegorical Fable, of which there are perhaps more Copies and Imitations than of any other whatever. Her offering a Cup, fill'd with intoxicating Liquor, to her Guests; her mingling Poison with their Food, and then by magical Arts turning them into the Shapes of Swine; and *Ulysses* resisting her Charms by the Virtue of an Herb call'd *Moly*, which he had receiv'd from the God *Mercury*, and restoring his Companions to their true Persons, are all Fictions of the last kind I have mention'd. The Person of the Goddess is likewise fictitious, and out of the Circle of the *Grecian* Divinities; and the Adventures are not to be understood but in a mystical Sense. The Episode of *Calypso*, tho somewhat of the same kind, approaches nearer to Nature and Probability: But the Story of *Dido* in the *Aeneis*, tho copy'd from the *Circe* and *Calypso*, and form'd on the same Moral, namely, to represent a Hero obstructed by the Allurements of Pleasure, and at last breaking from them; and tho *Mercury* likewise assists in it to dissolve the Charm, yet is not necessarily to be look'd upon as an Allegory; the Fable does not appear merely imaginary or emblematical: the Persons are natural, and, excepting the Distance of Time which the Criticks have noted between the real *Aeneas* and *Dido*, (a Circumstance which *Virgil*, not being bound to Historical Truth, wilfully neglected) there is nothing which might not really have happen'd. *Ariosto's Alcina*, and the *Armida* of *Tasso*, are Copies from the same Original: These again are plainly Allegorical. The whole literal Sense of the latter is a kind of Vision, or a Scene of Imagination, and is every where transparent, to shew the moral Sense which is under it. The Bower of Bliss, in the Second Book of the *Fairy Queen*, is in like manner a Copy from *Tasso*; but the Ornaments of Description, which *Spenser* has transplanted out of the *Italian* Poem, are more proper in his Work, which was design'ed to be wholly Allegorical, than in an Epick Poem, which is superior in its Nature to such lavish Embellishments. There is another Copy of the *Circe*, in the Dramatick way, in a Mask, by our famous *Milton*; the whole Plan of which is Allegorical, and is written with a very Poetical Spirit on the same Moral, tho with different Characters.

I have here instanc'd in one of the most antient and best-imagin'd Allegories extant. *Scilla*, *Charibdis*, and the *Syrens*, in the same Poem, are of the same Nature, and are Creatures purely Allegorical: But the *Harpies* in *Virgil*, which disturb'd *Aeneas* and his Followers at their Banquet, as they do not seem to exhibit any certain Moral, may probably have been thrown in by the Poet only as an Omen, and to raise what is commonly call'd *the Wonderful*; which is a Property as essential to Epick Poetry, as Probability. *Homer's* giving Speech to the River *Xanthus* in the Iliad, and to the Horses of *Achilles*, seem to be Inventions of the same kind, and might be design'd to fill the Reader with Astonishment and Concern, and with an Apprehension of the Greatness of an Occasion, which by a bold Fiction of the Poet is suppos'd to have produc'd such extraordinary Effects.

As Allegory sometimes, for the sake of the moral Sense couch'd under its Fictions, gives Speech to Brutes, and sometimes introduces Creatures which are out of Nature, as Goblins, Chimaera's, Fairies, and the like; so it frequently gives Life to Virtues and Vices, Passions and Diseases, to natural and moral Qualities; and represents them acting as divine, human, or infernal Persons. A very ingenious Writer calls these Characters *shadowy Beings**, and has with good reason censur'd the employing them in just Epick Poems: of this kind are Sin and Death, which I mention'd before in *Milton*; and Fame in *Virgil*. We find likewise a large Groupe of these shadowy Figures plac'd in the Sixth Book of the *Aeneis*, at the Entrance into the infernal Regions; but as they are only shewn there, and have no share in the Action of the Poem, the Description of them is a fine Allegory, and extremely proper to the Place where they appear.

[quotes *Aeneid* vi. 273–84]

As Persons of this imaginary Life are to be excluded from any share of Action in Epick Poems, they are yet less to be endur'd in the *Drama*; yet we find they have sometimes made their Appearance on the antient Stage. Thus in a Tragedy of *Aeschylus*, *Strength* is introduc'd assisting *Vulcan* to bind *Prometheus* to a Rock; and in one of *Euripides*, *Death* comes to the House of *Admetus* to demand *Alcestis*, who had offer'd her

* *Spectator*, Vol. IV. No. 273.

self to die to save her Husband's Life. But what I have here said of Epick and Dramatick Poems does not extend to such Writings, the very Frame and Model of which is design'd to be Allegorical; in which therefore, as I said before, such unsubstantial and symbolical Actors may be very properly admitted.

Every Book of the *Fairy Queen* is fruitful of these visionary Beings, which are invented and drawn with a surprizing Strength of Imagination. I shall produce but one Instance here, which the Reader may compare with that just mention'd in *Virgil*, to which it is no way inferior: It is in the Second Book, where *Mammon* conducts *Guyon* thro a Cave under Ground to shew him his Treasure.

[quotes *Faerie Queene* II. vii. 21–3]

The Posture of Jealousy, and the Motion of Fear in this Description, are particularly fine. These are Instances of Allegorical Persons, which are shewn only in one transient View. The Reader will every where meet with others in this Author, which are employ'd in the Action of the Poem, and which need not be mention'd here.

Having thus endeavour'd to give a general Idea of what is meant by Allegory in Poetry, and shewn what kind of Persons are frequently employ'd in it; I shall proceed to mention some Properties which seem requisite in all well-invented Fables of this kind.

There is no doubt, but Men of Critical Learning, if they had thought fit, might have given us Rules about Allegorical Writing, as they have done about Epick, and other kinds of Poetry; but they have rather chosen to let this Forest remain wild, as if they thought there was something in the Nature of the Soil, which cou'd not so well be restrain'd and cultivated in Inclosures. What Sir *William Temple* observes about Rules in general, may perhaps be more particularly applicable of this; that *they may possibly hinder some from being very bad Poets, but are not capable of making any very good one.* Notwithstanding this, they are useful to help our Observation in distinguishing the Beauties and the Blemishes, in such Works as have been already produc'd. I shall therefore beg leave to mention four Qualities, which I think are essential to every good Allegory: the three first of which relate to the Fable, and the last to the Moral.

The first is, that it be lively, and surprizing. The Fable, or literal Sense, being that which most immediately offers it self to the Reader's Observation, must have this Property, in order to raise and entertain his Curiosity. As there is therefore more Invention employ'd in a

Work of this kind, than in meer Narration, or Description, or in general Amplifications on any Subject, it consequently requires a more than ordinary Heat of Fancy in its first Production. If the Fable, on the contrary, is flat, spiritless, or barren of Invention, the Reader's Imagination is not affected, nor his Attention engag'd, tho the Instruction convey'd under it be ever so useful or important.

The second Qualification I shall mention is Elegance, or a beautiful Propriety, and Aptness in the Fable to the Subject on which it is employ'd. By this Quality the Invention of the Poet is restrain'd from taking too great a Compass, or losing it self in a Confusion of ill-sorted Ideas; such Representations as that mention'd by *Horace*, of *Dolphins in a Wood*, or *Boars in the Sea*, being fit only to surprize the Imagination, without pleasing the Judgment. The same Moral may likewise be express'd in different Fables, all of which may be lively and full of Spirit, yet not equally elegant; as various Dresses may be made for the same Body, yet not equally becoming. As it therefore requires a Heat of Fancy to raise Images and Resemblances, it requires a good Taste to distinguish and range them, and to chuse the most proper and beautiful, where there appears an almost distracting Variety. I may compare this to *Aeneas* searching in the Wood for the Golden Bough; he was at a loss where to lay his Hand, till his Mother's Doves, descending in his sight, flew before him, and pearch'd on the Tree where it was to be found.

Another essential Property is, That the Fable be every where consistent with it self. As licentious as Allegorical Fiction may seem in some Respects, it is nevertheless subject to this Restraint. The Poet is indeed at liberty in chusing his Story, and inventing his Persons; but after he has introduc'd them, he is oblig'd to sustain them in their proper Characters, as well as in more regular kinds of Writing. It is difficult to give particular Rules under this Head; it may suffice to say that this wild Nature is however subject to an Oeconomy proper to it self, and tho it may sometimes seem extravagant, ought never to be absurd. Most of the Allegories in the *Fairy Queen* are agreeable to this Rule; but in one of his other Poems, the Author has manifestly transgress'd it: the Poem I mean, is that which is call'd *Prothalamion*. In this, the two Brides are figur'd by two beautiful Swans sailing down the River *Thames*. The Allegory breaks before the Reader is prepar'd for it; and we see them, at their landing, in their true Shapes, without knowing how this sudden Change is effected. If this had been only a Simile, the Poet might have dropp'd it at pleasure; but as it is an Allegory, he ought to have made it of a piece, or to have invented some probable means of coming out of it.

The last Property I shall mention, is, That the Allegory be clear and intelligible: the Fable being design'd only to clothe and adorn the Moral, but not to hide it, should methinks resemble the Draperies we admire in some of the antient Statues; in which the Folds are not too many, nor too thick, but so judiciously order'd, that the Shape and Beauty of the Limbs may be seen thro them.

It must be confess'd, that many of the antient Fables appear to us at this Distance of Time very perplex'd and dark; and if they had any Moral at all, it is so closely couch'd, that it is very difficult to discover it. Whoever reads the Lord *Bacon*'s *Wisdom of the Antients*, will be convinc'd of this. He has employ'd a more than ordinary Penetration to decypher the most known Traditions in the Heathen Mythology; but his Interpretations are often far fetch'd, and so much at random, that the Reader can have no Assurance of their Truth. It is not to be doubted that a great part of these Fables were Allegorical, but others might have been Stories design'd only to amuse, or to practise upon the Credulity of the Vulgar; or the Doctrines they contain'd might be purposely clouded, to conceal them from common Knowledg. But tho, as I hinted in the former part of this Discourse, this may have been a Reason among Philosophers, it ought not to be admitted among Poets. An Allegory, which is not clear, is a Riddle, and the Sense of it lies at the Mercy of every fanciful Interpreter.

Tho the Epick Poets, as I have shewn, have sprinkled some Allegories thro their Poems, yet it wou'd be absurd to endeavour to understand them every where in a mystical Sense. We are told of one *Metrodorus Lampsacenus*, whose Works are lost, that turn'd the whole Writings of *Homer* into an Allegory: it was doubtless by some such means that the Principles of all Arts and Sciences whatever were discover'd in that single Author; for nothing can escape an Expositor, who proceeds in his Operations like a *Rosycrucian*, and brings with him the Gold he pretends to find.

It is surprizing that *Tasso*, whose *Jerusalem* was, at the time when he wrote, the best Plan of an Epick Poem after *Virgil*, shou'd be possess'd with this Affectation, and shou'd not believe his Work perfect till he had turn'd it into a Mystery. I cannot help thinking that *the Allegory*, as it is call'd, which he has printed with it, looks as if it were invented after the Poem was finish'd. He tells us, that the Christian Army represents Man; the City of *Jerusalem*, Civil Happiness; *Godfrey*, the

Understanding; *Rinaldo* and *Tancred*, the other Powers of the Soul; and that the Body is typify'd by the common Soldiers; with a great deal more that carries in it a strong Cast of Enthusiasm. He is indeed much more intelligible, when he explains the Flowers, the Fountains, the Nymphs, and the musical Instruments, to figure to us sensual Pleasures, under the false Appearance of Good: But for the rest, I appeal to any one who is acquainted with that Poem, whether he wou'd ever have discover'd these Mysteries, if the Poet had not let him into them; or whether even after this, he can keep them long in his Mind while he is reading it.

Spenser's Conduct is much more reasonable; as he design'd his Poem upon the Plan of the Vertues by which he has entitled his several Books, he scarce ever loses sight of this Design, but has almost every where taken care to let it appear. Sir *William Temple* indeed censures this as a Fault, and says, That tho his Flights of Fancy were very noble and high, yet his Moral lay so bare, that it lost the Effect: But I confess I do not understand this. A Moral which is not clear, is in my Apprehension next to no Moral at all.

It wou'd be easy to enumerate other Properties, which are various, according to the different kinds of Allegory, or its different Degrees of Perfection. Sometimes we are surpriz'd with an uncommon Moral, which ennobles the Fable that conveys it; and at other times we meet with a known and obvious Truth, plac'd in some new and beautiful Point of Light, and made surprizing by the Fiction under which it is exhibited. I have thought it sufficient to touch upon such Properties only as seem to be the most essential; and perhaps many more might be reduc'd under one or other of these general Heads.

I might here give Examples of this noble and antient kind of Writing, out of the Books of Holy Writ, and especially the *Jewish* Prophets, in which we find a Spirit of Poetry surprizingly sublime and majestick: But these are obvious to every one's reading. The East seems indeed to have been principally the Region of these figurative and emblematical Writings. Sir *John Chardin* in his Travels has given us a Translation of several Pieces of modern *Persian* Poetry; which shew that there are Traces of the same Genius remaining among the present Inhabitants of those Countries. But, not to prolong this Discourse, I shall only add one Instance of a very antient Allegory which has all the Properties in it I have mention'd: I mean that in *Xenophon*, of the Choice of *Hercules* when he is courted by Virtue and Pleasure, which is said to have been the Invention of *Prodicus*. This Fable is full of Spirit and

Elegance; the Characters are finely drawn, and consistent; and the Moral is clear. I shall not need to say any thing more of it, but refer the Reader to the Second Volume of the *Tatler*, where he will find it very beautifully translated.

After what has been said, it must be confess'd, that, excepting *Spenser*, there are few extraordinary Instances of this kind of Writing among the Moderns. The great Mines of Invention have been open'd long ago, and little new Oar seems to have been discover'd or brought to light by latter Ages. With us the Art of framing Fables, Apologues and Allegories, which was so frequent among the Writers of Antiquity, seems to be, like the Art of Painting upon Glass, but little practis'd, and in a great measure lost. Our Colours are not so rich and transparent, and are either so ill prepar'd, or so unskilfully laid on, that they often sully the Light which is to pass thro them, rather than agreeably tincture and beautify it. *Boccalini* must be reckon'd one of the chief modern Masters of Allegory; yet his Fables are often flat and ill chosen, and his Invention seems to have been rather fruitful than elegant. I cannot however conclude this Essay on Allegory without observing, that we have had the satisfaction to see this kind of Writing very lately reviv'd by an excellent Genius among our selves, in the true Spirit of the Antients. I need only mention the Visions in the *Tatler* and *Spectator*, by Mr. *Addison*, to convince every one of this. The Table of Fame, the Vision of Justice; that of the different Pursuits of Love, Ambition, and Avarice; the Vision of *Mirza*, and several others; and especially that admirable Fable of the two Families of Pain and Pleasure, which are all imagin'd, and writ with the greatest Strength and Delicacy, may give the Reader an Idea more than any thing I can say of the Perfection to which this kind of Writing is capable of being rais'd. We have likewise in the Second Volume of the *Guardian* a very good Example given us by the same Hand, of an Allegory, in the particular manner of *Spenser*.

(b) *Remarks on the 'Faerie Queene', ibid.*, pp. lviii–xciii (that is, excluding the closing remarks on Spenser's language):

By what has been offer'd in the foregoing Discourse on *Allegorical Poetry*, we may be able, not only to discover many Beauties in the *Fairy Queen*, but likewise to excuse some of its Irregularities. The chief Merit of this Poem consists in that surprizing Vein of fabulous Invention, which runs thro it, and enriches it every where with Imagery and Descriptions more than we meet with in any other modern Poem. The Author seems to be possess'd of a kind of Poetical Magick; and the Figures he calls up to our View rise so thick upon us, that we are at once pleased and distracted by the exhaustless Variety of them; so that his Faults may in a manner be imputed to his excellencies: His Abundance betrays him into Excess, and his Judgment is overborne by the Torrent of his Imagination.

That which seems the most liable to Exception in this Work, is the Model of it, and the Choice the Author has made of so romantick a Story. The several Books appear rather like so many several Poems, than one entire Fable: Each of them has its peculiar Knight, and is independent of the rest; and tho some of the Persons make their Appearance in different Books, yet this has very little Effect in connecting them. Prince *Arthur* is indeed the principal Person, and has therefore a share given him in every Legend; but his Part is not considerable enough in any one of them: He appears and vanishes again like a Spirit; and we lose sight of him too soon, to consider him as the Hero of the Poem.

These are the most obvious Defects in the Fable of the *Fairy Queen*. The want of Unity in the Story makes it difficult for the Reader to carry it in his Mind, and distracts too much his Attention to the several Parts of it; and indeed the whole Frame of it wou'd appear monstrous, if it were to be examin'd by the Rules of Epick Poetry, as they have been drawn from the Practice of *Homer* and *Virgil*. But as it is plain the Author never design'd it by those Rules, I think it ought rather to be consider'd as a Poem of a particular kind, describing in a Series of Allegorical Adventures or Episodes the most noted Virtues and Vices: to compare it therefore with the Models of Antiquity, wou'd be like drawing a Parallel between the *Roman* and the *Gothick* Architecture. In the first there is doubtless a more natural Grandeur and Simplicity: in the latter, we find great Mixtures of Beauty and Barbarism, yet assisted by the Invention of a Variety of inferior Ornaments; and tho the former is more majestick in the whole, the latter may be very surprizing and agreeable in its Parts.

It may seem strange indeed, since *Spenser* appears to have been well acquainted with the best Writers of Antiquity, that he has not imitated them in the Structure of his Story. Two Reasons may be given for this: The first is, That at the time when he wrote, the *Italian* Poets, whom he has chiefly imitated, and who were the first Revivers of this

Art among the Moderns, were in the highest vogue, and were universally read and admir'd. But the chief Reason was probably, that he chose to frame his Fable after a Model which might give the greatest Scope to that Range of Fancy which was so remarkably his Talent. There is a Bent in Nature, which is apt to determine Men that particular way in which they are most capable of excelling; and tho it is certain he might have form'd a better Plan, it is to be question'd whether he cou'd have executed any other so well.

It is probably for the same reason, that among the *Italian* Poets, he rather follow'd *Ariosto*, whom he found more agreeable to his Genius, than *Tasso*, who had form'd a better Plan, and from whom he has only borrow'd some particular Ornaments; yet it is but Justice to say, that his Plan is much more regular than that of *Ariosto*. In the *Orlando Furioso*, we every where meet with an exuberant Invention, join'd with great Liveliness and Facility of Description, yet debas'd by frequent Mixtures of the comick Genius, as well as many shocking Indecorums. Besides, in the Huddle and Distraction of the Adventures, we are for the most part only amus'd with extravagant Stories, without being instructed in any Moral. On the other hand, *Spenser*'s Fable, tho often wild is, as I have observ'd, always emblematical: And this may very much excuse likewise that Air of Romance in which he has follow'd the *Italian* Author. The perpetual Stories of Knights, Giants, Castles, and Enchantments, and all that Train of Legendary Adventures, wou'd indeed appear very trifling, if *Spenser* had not found a way to turn them all into Allegory, or if a less masterly Hand had fill'd up his Draught. But it is surprizing to observe how much the Strength of the Painting is superior to the Design. It ought to be consider'd too, that at the time when our Author wrote, the Remains of the old *Gothick* Chivalry were not quite abolish'd: It was not many Years before, that the famous Earl of *Surry*, remarkable for his Wit and Poetry in the Reign of King *Henry* the Eighth, took a romantick Journey to *Florence*, the Place of his Mistress's Birth, and publish'd there a Challenge against all Nations in Defence of her Beauty. Justs and Turnaments were held in *England* in the Time of Queen *Elizabeth*. Sir *Philip Sidney* tilted at one of these Entertainments, which was made for the *French* Ambassador, when the Treaty of Marriage was on foot with the Duke of *Anjou*: and some of our Historians have given us a very particular and formal Account of Preparations, by marking out Lists, and appointing Judges, for a Tryal by Combat, in the same Reign, which was to have decided the Title to a considerable Estate; and in which the whole Ceremony was perfectly agreeable to the fabulous Descriptions in Books of Knight-Errantry. This might render his Story more familiar to his first Readers; tho Knights in Armour, and Ladies Errant are as antiquated Figures to us, as the Court of that time wou'd appear, if we cou'd see them now in their Ruffs and Fardingales.

There are two other Objections to the Plan of the *Fairy Queen*, which, I confess, I am more at a loss to answer. I need not, I think, be scrupulous in mentioning freely the Defects of a Poem, which, tho it was never suppos'd to be perfect has always been allow'd to be admirable.

The first is, that the Scene is laid in *Fairy-Land*, and the chief Actors are *Fairies*. The Reader may see their imaginary Race and History in the Second Book, at the end of the Tenth Canto: but if he is not prepar'd before-hand, he may expect to find them acting agreeably to the common Stories and Traditions about such fancy'd Beings. Thus *Shakespear*, who has introduc'd them in his *Midsummer-Night's Dream*, has made them speak and act in a manner perfectly adapted to their suppos'd Characters; but the *Fairies* in this Poem are not distinguish'd from other Persons. There is this Misfortune likewise attends the Choice of such Actors, that having been accustom'd to conceive of them in a diminutive way, we find it difficult to raise our Ideas, and to imagine a *Fairy* encountring with a Monster or a Giant. *Homer* has pursu'd a contrary Method, and represented his Heroes above the Size and Strength of ordinary Men; and it is certain that the Actions of the Iliad wou'd have appear'd but ill proportion'd to the Characters, if we were to have imagin'd them all perform'd by Pigmies.

But as the Actors our Author has chosen, are only fancy'd Beings, he might possibly think himself at liberty to give them what Stature, Customs and Manners he pleas'd. I will not say he was in the right in this: but it is plain that by the literal Sense of *Fairy-Land*, he only design'd an *Utopia*, an imaginary Place; and by his *Fairies*, Persons of whom he might invent any Action proper to human Kind, without being restrain'd, as he must have been, if he had chosen a real Scene and historical Characters. As for the mystical Sense, it appears both by the Work it self, and by the Author's★ Explanation of it, that his *Fairy-Land* is *England*, and his *Fairy-Queen*, Queen *Elizabeth*; at whose Command the Adventure of every Legend is suppos'd to be undertaken.

The other Objection is, that having chosen an historical Person, Prince *Arthur*, for his principal Hero; who is no *Fairy*, yet is mingled

★ *Vid. Letter to Sir* W. Raleigh.

with them: he has not however represented any part of his History. He appears here indeed only in his Minority, and performs his Exercises in *Fairy-Land*, as a private Gentleman; but we might at least have expected, that the fabulous Accounts of him, and of his Victories over the *Saxons*, shou'd have been work'd into some beautiful Vision or Prophecy: and I cannot think *Spenser* wou'd wholly omit this, but am apt to believe he had done it in some of the following Books which were lost.

In the moral Introductions to every Book, many of which have a great Propriety and Elegance, the Author has follow'd the Example of *Ariosto*. I will only beg leave to point out some of the principal Beauties in each Book, which may yet more particularly discover the Genius of the Author.

If we consider the First Book as an entire Work of it self, we shall find it to be no irregular Contrivance: There is one principal Action, which is compleated in the Twelfth Canto; and the several Incidents or Episodes are proper, as they tend either to obstruct or promote it. The same may be said of some other of the following Books, tho I think they are not so regular as this. The Author has shewn Judgment in making his Knight of the *Red Cross*, or St. *George*, no perfect Character; without which, many of the Incidents cou'd not have been represented. The Character of *Una*, or *Truth*, is very properly oppos'd by those of *Duessa*, or *Falshood*, and *Archimago*, or *Fraud*. *Spenser*'s particular manner, which (if it may be allow'd) I wou'd call his Painter-like Genius, immediately shews it self in the Figure of *Error*, who is drawn as a Monster, and that of *Hypocrisy*, as a Hermit. The Description of the former of these, in the mix'd Shape of a Woman and a Serpent, surrounded with her Offspring, and especially that Circumstance of their creeping into her Mouth on the sudden Light which glanced upon them from the Knight's Armour, incline one to think that our Great *Milton* had it in his eye when he wrote his famous Episode of Sin and Death. The Artifices of *Archimago* and *Duessa*, to separate the Knight from *Una*, are well invented, and intermingled with beautiful Strokes of Poetry; particularly in that Episode where the Magician sends one of his Spirits to fetch a false Dream from the House of *Morpheus*:

[quotes *Faerie Queene* I. i. 39⁴⁻⁶]

Mr. *Rhimer*, as I remember, has, by way of Comparison, collected from most of the antient and modern Poets, the finest Descriptions of the Night; among all which, he gives the Preference to the *English* Poets: This of *Morpheus*, or Sleep, being a Poetical Subject of the same kind, might be subjected to a like Trial; and the Reader may particularly compare it with that in the Eleventh Book of *Ovid*'s *Metamorphoses*; to which, I believe, he will not think it inferior.

The miraculous Incident of a Tree shedding Drops of Blood, and a Voice speaking from the Trunk of it, is borrow'd from that of *Polidorus* in the Third Book of *Virgil*'s *Aeneis*. *Ariosto* and *Tasso* have both copy'd the same Story, tho in a different manner. It was impossible that the modern Poets, who have run so much into the Taste of Romance, should let a Fiction of this kind escape their Imitation.

The Adventures which befal *Una*, after she is forsaken by the Knight; her coming to the House of *Abessa*, or *Superstition*; the Consternation occasion'd by that Visit; her Reception among the Savages; and her civilizing them, are all very fine Emblems. The Education of *Satyrane*, a young Satyr, is describ'd on this Occasion with an agreeable Wildness of Fancy.

But there is one Episode in this Book, which I cannot but particularly admire; I mean that in the Fifth Canto, where *Duessa* the Witch seeks the Assistance of *Night*, to convey the Body of the wounded *Pagan* to be cured by *Aesculapius* in the Regions below. The Author here rises above himself, and is got into a Track of imitating the Antients, different from the greatest part of his Poem. The Speech in which *Duessa* addresses *Night*, is wonderfully great, and stained with that impious Flattery, which is the Character of *Falshood*, who is the Speaker:

[quotes *Faerie Queene* I. v. 22$^{2-6}$]

As *Duessa* came away hastily on this Expedition, and forgot to put off the Shape of Truth, which she had assum'd a little before, *Night* does not know her: This Circumstance, and the Discovery afterwards, when she owns her for her Daughter, are finely emblematical. The Images of *Horror* are rais'd in a very masterly manner; *Night* takes the Witch into her Chariot; and being arriv'd where the Body lay, they alight.

[quotes *Faerie Queene* I. v. 30]

They steal away the Body, and carry it down thro the Cave *Avernus*, to the Realms of *Pluto*. What Strength of Painting is there in the following Lines!

[quotes *Faerie Queene* I. v. 32⁴⁻⁹]

Longinus commending a Description in *Euripides* of *Phaeton*'s Journey thro the Heavens, in which the Turnings and Windings are mark'd out in a very lively manner, says, That the Soul of the Poet seems to mount the Chariot with him, and to share all his Dangers. The Reader will find himself in a like manner transported throughout this whole Episode; which shews that it has in it the Force and Spirit of the most sublime Poetry.

The first Appearance of Prince *Arthur* in this Book is represented to great Advantage, and gives occasion to a very finish'd Description of a martial Figure. How sprightly is that Image and Simile in the following Lines!

[quotes *Faerie Queene* I. vii. 32]

I must not omit mentioning the House of *Pride*, and that of *Holiness*, which are beautiful Allegories in different Parts of this Book. In the former of these there is a minute Circumstance which is very artificial; for the Reader may observe, that the six Counsellors which attend *Pride* in her Progress, and ride on the Beasts which draw her Chariot, are plac'd in that Order in which the Vices they represent, naturally produce and follow each other. In the Dungeon among the Captives of *Pride*, the Poet has represented *Nebuchadnezzar*, *Croesus*, *Antiochus*, *Alexander*, and serveral other eminent Persons, in Circumstances of the utmost Ignominy. The Moral is truly noble; for upon the sight of so many illustrious Slaves, the Knight hastens from the Place, and makes his Escape.

The Description of *Despair* in the Ninth Canto, is that which is said to have been taken notice of by Sir *Philip Sidney*. But I think the Speech of *Despair*, in which the distemper'd Reasonings, that are apt to agitate the Heart of a Man abandon'd to this Passion, are so pathetically represented, is much superior to the Description.

Among the Allegories in the Tenth Canto, it is impossible not to distinguish that venerable Figure of Contemplation, in his Hermitage on the Top of a Hill, represented as an old Man almost wasted away in Study:

[quotes *Faerie Queene* I. x. 48²⁻⁴]

The Knight and his Companion enquire of him:

[quotes *Faerie Queene* I. x. 50⁴⁻⁶]

This is extremely noble, as well as the old Man's shewing him from the Top of the Hill, the heavenly *Jerusalem*; which was proper to animate the Hero against the Combat, in which he is presently after engag'd: His Success in that Combat, and his marrying *Una*, are a very just Conclusion of this Book, and of its chief Allegory.

It would be easy to point out many Instances, besides those I have mention'd, of the Beauties in this Book; yet these few will give the Reader a Taste of that Poetical Spirit and Genius for Allegory, which every where shine in this Author. It wou'd be endless to take notice of the more minute Beauties of his Epithets, his Figures, and his Similes, which occur in almost every Page. I shall only mention one or two as a Specimen. That Image of *Strength*, in striking a Club into the Ground, which is illustrated by the following Smile, is very great.

[quotes *Faerie Queene* I. viii. 9]

As also that of a Giant's Fall,

[quotes *Faerie Queene* I. viii. 22J⁻⁹]

These are such Passages as we may imagine our excellent *Milton* to have study'd in this Author. And here by the way it is remarkable that as *Spenser* abounds with such Thoughts as are truly sublime, so he is almost every where free from the Mixture of little Conceits, and that low Affectation of Wit which so much infected both our Verse and Prose afterwards; and from which scarce any Writer of his own Time, besides himself, was free.

I shall shorten my Remarks on the following Books; yet the Beauties in them rise so thick, that I must not pass them by without mentioning some. The Second Legend is fram'd on the Vertue of *Temperance*, which gives the Author opportunity to lay out in Description all the most luxurious Images of Pleasure, Riches and Riot which are oppos'd to it, and consequently makes it one of the most Poetical Books of this whole Work. Sir *Guyon* is the Hero, and the Poet has given him Sobriety in the Habit of a Palmer for his Guide and Counsellor; as *Homer* has suppos'd *Minerva* or *Wisdom* in the Shape of *Mentor* to attend *Telemachus* in his Travels, when he is seeking out his Father *Ulysses*. That shining Description of *Belphoebe*, as a Huntress, like *Venus* in *Virgil* appearing to her Son *Aeneas*, is design'd as a Complement on Queen *Elizabeth*, and is therefore wrought up with the most finish'd Beauty. Her Speech in praise of that true Glory, which is

only attain'd by Labour and Study, is not only extremely proper to the
Subject of this Book, but admirable, if we consider it as the Sense of that
Princess, and as a short Character of so active and glorious a Reign;

[quotes *Faerie Queene* II. iii. 40$^{8-9}$, 41]

Such Passages as these kindle in the Mind a generous Emulation, and
are an Honour to the Art of Poetry, which ought always to recom-
mend worthy Sentiments. The Reader may see in the Sixth Canto a
Character quite opposite to this, in that of *Idleness*; who draws Sir
Guyon for a while from his Guide, and lays him asleep in her Island.
Her Song with which she charms him into a Slumber,

[quotes *Faerie Queene* II. vi. 15$^{1-2}$]

is very artfully adapted to the Occasion; and is a Contrast to that Speech
of *Belphoebe*, I have just quoted.

The Episode of *Mammon*, who in the Palmer's Absence leads Sir
Guyon into his Cave, and tempts him with a Survey of his Riches, very
properly diversifies the Entertainment in this Book; and gives occasion
to a noble Speech against Riches, and the mischevous Effects of them.
I have, in the Discourse on Allegory, taken notice of the Fiends and
Spectres, which are plac'd in Crouds at the Entrance to this Place. The
Author supposes the House of Riches to lie almost contiguous to Hell;
and the Guard he sets upon it, expresses a very just Moral.

[quotes *Faerie Queene* II. vii. 25$^{1-2}$]

The Light which is let into this Place,

[quotes *Faerie Queene* II. vii. 29$^{7-8}$]

The Smoakiness of it, and the Slaves of *Mammon* working at an
hundred Furnaces, are all describ'd in the most lively manner: As their
sudden looking at Sir *Guyon* is a Circumstance very naturally represented. The Walks thro which *Mammon* afterwards leads the Knight, are
agreeably vary'd. The Description of *Ambition*, and of the Garden of
Proserpine, are good Allegories; and Sir *Guyon*'s falling into a Swoon
on his coming into the open Air, gives occasion to a fine Machine of
the Appearance of an heavenly Spirit in the next Canto; by whose
Assistance he is restor'd to the Palmer.

I cannot think the Poet so succesful in his Description of the House of
Temperance; in which the Allegory seems to be debas'd by a Mixture
of too many low Images, as *Diet, Concoction, Digestion*, and the like;

SPENSER

which are represented as Persons. But the Allegorical Description of *Memory*, which follows soon after, is very good.

The *Ninth* Canto, in which the Author has made an Abridgment of the old *British* History, is a very amusing Digression; but might have been more artfully introduc'd. *Homer* or *Virgil* wou'd not have suffer'd the Action of the Poem to stand still whilst the Hero had been reading over a Book; but wou'd have put the History into the Mouth of some proper Person to relate it. But I have already said, that this Work is not to be examin'd by the strict Rules of Epick Poetry.

The last Canto of this Second Book being design'd to shew the utmost Tryal of the Vertue of *Temperance*, abounds with the most pleasurable Ideas and Representations which the Fancy of the Poet cou'd assemble together; but from the fifty eighth Stanza to the end, it is for the most part copy'd, and many whole Stanza's translated, from the famous Episode of *Armida* in *Tasso*. The Reader may observe, that the *Italian* Genius for Luxury appears very much in the Descriptions of the Garden, the Fountain, and the Nymphs; which however are finely amplify'd and improv'd by our *English* Poet. I shall give but one Instance in the following celebrated Stanza; which, to gratify the Curiosity of those who may be willing to compare the Copy with the Original, I shall set down in *Italian*.

[quotes *La Gerusalemme Liberata* xvi. 12]

Spenser has two Stanza's on this Thought; the last of which only is an Imitation of *Tasso*, but with finer Turns of the Verse: which are so artificial, that he seems to make the Musick he describes.

[quotes *Faerie Queene* II. xii. 70–1]

Sir *Guyon* and the Palmer, rescuing the Youth who was held Captive by *Acrasia* in this delightful Mansion, resembles that of the two Warriors recovering *Rinaldo* from the Charms of *Armida* in the *Italian* Poem.

In the Third Book, the Character of *Britomartis*, a Lady errant, who is the Heroine, and performs the chief Adventure, resembles *Ariosto*'s *Bradamante*, and *Tasso*'s *Clorinda*; as they are all Copies of the *Camilla* in *Virgil*.

Among the chief Beauties in this Book, we may reckon that Episode in which *Britomartis* goes to the Cave of *Merlin*, and is entertain'd with a prophetical Account of her future Marriage and Offspring. This

THE CRITICAL HERITAGE

Thought is remotely taken from *Virgil*, but more immediately from *Ariosto*; who has represented *Bradamante* on the like occasion making a Visit to the Tomb of *Merlin*; which he is forc'd for that purpose to suppose to be in *Gaul*: where she sees in like manner, in a Vision, the Heroes and Captains who were to be her Descendents.

The Story of *Marinel*, and that of the Birth of *Belphoebe* and *Amoret*, in which the manner of *Ovid* is well imitated, are very amusing. That Complaint against *Night*, at the end of the Fourth Canto,

[quotes *Faerie Queene* III. iv. 55¹⁻²]

tho it were only consider'd as detach'd from the rest, might be esteem'd a very fine Piece of Poetry. But there is nothing more entertaining in this whole Book, than the Prospect of the Gardens of *Adonis*, which is vary'd from the *Bower of Bliss* in the former Book, by an agreeable Mixture of Philosophical Fable. The Figure of Time walking in this Garden, spoiling the Beauty of it, and cutting down the Flowers, is a very fine and significant Allegory.

I cannot so much commend the Story of *the Squire of Dames*, and the Intrigue between *Paridel* and *Hellenore*: These Passages savour too much of the coarse and comick Mixtures in *Ariosto*. But that Image of *Jealousy*, at the end of the tenth Canto, grown to a Savage, throwing himself into a Cave, and lying there without ever shutting one Eye, under a craggy Clift just threatning to fall, is strongly conceiv'd and very poetical. There is likewise a great Variety of Fancy in drawing up and distinguishing, by their proper Emblems, the Visionary Persons in the Masque of *Cupid*, which is one of the chief Embellishments of this Book.

In the Story of *Cambel* and *Canace*, in the Fourth Book, the Author has taken the Rise of his Invention from the *Squire's Tale* in *Chaucer*, the greatest part of which was lost. The Battel of *Cambel* with the three Brethren, and the sudden parting of it by that beautiful Machine of the Appearance of *Concord*; who by a Touch of her Wand charms down the Fury of the Warriors, and converts them into Friends; is one of the most shining Passages in this Legend. We may add to this the Fiction concerning the Girdle of *Florimel*, which is a good Allegory; as also the Description of *Ate*, or *Discord*: That of *Care*, working like a Smith, and living amidst the perpetual Noise of Hammers; and especially the Temple of *Venus*, which is adorn'd with a great Variety of Fancy. The Prayer of a Lover in this Temple, which begins,

Great Venus, *Queen of Beauty and of Grace,*
[*Faerie Queene IV.* x. 44–7]

is taken from *Lucretius*'s Invocation of the same Goddess in the beginning of his Poem, and may be reckon'd one of the most elegant
Translations in our Language. The Continuation of the Fable of
Marinel, tho not so strictly to the Subject of this Legend, gives occasion
to the Poet to introduce that admirable Episode of *the Marriage of the*
Thames *and the* Medway; with the Train of the Sea-Gods, Nymphs,
and Rivers, and especially those of *England* and *Ireland*, that were present
at the Ceremony: all which are describ'd with a suprizing Variety, and
with very agreeable Mixtures of Geography; among which *Spenser*
has not forgot to mention his *Mulla*, the River which ran thro his own
Grounds.

Besides the general Morals and Allegories in the *Fairy Queen*, there
are some parallel Passages and Characters, which, as I have said, were
design'd to allude to particular Actions and Persons; yet no part is so
full of them as the Fifth Book, which being fram'd on the Vertue of
Justice, is a kind of figurative Representation of Queen *Elizabeth*'s
Reign. Here we meet with her again, under the Name of *Mercilla*; we
see her sending Relief to *Belge*, or the *Netherlands*, and reducing the
tyrannical Power of *Geryoneo*, or *Spain*. Her Court and Attendants are
drawn with a Majesty sutable to her Character. The Reader will
easily perceive that the Trial of the Queen of *Scots* is shadow'd in the
Ninth Canto: but the Poet has avoided the Catastrophe of her Death,
and has artfully touch'd on the Queen's Reluctance and Tenderness in
that Affair; by which he has turned the Compliment on her Justice,
into another on her Mercy.

Talus with his Iron Flail, who attends *Arthegal*, is a bold Allegorical
Figure, to signify the Execution of Justice.

The next Book, which is the Sixth, is on the Subject of *Courtesy*. I shall
not prolong this Discourse to trace out particular Passages in it, but only
mention that remarkable one in the Tenth Canto; where the Author
has introduc'd himself under the Person of *Colin Clout*. That Vein of
Pastoral which runs thro this part of the Work, is indeed different
from the rest of the Poem. But *Tasso*, in a more regular Plan, has
mingled the Pastoral Taste with the Heroick, in his Representation of
Erminia among the Shepherds. The Picture which *Spenser* has here
given us of his Mistress, dancing among the Graces, is a very agreeable

one, and discovers all the skill of the Painter, assisted by the Passion of the Lover.

Tho the remaining Six Books, which were to have compleated this beautiful and moral Poem, are lost; we have a noble Fragment of them preserv'd in the Two Canto's of *Mutability*: This is, in my Opinion, the most sublime and best-invented Allegory in the whole Work. The Fable of *Arlo-Hill*, and of the River *Molanna*, which is a Digression on this Occasion, has all the Beauty we admire in the *Metamorphoses* of *Ovid*. But the Pedegree of *Mutability*, who is represented as a Giantess; her Progress from the Earth to the Circle of the Moon; the Commotion she raises there, by endeavouring to remove that Planet from the sky; and the Shadow, which is cast, during the Attempt, on the Inhabitants of the Earth, are greatly imagin'd. We find several Strains of Invention in this Fable, which might appear not unworthy even of *Homer* himself. *Jupiter* is alarm'd, and sends *Mercury* to know the Reason of this Strife, and to bring the Offender before him. How *Homer*-like are those Lines, after he has concluded his Speech among the Gods?

[quotes *Faerie Queene* VII. vi. 22$^{1-5}$]

And afterwards:

[quotes *Faerie Queene* VII. vi. 30$^{6-9}$]

The Simile likewise, in which the Gods are represented looking on *Mutability* with Surprize,

[quotes *Faerie Queene* VII. vi. 28$^{6-8}$]

is very much in the Simplicity of that old Father of Heroick Poetry. *Mutability* appeals from *Jupiter* to *Nature*, before whom she obtains a Hearing. The Poet on this Occasion has with a most abundant Fancy, drawn out to a Review the Four Seasons, the Months, Day and Night, the Hours, Life and Death; *Change* asserts her Dominion over them all, and over the Heavens themselves. All Creatures are represented looking up in the Face of Nature, in expectation of the Sentence. The Conclusion is great, and contains a noble Moral; That tho all things are vary'd and shift their Forms, they do not perish, but return to their first Beings; and that *Mutability* only shall be at last entirely destroy'd, and the time shall come in which *Change shall be no more*.

(c) *Remarks on the Shepherd's Calendar, &c., ibid.*, pp. xcvii–cx (that is, excluding the remarks on Spenser orthography and the like):

In the Remarks of the *Fairy Queen*, I have chiefly consider'd our Author as an Allegorical Writer; and his Poem as fram'd after a Model of a particular kind. In some of his other Writings, we find more Regularity, tho less Invention. There seems to be the same difference between the *Fairy Queen* and the *Shepherd's Calendar*, as between a Royal Palace and a little Country Seat. The first strikes the Eye with more Magnificence; but the latter may perhaps give the greatest Pleasure. In this Work the Author has not been misled by the *Italians*; tho *Tasso's Aminta* might have been at least of as good Authority to him in the Pastoral, as *Ariosto* in the greater kind of Poetry. But *Spenser* rather chose to follow Nature it self, and to paint the Life and Sentiments of Shepherds after a more simple and unaffected manner.

The two things which seem the most essential to Pastoral, are Love, and the Images of a Country Life: and to represent these, our Author had little more to do, than to examine his own Heart, and to copy the Scene about him; for at the time when he wrote the *Shepherd's Calendar*, he was a passionate Lover of his *Rosalind*: and it appears that the greatest part of it, if not the whole, was compos'd in the Country on his first leaving the University; and before he had engag'd in Business, or fill'd his Mind with the Thoughts of Preferment in a Life at Court. Perhaps too there is a certain Age most proper for Pastoral Writing; and tho the same Genius shou'd arise afterwards to greater Excellencies, it may grow less capable of this. Accordingly in the Poem call'd *Colin Clout's come home again*, which was written a considerable time after, we find him less a Shepherd than at first: He had then been drawn out of his Retirement, had appear'd at Court, and been engag'd in an Employment which brought him into a Variety of Business and Acquaintance, and gave him a quite different Sett of Ideas. And tho this Poem is not without its Beauties; yet what I wou'd here observe so that in the Pastoral Kind it is not so simple and unmix'd, and consequently not so perfect as the *Eclogues*, of which I have perhaps given the Reason.

But I am sensible that what I have mention'd as a Beauty in *Spenser's* Pastorals, will not seem so to all Readers; and that the Simplicity which appears in them may be thought to have too much of the *Merum Rus*. If our Author has err'd in this, he has at least err'd on the right hand. The true Model of Pastoral Writing seems indeed not to be yet fix'd

by the Criticks; and there is room for the best Judges to differ in
their Opinions about it: Those who wou'd argue for the Simplicity
of Pastoral, may say, That the very Idea of this kind of Writing is the
Representation of a Life of Retirement and Innocence, made agreeable
by all those Pleasures and Amusements, which the Fields, the Woods
and the various Seasons of the Year afford to Men, who live according
to the first Dictates of Nature, and without the artificial Cares and
Refinements, which Wealth, Luxury, and Ambition, by multiplying
both our Wants and Enjoyments, have introduc'd among the Rich and
the Polite: That therefore as the Images, Similies, and Allusions are to
be drawn from the Scene; so the Sentiments and Expressions ought no
where to taste of the City, or the Court, but to have such a kind of
plain Elegance only, as may appear proper to the Life and Characters
of the Persons introduc'd in such Poems: That this Simplicity, skilfully
drawn, will make the Picture more natural, and consequently more
pleasing: That even the low Images in such a Representation are
amusing, as they contribute to deceive the Reader, and make him fancy
himself really in such a Place, and among such Persons as are describ'd;
the Pleasure in this case being like that express'd by *Milton* of one
walking out into the Fields:

[quotes *Paradise Lost* IX. 445–51]

This indeed seems to be the true Reason of the Entertainment which
Pastoral Poetry gives to its Readers: for as Mankind is departed from
the Simplicity, as well as the Innocence, of a State of Nature, and is
immers'd in Cares and Pursuits of a very different kind; it is a wonderful Amusement to the Imagination, to be sometimes transported, as it
were, out of modern Life, and to wander in these pleasant Scenes which
the Pastoral Poets provide for us, and in which we are apt to fancy our
selves reinstated for a time in our first Innocence and Happiness.

Those who argue against the strict Simplicity of Pastoral Writing,
think there is something too low in the Characters and Sentiments of
mere Shepherds, to support this kind of Poetry, if not rais'd and improv'd by the Assistance of Art; or at least that we ought to distinguish
between what is simple, and what is rustick, and take care that while
we represent Shepherds, we do not make them Clowns: That it is a
Mistake to imagine that the Life of Shepherds is incapable of any
Refinement, or that their Sentiments may not sometimes rise above
the Country. To justify this, they tell us, that we conceive too low an
Idea of this kind of Life, by taking it from that of modern Shepherds,

who are the meanest and poorest sort of People among us. But in the first Ages of the World it was otherwise; that Persons of Rank and Dignity honour'd this Employment; that Shepherds were the Owners of their own Flocks; and that *David* was once a Shepherd, who became afterwards a King, and was himself too the most sublime of Poets. Those who argue for the first kind of Pastoral, recommend *Theocritus* as the best Model; and those who are for the latter, think that *Virgil*, by raising it to a higher Pitch, has improv'd it. I shall not determine this Controversy, but only observe, that the Pastorals of *Spenser* are of the former kind.

It is for the same Reason that the Language of the *Shepherd's Calendar*, which is designed to be rural, is older than that of his other Poems. Sir *Philip Sidney* however, tho he commends this Work in his *Apology for Poetry*, censures the Rusticity of the Stile as an Affectation not to be allow'd. The Author's profess'd Veneration for *Chaucer* partly led him into this; yet there is a difference among the Pastorals, and the Reader will observe, that the Language of the Fifth and Eighth is more obsolete than that of some others; the reason of which might be, that the Design of those two Eclogues being Allegorical Satire, he chose a more antiquated Dress, as more proper to his Purpose. But however faulty he may be in the Excess of this, it is certain that a sprinkling of the rural Phrase, as it humours the Scene and Characters, has a very great Beauty in Pastoral Poetry; and of this any one may be convinc'd, by reading the Pastorals of Mr. *Philips*, which are written with great Delicacy of Taste, in the very Spirit and Manner of *Spenser*.

Having said that *Spenser* has mingled Satire in some of his Eclogues, I know not whether this may not be another Objection to them: it may be doubted whether any thing of this kind shou'd be admitted to disturb the Tranquillity and Pleasure which shou'd every where reign in Pastoral Poems; or at least nothing shou'd be introduc'd more than the light and pleasant Railleries or Contentions of Shepherds about their Flocks, their Mistresses, or their Skill in piping and singing. I cannot wholly justify my Author in this, yet must say that the Excellency of the Moral in those Pastorals does in a great measure excuse his transgessing the strict Rules of Criticism. Besides, as he design'd under an Allegory to censure the vicious Lives of bad Priests, and to expose their Usurpation of Pomp and Dominion, nothing cou'd be more proper to this purpose than the Allegory he has chosen; the Author of our Holy Religion having himself dignify'd the Parable of a *good Shepherd*; and the natural Innocence, Simplicity, Vigilance, and

Freedom from Ambition, which are the Characters of that kind of Life, being a very good Contrast to the Vices and Luxury, and to that Degeneracy from their first Pattern, which the Poet wou'd there reprehend.

I have already mention'd the Poem call'd, *Colin Clout's come home again*; which, tho not so perfectly Pastoral as the *Shepherd's Calendar*, is yet very agreeable and amusing. In this Piece the Author has taken occasion to celebrate the reigning Wits and Beauties of that Age; but Time has blended them both in that common Obscurity, that we can trace out but few of them by their true Names. The Reader will perceive, that by the *Shepherd of the Ocean* is meant Sir *Walter Raleigh*; who, as I have said in the Life of the Author, was newly become *Spenser's* Friend, and was at that time rising into great Favour at Court. The Name of *Cynthia*, given to Queen *Elizabeth*, is the same under which *Raleigh* himself had celebrated her in a Poem commended more than once by our Author. By *Astrophel* is meant Sir *Philip Sidney*, who dy'd about four Years before this Poem was written; by *Urania*, his Sister, the Countess of *Pembroke*; by *Stella*, the Lady *Rich*, whom *Sidney* himself has celebrated in his Poems; and by *Mansilia*, the Marchioness of *Northampton*: Mr. *Daniel*, the Poet and Historian, is mention'd by his own Name; as also *William Alabaster*, the Author of a Poem call'd *Eliseis*, on which *Spenser* has bestow'd such unparallel'd Praises, that I wish I cou'd give the Reader any further Information about it, than only that this Person is likewise mention'd by *Anthony a Wood* in his *Athenae Oxonienses*, who says he left a *Latin* Poem, under that Title, unfinish'd at his Death; but I do not find it has ever been publish'd.

In the Poem call'd *Mother* Hubberd's *Tale*, we have a Specimen of our Author's Genius in Satire, a Talent he very seldom exercis'd. This Fable is after the old manner of *Chaucer*, of whom it is an excellent Imitation; and perhaps the antiquated Stile has no ill Effect in improving the Humour of the Story. The Morality of it is admirable. Every one will observe that Keenness of Wit with which he has represented the Arts of ill Courtiers. In the Description of a good Courtier, which is so finely set off by the contrary Characters, it is believ'd the Author had in his View Sir *Philip Sidney*, of whom this seems to be a very just as well as beautiful Picture.

There are several other Pieces of our Author which appear not un-

275

worthy of the same Genius, especially that admirable *Epithalamion* on his own Marriage; his *Hymns*; his *Daphnaida*; and his *Elegies on Sir Philip Sidney*: but these I shall leave to the Reader's own Observation, and only say something of the *Sonnets*, a Species of Poetry so entirely disus'd, that it seems to be scarce known among us at this time. Here again we find our Author copying the *Italians*. The *Sonnet* consists generally of one Thought, and that always turn'd in a single Stanza, of fourteen Lines, of the Length of our Heroicks, the Rhime being interchang'd alternately; and in this it differs from the *Canzone*, which are not confin'd to any Number of Lines or Stanza's. The famous *Petrarch* is the Original of this kind of little Odes, and has fill'd a whole Book with them in honour of his *Laura*, with whom he was in Love, as himself tells us,* for twenty one Years; and whose Death he lamented, with the same Zeal, for ten Years afterwards. The uncommon Ardor of his Passion, as well as the Fineness of his Wit and Language, establish'd him the Master of Love-Poetry among the Moderns. Accordingly we find his Manner of Writing copy'd soon after by the Wits of *Spain*, *France*, and *England*; and the *Sonnet* grown so much into fashion, that *Sidney* himself, who had written a great Number on his beloved *Stella*, has pleasantly rally'd his Cotemporaries in the following one; which for the Sprightliness of it, and the beautiful Turn in the Close, the Reader may not be displeas'd to find here inserted.

[quotes *Astrophil and Stella*, Sonnet 15]

I have the rather set down the foregoing Lines, because the Thought they are turn'd upon is likewise the Rule for this kind of Writings, which are only recommended by their natural Tenderness, Simplicity and Correctness. Most of *Spenser*'s *Sonnets* have this Beauty. *Milton* has writ some, both in *Italian* and *English*, and is, I think, the last who has given us any Example of them in our own Language.

As for the Poem call'd *Britain*'s *Ida*, tho it has formerly appear'd with our Author's Works, and is therefore now reprinted, I am apt to believe, notwithstanding the Opinion of its first Publisher, that it is not *Spenser's*.

---

* *Tennemi amor anni vent'uno ardendo*
Lieto nel foco, e nel duol pien di speme;
Poi che Madonna, e'l mio cor seco inseme
Saltro al Ciel, dieci altri anni piangendo. &c.
Sonetto 313.

See Introduction pp. 22–4. Where linguistic and stylistic comment is incidental to some more general argument, it will be found in the earlier sections of the book. See in particular Nos. 1, 2, 4, 56, 57, 71, 87, 88, 96, 97, 99, 103, 110, 122. Most of this early comment is misdirected, and the reader should at least be aware of the works listed in Dorothy Atkinson's *Bibliographical Supplement*.

132. Gabriel Harvey

1580

See headnote to No. 3.

(a) From the *Marginalia*, ed. G. C. Moore Smith (Stratford-upon-Avon, 1913), p. 168 (to Gascoigne's *Certaine notes of Instruction*):

The difference of *the* last verse from *the* rest in euerie Stanza, a grace in *the* Faerie Queen.

Ibid., pp. 168–9.

The reason of manie a good uerse, marred in Sir Philip Sidney, M. Spenser, M. Fraunce, & in a manner all our excellentest poets: in such words, as heauen, euil, diuel, & *the* like; made dyssyllables, contrarie to their natural pronunciation.

So M. Spenser, & Sir Philip, for *the* most part (write lines with unequal numbers of syllables, such that the fewer the syllables, the longer the line will seem to the ear).

Our poems only Rymes, and not Verses.

Aschami querela. Et mea post illum Reformatio; post me, Sidneius, Spencerus, Francius.[1]

... Monosyllables ar good to make upp A hobbling and hudling verse. Sir Philip Sydney, & M. Spenser of mie opinion.

Ibid., pp. 169–70:

Spenser hath reuiued, vncouth, whilom, of yore, for thy.

All theise in Spenser (ydone, adowne, tane, power for powre, heauen for heavn, thewes for good qualities), & manie like: but with discretion: & tolerably, thowgh sumtime not greatly commendably.

(b) From *Two Other very commendable Letters* ... (1580); repr. *Variorum Spenser: Prose Works*, pp. 442–3:

Your Englisshe *Trimetra* I lyke better, than perhappes you will easily beleeue: and am to requite them better, or worse, at more conuenient leysure. Marry, you must pardon me, I find not your warrant so sufficiently good, and substantiall in Lawe, that it can persuade me, they are all, so precisely perfect for the Feet, as your selfe ouer-partially weene, and ouer confidently auouche: especiallye the thirde, whych hath a foote more than a Lowce (a wonderous deformitie in a righte and pure Senarie) and the sixte, which is also in the same Predicament, vnlesse happly one of the feete be sawed off wyth a payre of *Syncopes*: and then shoulde the Orthographie haue testified so muche: and in steade of *Hēauenli Virgnīals*, you should haue written, *Heaūnlĭ Virgnāls*: & *Virgnāls* againe in the ninth, & should haue made a Curtoll of *Immĕrĭtō* in the laste: being all notwithstandying vsuall, and tollerable ynoughe, in a mixte, and licentious *Iambicke*: and of two euilles, better (no doubte) the fyrste, than the laste: a thyrde superfluous sillable, than a dull *Spondee*. Then me thinketh, you haue in my fancie somwhat too many *Spondees* beside: and whereas *Trochee* sometyme presumeth in the firste place, as namely in the second Verse, *Make thy*, whiche *thy*, by youre Maistershippes owne authoritie muste needes be shorte, I shall be faine to supplye the office of the Arte Memoratiue, and putte you in minde of a pretty Fable in *Abstemio* the Italian, implying thus much, or rather thus little in effect.

A certaine lame man beyng inuited to a solempne Nuptiall Feaste,

[1] Ascham's argument. And after him, my own reform; and after me, Sidney, Spenser and Fraunce.

made no more adoe, but sate me hym roundlye downe foremoste at the hyghest ende of the Table. The Master of the feast, suddainly spying his presumption, and hansomely remoouing him from thence, placed me this haulting Gentleman belowe at the nether end of the bourd: alledging for his defence the common verse: *Sedes nulla datur, praeterquam sexta Trochaeo:* and pleasantly alluding to this foote, which standing vppon two syllables, the one long, the other short, (much like, of a like, his guestes feete) is always thrust downe to the laste place, in a true Hexameter, and quite thrust out of doores in a pure and iust *Senarie*. Nowe Syr, what thinke you, I began to thinke with my selfe, when I began to reade your warrant first: so boldly, and venterously set down in so formall, and autentique wordes, as these, *Precisely perfit, and not an inch from the Rule*? Ah Syrrha, and Iesu Lord, thought I, haue we at the last gotten one of whom his olde friendes and Companions may iustly glory, *In eo solum peccat, quod nihil peccat:* and that is yet more exacte, and precise in his English Comicall Iambickes, than euer *M. Watson*, himselfe was in his *Lattin* Tragicall Iambickes, of whom *M. Ascham* reporteth, that he would neuer to this day suffer his famous *Absolon* to come abrode, onely because *Anapaestus in Locis paribus*, is twice, or thrice vsed in stead of *Iambus?* A small fault, ywisse, and such a one in M. Aschams owne opinion, as perchaunce woulde neuer haue beene espyed, no neither in *Italy*, nor in *Fraunce*. But when I came to the curious scanning, and fingering of euery foote, & syllable: Lo here, quoth I, *M. Watsons Anapaestus* for all the worlde. A good horse that trippeth not once in a iourney: and *M. Immerito* doth, but as *M. Watson*, & in a manner all other *Iambici* haue done before him: marry he might haue spared his preface, or at *the* least, that same restrictiue, & streight laced terme, Precisely, and all had been well enough: and I assure you, of my selfe, I beleeue, no peece of a fault marked at all. But this is the Effect of warrantes and perhappes the Errour may rather proceede of his Master, *M. Drantes* Rule, than of himselfe. Howsoeuer it is, the matter is not great, and I always was, and will euer continue of this Opinion, *Pauca multis condonanda vitia Virtuitibus*, especially these being no *Vitia* neither, in a common and licencious *Iambicke*.

133. Sir Philip Sidney

c. 1583

Sir Philip Sidney (1554–86) was educated at Christ Church, Oxford. For a notice of his association with Spenser, see Aubrey (No. 172). Attempts to make the explicit poetics of *The Defence* square with the implicit poetics of the *Faerie Queene* are not particularly well augured by Sidney's only reference to Spenser here. See Shepherd's note in the edition cited below, p. 218. For the dating *c.* 1583, see the same edition, pp. 2–4.

From *The Defence of Poesie* ... *Printed for William Ponsonby*, (1595), sig. H3ᵛ; also *An Apologie for Poetrie* ... *Printed for Henry Olney* (1595); repr. in edition of Geoffrey Shepherd (1965), p. 133:

I account the Mirrour of Magistrates, meetly furnished of bewtiful partes. And in the Earle of *Surries Lirickes*, manie thinges tasting of a Noble birth, and worthie of a Noble minde. The Sheepheards Kallender, hath much *Poetrie* in his Egloges, indeed worthie the reading, if I be not deceiued. That same framing of his style to an olde rusticke language, I dare not allow: since neither *Theocritus* in Greeke, *Virgill* in Latine, nor *Sanazara* in Italian, did affect it. Besides these, I doo not remember to haue seene but fewe (to speake bodly) printed, that haue poeticall sinnewes in them.

134. Abraham Fraunce

1588

Abraham Fraunce (1560?–1633) studied at St Johns College, Cambridge, of which he became a Fellow, and Gray's Inn. Early he came under the aegis of Sidney, as whose protégé he would have met Spenser and Dyer and along with whom he championed the introduction of classical metres into English. Spenser calls him 'hablest wit of most I know this day' (*Colin Clout* l. 383) and whether or not as an able critical wit, Fraunce clearly had access to the *Faerie Queene* before its publication. *The Shepheardes Logike* (B.M. MS. Add. 34361, fols. 3–28; written 1580–85) uses the *Shepheards Calender* extensively for purposes of illustration as does its revision *The Lawiers Logike*, and it is in *The Arcadian Rhetorike* (1588) that we find the earliest quotation of the *Faerie Queene* (of II. iv. 35). In spite of Fraunce's dependence on Spenser for illustrative material (perhaps only out of friendly courtesy), the two sentences below make up his only sustained comment on anything of Spenser's.

From *The Lawiers Logike, exemplifying the praecepts of Logike by the practise of the Common Lawe* (1588), sigs. Ii.iij–Ii.iijᵛ:

For our Kalender, although shepheardes bee not woont to binde themselues to any ouerstrict methode in speaking, yet that song of *Colyn Clowt* rehearsed by *Hobbynoll* in May, may make us beleeuve, that euen shepheardes, by the light of nature, did, asmuch as in them lay, expresse this method in their speeches. For there he, after a poetical inuocation, and generall proposition of that which he hath in hand, I meane the prayses of *Elysa*, commeth nearer *the* matter, and first putteth downe the causes, then adi[u]nctes, and other arguments, incident to *Elysa*.

135. Henry Peacham

1593

Henry Peacham (*flor.* 1577) was the father of the Henry Peacham who wrote the *Compleat Gentleman*. The quotation below is from the second and augmented edition of the *Garden of Eloquence* (1593). The first edition of 1577 contains no mention of Spenser.

From *The Garden of Eloquence Conteining The Most Excellent Ornaments, Exornations, Lightes, flowers, and formes of speech* (1593), p. 15 (under Onomatopeia):

Touching this part I will refer the Reader to *Chaucer* & *Gower*, and to the new Shepherds calender, a most singular imitation of ancient speech.

136. Hadrian Dorrell

1594

Possibly Hadrian Dorrell is to be identified with Thomas Dorrell, who took his B.A. from Brasenose College in 1595. See *Willobie his Avisa*, ed. Charles Hughes (1904), p. xvi.

From the epistle *To the gentle & courteous Reader* prefatory to *Willobie his Auisa* (1594), sig. A2ᵛ; repr. in edition of G. B. Harrison (1926), pp. 14–15:

For the composition and order of the verse: Although hee (Henry Willobie) flye not alofte with the winges of *Astrophell*, nor dare to compare with the Arcadian shepheard, or any way match with the dainetie Fayry Queene; yet shall you find his wordes and phrases, neither Tryuiall nor absurd.

137. Sir John Harington

1596

See headnote to No. 15.

From *A New Discourse of a Stale Subiect, Called The Metamorphosis of Aiax* (1956), sigs. Aa^v–Aa2; repr. in edition of E. Donno (1962), p. 207:

They descanted of the new Faerie Queene and the olde both, and the greatest fault they coulde finde in it was that the last verse disordered their mouthes, and was lyke a trycke of xvii in a sinkapace.

138. William Lisle

c. 1596

See headnote to No. 71. Lisle's philological preoccupations are reflected in the passage below.

From the epistle *To the Readers*, prefatory to *Part of Du Bartas, English and French, and in his Owne Kinde of Verse* (1625; but written *c.* 1596), sigs. ¶¶4–¶¶4^v:

I was about to end; but may not forget to let you vnderstand, that this Bartassian verse (not vnlike herein to the Latin Pentameter) hath euer this propertie, to part in the mids betwixt two wordes; so much doe some French prints signifie, with a stroke interposed, as here in the first two pages you may see, for example. The neglect of this hath caused many a braue Stanza in the Faerie Queen to end but harshly, which might haue beene preuented at the first; but now the fault may be sooner found then amended.

139. Joseph Hall

1598

See headnote to No. 26. In view of Hall's enthusiasm for Spenser elsewhere, it may be better to take this couplet as referring to Stanyhurst.

From *Virgidemiarum*, p. 14 (Lib. I, sat. 6); repr. Grosart, p. 30:

Fie on the forged mint that did create
New coyne of words neuer articulate.

140. Francis Beaumont

1598

Francis Beaumont (d. 1598) was educated at Peterhouse and the Inner Temple. He was the father of the dramatist of the same name.

From the *Letter from Francis Beaumont to Thomas Speght* prefatory to Speght's edition of Chaucer (1598), sig. Aiii^v:

But yet so pure were Chaucers wordes in his owne daies, as *Lidgat:* that learned man calleth him *The Loadstarre of the English languagee* and so good they are in our daies, as Maister *Spencer*, following the counsaile of *Tullie* in *de Oratore*, for reuiuing of antient wordes, hath adorned his owne stile with that beauty and grauitie, which *Tully* speakes of: and his much frequenting of *Chaucers* antient speeches causeth many to allow farre better of him, than otherwise they would.

141. Charles Butler

1598

Charles Butler (d. 1647) was educated at Magdalen Hall, Oxford, and employed what leisure his clerical duties allowed as an English philologist. In 1633 he produced *The English Grammar*. The extract below is from an earlier effort.

From *Rhetoricae Libri Duo* (Oxford, 1598), sigs. C3ᵛ–C4:

Number in poetry is called rhythm or metre. Rhythm then is poetic number, containing a fixed total of syllables, and not contained by any quantitative principle. Natural rhythms of this sort are found in every nation and among all peoples. They are even to be discovered in Greece before Homer, and in Italy before Andronicus. And in modern times for the most part they rhyme, as in our Homer's poem. [quotes *RT* 11.400–406] And a little later [quotes *RT* 11.428–34] Careful reading in the best poets will show the different kinds of rhythm.

[Butler's note reads:] Those amongst our poets most deserving of comparison with Homer, Virgil, and Ovid, are Edmund Spenser, Samuel Daniel, Michael Drayton, and others, full of native talent and artistic skill (in both of which this age is fertile). First among them, the master of them all and the only lamp of his own dark age, is Master Geoffrey Chaucer.[1]

---

[1] Rhythmus Numerus *Numerus poeticus est rhythmus, aut metrum.* RHYTHMVS *est numerus poeticus certunsyllabarum numerum (nulla habita quantitatis ratione) continens. Tales rhythmi naturales sunt in omni natione atque gente: etiam in Graecia ante Homerum, & in Italia ante Andronicum reperti sunt. Hodie autem plerumque Epistrophen soni coniunctam habent: ut in illo Homeri nostri poemate.* [quotes R.T. 400–6]
& paulo post. [quotes R.T. 428–34]
Varia rhythmorum genera optimorum poetarum observatio optime premonstrabit.
[Butler's note reads:]
Quales sunt apud *nos* Homero, Maroni, & Ovidio *merito* aequiparandi, Edmvndvs Spencer, Samvel Daniel, & Michael Drayton: *aliiq, ingenio & arte florentes,* (*quorum haec aetas uberrima est*) *Atque inprimis horum omnium magister, unicum caligantis sui seculi lumen, dominus* Galfridvs Chavcer.

142. Everard Guilpin

1598

Everard Guilpin (*flor.* 1598) was educated at Emmanuel College, Cambridge, and Gray's Inn. For a full account, see R. E. Bennett, 'John Donne and Everard Guilpin', *RES*, XV (1939), 66–72.

From *Skialetheia, Or, A shadowe of Truth, in certain Epigrams and Satyres* (1598), sig. E (Satyra sexta); repr. in edition of A. B. Grosart, Occasional Issues, VI (Manchester, 1878), p. 63:

> Some blame deep *Spencer* for his grandam words
> Others protest that, in them he records
> His maister-peece of cunning giuing praise,
> And grauity to his profound-prickt layes.

143. A note on Spenser's failure to write 'trew Hexameters'

1599

The piece below makes clearer and more explicit Thomas Nashe's remarks in *Strange News* on why Chaucer and Spenser are 'farre ouerseene' by Homer and Virgil: see G. Gregory Smith, *Elizabethan Critical Essays* (Oxford, 1904), II. 240.

From *The First Booke of the Preservation of King Henry the vij when he was but Earle of Richmond* (1599), sig. A2ᵛ:

I confesse and acknowledge that we haue many excellent and singular good Poets in this our age, as Maister *Spencer*, that was, Maister *Gowlding*, Doctor *Phayer*, Maister *Harrington*, *Daniell*, and diuers others whom I reuerence in that kind of prose-rythme: wherein *Spencer* (with offence spoken) hath surpassed them all. I would to God they had done so well in trew Hexameters: for they had then beautified our language.

144. John Bodenham

1600

John Bodenham (*flor.* 1600) was, as it were, a great planner of projects and organized the production among other things of *Wits Commonwealth* and *Englands Helicon*. *Bel-vedere or The Garden of the Muses* has much in common as regards its broad intentions and, in particular, as regards its extensive use of Spenserian material, with *Englands Parnassus* compiled by Bodenham's friend Robert Allott. For details see Charles Crawford, '*Belvedere, or The Garden of the Muses*', *Englische Studien*, XLIII (1911), 207.

From *Bel-vedere or The Garden of the Muses* (1600), sigs. A3ᵛ–A6; repr. Spenser Society (1875), sigs. A3ᵛ–A6:

Concerning the nature and qualitie of these excellent flowres, thou seest that they are most learned, graue, and wittie sentences; each line being a seuerall sentence, and none exceeding two lines at the uttermost. All which, being subiected vnder apt and proper heads, as arguments what is then dilated and spoken of: euen so each head hath first his definition in a couplet sentence; then the single and double sentences by variation of letter do follow: and lastly Similies and Examples in the same nature likewise, to conclude euery Head or Argument handled ... I haue set down both how, whence, and where these flowres had their first springing, till thus they were drawne togither into the *Muses Garden*, that euery ground may challenge his owne, each plant his particular, and no one be iniured in the iustice of his merit ...

From diuers essayes of their Poetrie; some extent among other Honourable personages writings; some from priuate labours and translations.

> *Edmund Spencer*
> *Henry Constable Esquier*
> *Samuel Daniel* ...

145. Richard Carew

1602

See headnote to No. 28.

From *The Suruey of Cornwall* (1602), fol. 57:

... which termes [dialect words of Cornwall and Devon], as they expresse our meaning more directly, so they want but another *Spencer*, to make them passable.

146. Edmund Bolton

c. 1618

Edmund Bolton (1575–1633) studied at Trinity Hall, Cambridge, and the Inner Temple. He is best known as an antiquarian, but as a poet made some show as a contributor to *Englands Helicon*. Against the judgment printed below we must set that in Section 1 of *Addresse the Fourth* of the *Hypercritica* as preserved in Bodleian Rawlinson MS. Misc. 1, p. 13: among a list of writers commended by Bolton for their use of English is 'Edmund Spencer (the most learned Poet of our Nation,) very little for the vse of history'.

From *Hypercritica; or a Rule of Judgment for writing, or reading our History's* (written *c.* 1618, published Oxford, 1722), p. 235; repr. J. E. Spingarn, *English Critical Essays of the Seventeenth Century* (Oxford, 1908–9), I. 109:

In verse there are *Ed. Spencer's* Hymns. I cannot advise the allowance of other his Poems, as for practick *English*, no more that I can do *Jeff. Chaucer, Lydgate, Pierce Ploughman,* or *Laureat Skelton.*

147. Alexander Gill

1621

See headnote to No. 68. Almost all Gill's examples, as he himself says (p. 97), are taken from Spenser's *Faerie Queene*. The two below are a little less specific than most.

(a) From *Logonomia Anglica* (1621), p. 99; repr. in edition of O. L. Jiriczek (Strasburg, 1903), pp. 104–5:

[Gill is talking about metaphor.] From this source, rise all allegories and similes (also most proverbs and enigmas). For allegory is nothing but a continued metaphor. . . .

[quotes *Faerie Queene* III. iv. 8–9$^{1-3}$]

But all Spenser's poem is an allegory, by means of which he educates his readers morally with fables. Thus allegory, working like a metaphor, deals darkly with a whole world. . . . Proverb and enigma deal with it more obscurely yet. Simile operates more clearly, because the metaphor is first of all unfolded, and then set alongside its actual reference.

[quotes *Faerie Queene* I. ii. 16$^{1-7}$][1]

(b) *Ibid.*, p. 142; repr. Jiriczek, p. 146:

In Spenser's Epic or Heroic Poem, every ninth verse, for the sake of its weight and a certain sureness of stance, is a hexameter.[2]

---

[1] *Ab hoc fonte Allegoriae omnes, & Comparationes, Παροιμίαι etiam pleraeque; et ᾿Αινίγματα. Allegoria nihil enim est, quam continuata Metaphora. . . . Sed & totum Spenseri poema allegoria est, qua ethicen fabulis edocet. Sic Allegoria rem totam per Metaphoram obscure tractat: Paroimia & Aenigma multo obscurius: Comparatio dilucidius, quia primo Metaforam explicat, postea cum re componit.*

[2] *Spenceri tamen Epicum, siue Heroicum, nonum quemque versum habet hexametrum; ad grauitatem, & quandam stationis firmitudinem.*

293

148. Ben Jonson

1640

See headnote to No. 61. Compare also Virgil's speech on literary dietics in *Poetaster* V. iii.

From *Timber; or Discoveries*..., in *Workes*... *The Second Volume* (1640), pp. 116–17; repr. *Works*, ed. Herford and Simpson (Oxford, 1925–52), VIII. 618:

Spencer, in affecting the Ancients, writ no Language: Yet I would have him read for his matter; but as *Virgil* read *Ennius*.

Ibid., p. 119; repr. Herford and Simpson, VIII. 622:

Words borrow'd of Antiquity, doe lend a kind of Majesty to style, and are not without their delight sometimes. For they have the Authority of yeares, and out of their intermission doe win to themselves a kind of grace-like newnesse. But the eldest of the present, and newnesse of the past Language is the best. For what was the ancient Language, which some men so doate upon, but the ancient Custome? ... *Virgill* was most loving of Antiquity; yet how rarely doth hee insert *aquai*, and *pictai*! Lucretius is scabrous and rough in these; hee seekes 'hem: As some doe Chaucerismes with us, which were better expung'd and banish'd.

149. Nathaniel Sterry

c. 1650

Nathaniel Sterry (d. 1698) was educated at Emmanuel College, Cambridge. The piece below must date from before 1649, when he became a Fellow of Merton College, Oxford. See the letter by V. de S. Pinto in *TLS*, 31 August 1933.

From *A direction for a good and profitable proceeding in study, by Mr. N. Sterry of E.C.*, Bodleian Tanner MSS., vol. 88, no. 5:

After all this, if you can, before you are Batchelor read Spencer, & Daniels poems for the furnishing of your English tongue. for what good will all learning doe you, if you cannot make vse of it in the mother tongue? which excellency few looke after, which is an extraordinary folly.

150. John Davies

1653

John Davies of Kidwelly (1627?–93) was educated at Jesus College, Oxford, and St John's College, Cambridge. He is remembered as historian, critic and, best of all, as translator.

From the prefatory material to *The Extravagant Shepherd. Or, The History of the Shepherd Lysis* (1653), sig. A^v:

Nay, and thus many men not weighing discreetly the differences of *times*, *persons* and *places*, which they have had to represent, have fallen into error very misbecoming. The *Indecorum* of *Homers* gods, the fault in *Virgils* chronology, *Tasso* making Christians speak like *Heathens*, *Spencers* confusion, and different choice of names, are things never to be forgiven.

151. Edward Howard

1669, 1689

See headnote to No. 111.

(a) From *Preface to the Reader* in *The Brittish Princes: An Heroick Poem* (1669), sigs. A5ᵛ–A6:

And now to pay a due esteem to such Poets of our own Country, who are justly dignified by the Heroick muse . . . yet have these our Native Poets deservedly merited esteem, perhaps above those any other Nation has produced in the times they lived; and of these the most considerable, I think must be granted our famous Spencer, and the late Sir *William Davenant*, (not considering *Daniel*, *Drayton*, and the like, rather Historians than Epicke Poets) the first of whom is by many granted a parallel to most of the Antients, whose genius was in all degrees proportion'd for the work he accomplished, or for whatsoever structures his Muse had thought fit to raise, whose thoughts were like so many nerves and sinews ready with due motion and strength to actuate the body he produced; nor was the success of his Poem less worthy of Admiration, which notwithstanding it be frequent in words of obsolete signification, had the good fortune to have a reception suitable to its desert, which tells us the age he writ in, had a value for sense above words, though perhaps he may have received deservedly some censure in that particular, since our Language (when he writ) was held much improved, that it has been the wonder as well as the pity of some, that so famous a Poet should so much obscure the glory of his thoughts, wrapt up in words and expressions, which time and use had well nigh exploded: And though words serve our uses but like Counters or numbers to summe our intellectual Products, yet they must be currant as the money of the Age, or they will hardly pass: Nor is it less ridiculous to see a man confidently walk in the antiquated and mothy Garments of his Predecessors, out of an obstinate contempt of the present Mode, than to imitate the expressions of obsolete

297

Authors, which renders even Wit barbarous, and looks like some affront to the present Age, which expects from Writers due esteem of the tongue they speak. But this objection which I have presumed to mention against Renowned *Spencer*, (though it be a Common one, and the most is laid to his charge,) shows us that his building was rather mighty than curious, and like the Pyramids of Egypt, may expect to be a long Companion of times.

(b) From *Caroloiades, or, The Rebellion of Forty One* (1689), p. 137:

> Of which he *Chaucer, Spencer*, much beheld,
> And where their Learned Poems most excell'd.
> Tho' words now obsolete express their Flame,
> Like Gemms that out of Fashion value Claim.

152. Sir Thomas Culpepper

1671

Sir Thomas Culpepper (1626–97) was a Fellow of All Souls. His objections to Spencer's archaism are the standard neo-classical ones.

From *Essayes or Moral Discourses On several Subjects* (1671), p. 118:

Some have thought to honour Antiquity by using such (words) as were obsolete, as hath been done by our famous *Spencer*, and others, though the times past are no more respected by an unnecessary continuing of their words then if wee wore constantly the same trimming to our Cloaths as they did, for it is not Speech, but things which render antiquity venerable, besides the danger of expressing no Language, if as *Spencer* made use of *Chaucers*, we should likewise introduce his.

153. Edward Phillips

1675

See headnote to No. 97, and also No. 173.

(a) From *The Preface* to *Theatrum Poetarum, or a Compleat Collection of the Poets* (1675), sigs. **3ᵛ–**4; repr. J. E. Spingarn, *Critical Essays of the Seventeenth Century* (Oxford, 1908–9) II. 265:

There is certainly a decency in one sort of Verse more than another which custom cannot really alter, only by familiarity make it seem better; how much more stately and Majestic in Epic Poems, especially of Heroic Argument, *Spencer*'s Stanza (which I take to be but an Improvement upon *Tasso*'s *Ottava Rima*, or the Ottava Rima it self, used by many of our once esteemed Poets) is above the way either of Couplet or Alternation of four Verses only, I am persuaded, were it revived, would soon be acknowledg'd.

(b) *Ibid.*, sigs. **9–**9ᵛ; repr. Spingarn, II. 271:

Nay, though all the Laws of *Heroic Poem*, all the Laws of *Tragedy* were exactly observed, yet still this *tour entrejeant*, this Poetic *Energie*, if I may so call it, would be required to give life to all the rest, which shines through the roughest most unpolish't and antiquated Language, and may happly be wanting, in the most polite and reformed: let us observe *Spencer*, with all his Rustie, obsolete words, with all his rough-hewn clowterly Verses; yet take him throughout, and we shall find in him a graceful and Poetic Majesty.

154. John Oldham

1681

John Oldham (1653–83) was educated at St Edmund Hall, Oxford, and before his comparatively early death achieved considerable reputation as a poet.

From *Horace His Art of Poetry, Imitated in English* in *Some New Pieces Never before Publisht. By the Author of the Satyrs upon the Jesuits* (1681), p. 6:

> If *Spencer*'s Muse be justly so ador'd
> For that rich copiousness, wherewith he stor'd
> Our Native Tongue; for Gods sake why should I ⎫
> Straight be thought arrogant, if modestly　　⎬
> I claim and use the self-same liberty?　　　 ⎭

155. John Dryden

1685–97

See headnote to No. 100.

(a) From *The Preface* to *Sylvae: or, the Second Part of Poetical* Miscellanies (1685), sig. a6; repr. *Works*, ed. Walter Scott (1808), rev. George Saintsbury (Edinburgh, 1882–93), XII. 298:

Even his Dorick Dialect has an incomparable sweetness in its Clownishness, like a fair Shepherdess in her Country Russet, talking in a *Yorkshire* Tone. This was impossible for Virgil to imitate; because the severity of the *Roman* Language denied him that advantage. *Spencer* has endeavour'd it in his Shepherds Calendar; but neither will it succeed in *English*, for which reason I forbore to attempt it.

(b) From the *Dedication to the Right Honourable Charles Earl of Dorset and Middlesex* in *The Satires of Decimus Junius Juvenalis. Translated into English Verse* (1693), p. 1; repr. Scott-Saintsbury, XIII. 117:

I consulted . . . *Milton* . . . I found in him a true sublimity, lofty thoughts, which were cloath'd with admirable *Grecisms*, and ancient words, which he had been digging from the Mines of *Chaucer*, and of *Spencer*, and which, with all their rusticity, had somewhat of Venerable in them. But I found not there neither for which I look'd. At last, I had recourse to his Master, *Spencer*, the Author of that immortal Poem call'd the *Fairy Queen*; and there I met with that which I had been looking for so long in vain. *Spencer* had studi'd *Virgil* to as much advantage as *Milton* had done *Homer*. And amongst the rest of his Excellencies had Copy'd that.

(c) From the Dedication of the *Aeneid, To the Right Honourable John, Lord Marquess of Normanby, Earl of Mulgrave* in *The Works of Virgil* . . .

Translated into English Verse (1697), p. 237; repr. Scott-Saintsbury, XIV. 208:

I must acknowledge that *Virgil* in Latin, and *Spencer* in English, have been my Masters. *Spencer* has also given me the boldness to make use sometimes of his *Alexandrin* Line, which we call, though improperly, the *Pindarick*; because Mr Cowley has often employ'd it in his Odes.

Ibid., p. 243; repr. Scott-Saintsbury, XIV. 221:

Spencer is my Example for both these priviledges of *English* Verses [Pindaric lines and triplet rhymes].

Ibid., pp. 243–4; repr. Scott-Saintsbury, XIV. 222:

There is another thing in which I have presum'd to deviate from him [Cowley] and *Spencer*. They both make Hemysticks (or half Verses) breaking off in the middle of a Line. I confess there are not many such in the *Fairy Queen*: And even those few might be occasion'd by his unhappy choice of so long a Stanza.

156. Francis Atterbury

1690

Francis Atterbury (1662–1732) was educated at Westminster School and Christ Church, Oxford. He combined his duties as Bishop of Rochester with those of a man of letters, and was a friend of Swift and Pope.

From the Preface to *The Second Part of Mr Waller's Poems* (1690), sig. A4ᵛ:

In the meantime, 'tis a surprising Reflection, that between what

Spencer wrote last, and *Waller* first, there should not be much above twenty years distance: and yet the one's Language, like the Money of that time, is as current now as ever; whilst the other's words are like old Coyns, one must go to an Antiquary to understand their true meaning and value. Such advances may a great Genius make, when it undertakes any thing in earnest!

157. James Harrington

1691

James Harrington (1664–93) was educated at Christ Church, the Inner Temple and Lincoln's Inn. It is of course on his status as a political philosopher that his reputation rests.

From the Preface to Anthony Wood's *Athenae Oxonienses* (1691), sig. Aᵛ; repr. in the edition of Philip Bliss (1813), I. clix–clx:

An old word is retain'd by an Antiquary with as much Religion as a Relick; and few are by him receiv'd as English, but such as have been naturaliz'd by *Spencer*.

158. Sir Thomas Pope Blount

1694

Sir Thomas Pope Blount (1649–97) was privately educated by his father. His major compendium of literature, the *Censura Celebrorum Authorum* (1690), contains no mention of Spenser. The extended account in *De Re Poetica* is, as he acknowledges, wholly derivative. See also No. 177.

(a) From *De Re Poetica: or, Remarks upon Poetry . . . with Characters and Censures of the most Considerable Poets* (1694), II. 135–7:

Dryden tells us That in *Epique* Poetry, the *English* have only to boast of *Spencer* and *Milton*; neither of whom wanted either *Genius* or *Learning*, to have been perfect Poets; and yet both of them are liable to many Censures. . . . His (Milton's) Antiquated Words were his Choice, not his Necessity; for therein he imitated *Spencer*, as *Spencer* did *Chaucer*. And tho', perhaps, the love of their Masters, may have transported *both* too far, in the frequent use of them; yet in my Opinion, says *Dryden*, *Obsolete* words may then be laudably reviv'd, when either they are more *Sounding*, or more *Significant* than those in practice: And when their Obscurity is taken away, by joyning other words to them which clear the Sense; according to the Rule of *Horace*, for the admission of New words. . . . *Dryd. Dedic:* before the *Translat.* of *Juvenal*, pag. 8, 9.

I consulted (says Dryden) a greater Genius than *Cowley*, (without offence to the *Manes* of that Noble Author) I mean *Milton*, for the *Beautiful Turns* of *Words* and *Thoughts*. But as he endeavours every where to express *Homer*, whose Age had not arriv'd to that *fineness*, I found in him (says *Dryden*) a true Sublimity, lofty Thoughts, which were cloath'd with admirable *Grecisms*, and *Ancient Words*, which he had been digging from the Mines of *Chaucer*, and of *Spencer*, and which, with all their *Rusticity*, had somewhat of *Venerable* in them: But, says *Dryden*, I found not *there* what I look'd for, *viz.* any *Elegant Turns*,

---

either on the *Word*, or on the *Thought*. *Dryd. Ibid. page* 50. (*cf.* 1693. John Dryden, above).

(b) *Ibid.*, II. 232:

Even his [Theocritus's] *Dorick* Dialect has an incomparable Sweetness in its *Clownishness*, like a *fair Shepherdess* in her *Country Russet*, talking in a *Yorkshire* Tone. This (says *Dryden*) was impossible for *Virgil* to imitate; because the severity of the *Roman* Language denied him that advantage. *Spencer* has endeavoured it in his *Shepherds Calendar*; but neither will it succeed in English, for which reason, *Dryden* says, he forbore to attempt it.

159. John Hughes

1698, 1715

See headnote to No. 131, and also 178.

(a) From *Of Style* in *Poems on Several Occasions. With some Select Essays in Prose* (written 1698, published 1735), I. 249–50; repr. in *Critical Essays of the Eighteenth Century*, ed. Willard H. Durham (New Haven, 1915), p. 81:

There is another particular which I shall mention here, because I think it differs but little from *Propriety*, and that is *Purity*, which I take more particularly to respect the Language, as it is now spoke or written. The Rule of this is *modern Use*, according to that of *Horace*.

> *Multa renascentur quae jam cecidere, cadentque*
> *Quae nunc sunt in honore vocabula, si volet usus,*
> *Quem penes arbitrium est, & jus & norma loquendi.*
> [*Ars Poetica* 70–2]

By this Rule, all obsolete Words are to be avoided. But to a Man of long Practice and Reputation in the Language, the Privilege may be allow'd sometimes of reviving old, or bringing in new Words, where the common ones are deficient. For this reason, we dare not censure so great a Man as *Milton* for his antiquated Words, which he took from *Spencer*.

(b) From *Remarks on the 'Faerie Queene'*, in his edition of Spenser's *Works* (1715), I. xciii–xcvi:

I have not yet said any thing concerning *Spencer*'s Versification; in which, tho he is not always equal to himself, it may be affirm'd, that he is superior to all his Cotemporaries, and even to those that follow'd him for some time, except *Fairfax*, the applauded Translator of *Tasso*. In this he commendably study'd the *Italians*, and must be allow'd to have been a great Improver of our *English* Numbers: Before his time, Musick seems to have been so much a Stranger to our Poetry, that, excepting the Earl of *Surry*'s Lyricks, we have very few Examples of Verses that had any tolerable Cadence. In *Chaucer* there is so little of this, that many of his Lines are not even restrain'd to a certain Number of Syllables. Instances of this loose Verse are likewise to be found in our Author, but it is only in such Places where he has purposely imitated *Chaucer*, as in the second Eclogue, and some others. This great Defect of Harmony put the Wits in Queen *Elizabeth*'s Reign upon a Design of totally changing our Numbers, not only by banishing Rhime, but by new moulding our Language into the Feet and Measures of the *Latin* Poetry. Sir *Philip Sidney* was at the Head of this Project, and has accordingly given us some Hexameter and Pentameter Verses in his *Arcadia*. But the Experiment soon fail'd; and tho our Author, by some Passages in his Letters to Mr *Harvey*, seems not to have disapprov'd it, yet it does not appear by those Poems of his, which are preserv'd, that he gave it any Authority by his Example.

As to the Stanza in which the *Fairy Queen* is written, tho the Author cannot be commended for his Choice of it, yet it is much more harmonious in its kind than the Heroick Verse of that Age. It is almost the same with what the *Italians* call their *Ottave Rime*, which is us'd both by *Ariosto* and *Tasso*, but improv'd by *Spenser*, with the Addition of a Line more in the Close, of the Length of our Alexandrines. The Defect of it, in long or narrative Poems, is apparent. The same Measure, closed always by a full Stop, in the same Place, by which every Stanza is made as it were a distinct Paragraph, grows tiresom by continual Repetition, and frequently breaks the Sense, when it ought to be carry'd on without Interruption. With this Exception, the Reader will however find it harmonious, full of well-sounding Epithets, and of such elegant Turns on the Thought and Words, that *Dryden*★ himself owns he learn'd these Graces of Verse chiefly from our Author; and does not scruple to say, that in this Particular *only* Virgil *surpass'd him among the* Romans, *and only Mr* Waller *among the* English.

(c) From *Remarks on the Writings of Spenser, ibid.*, pp. cx–cxiii:

I shall only add a few Words concerning the Edition, in which these several Pieces now appear. It is hoped the Reader will find it much more correct than some former Editions. The *Shepherd's Calendar* had been so extremely corrupted, that it is now in a manner wholly restor'd. Care has been taken not only to collect every thing of this Author which has appear'd before, and to preserve the Text entire, but to follow likewise, for the most part, the old Spelling. This may be thought by some too strict and precise; yet there was a Necessity for it, not only to shew the true State of our Language, as *Spenser* wrote it, but to keep the exact Sense, which wou'd sometimes be chang'd by the Variation of a Syllable or a Letter. It must be own'd however that *Spenser* himself is irregular in this, and often writes the same Word differently, especially at the end of a Line; where, according to the Practice of that Age, he frequently alters the Spelling for the sake of the Rhime, and even sometimes only to make the Rhime appear more exact to the Eye of the Reader. In this, the old Editions are not every where follow'd; but when the Sense is render'd obscure by such Alterations, the Words are restor'd to their proper Orthography.

The *Glossary*, which is here added, contains the greatest part of the old or obscure Words; some of which, for the Satisfaction of the Curious, are illustrated by their Etymologies. Yet I must observe, that in this way of explaining the Language of an Author, there is need of great Caution; for Words are often vary'd by Time from their original Sense, as Tides from the Sea wear away their first Tincture by the Length of their Course, and by mingling with the fresh Waters that fall in with them. *Spenser*'s old Words are of a mix'd Derivation, from the *Latin, Saxon, Runick, French* and *German* Languages; many of these he receiv'd from *Chaucer*; and many others are of his own

★ *Dedication to* Juvenal.

making. He likewise uses the same Word in different Senses; so that it wou'd not be sufficient to explain him by the help of Dictionaries only, without permitting him to be his own Interpreter. The liberty he has taken is indeed very great, and the *Poetical Licences*, such as lengthning or contracting Words, by the adding or dropping a Syllable (a Practice he seems to have learn'd from the *Italians*) wou'd be unpardonable in a Writer of less Merit. Yet, with all its Imperfections, it must be said, that his Diction is, for the most part, strong, significant and harmonious; and much more sublime and beautiful than that of any *English* Poet, who had written before him.

160. Luke Milbourne

1698

See also No. 117.

From *Notes on Dryden's Virgil. In a Letter to a Friend* (1698), p. 25:

The Alexandrine *Line, which we call, tho' improperly the* Pindarick; tho' *sillily,* he means sure; for none who understood any thing of *Pindaric Poetry,* could call that the *Pindaric Line* in contradistinction to Lines of other Measures: And since Mr *Spencer* uses it to close his *Stanza,* without any Thought of *Pindarizing* in it, why should Mr *Cowley's* using it give it that Name now.

161. Richard Bentley

1699

Richard Bentley (1662–1742) conceived the *Dissertation* in the first place as a contribution to the battle of the Ancients and the Moderns, but it is of course more than that, and may fairly be considered to mark the beginnings of modern English Classical scholarship. Bentley's immediate reward was the Mastership of Trinity.

From *A Dissertation upon the Epistles of Phalaris*, second edition (1699), p. 406:

Nay even *Oppian* himself, who took the allow'd privilege of using antiquated Words (as among Us *Spencer* and *Milton* did, though a little more sparingly) could not be understood in his own Town, except by the Learned.

162. Samuel Wesley

1700

See headnote to No. 119.

From *An Epistle to A Friend concerning Poetry* (1700), p. 12:

SPENCER more *smooth* and *neat* than Chaucer, and none than He
Could better skill of *English Quantity*;
Tho by his *Stanza* cramp'd, his *Rhimes* less chast,
And *antique Words* affected all disgrac'd;
Yet *vast* his *Genius, noble* were his *Thoughts,*
Whence equal Readers wink at *lesser* faults.

163. Matthew Prior

1706

See headnote to No. 125.

From *The Preface to An Ode, Humbly Inscrib'd to the Queen* . . . *Written in Imitation of Spenser's Stile* (1706), sigs. A–Aᵛ; repr. *The Literary Works*, ed. H. B. Wright and M. K. Spears (Oxford, 1959), I. 230–1:

As to the Style, the Choice I made of following the *Ode* in *Latin,* determin'd Me in *English* to the *Stanza*; and herein it was impossible not to have a Mind to follow Our great Countryman SPENSER; which I have done (as well at least as I could) in the Manner of my Expression, and the Turn of my Number: having only added one Verse to his Stanza, which I thought made the Number more Harmonious; and avoided such of his Words as I found too obsolete. I have however retain'd some few of them, to make the Colouring look more like SPENSER's. *Behest*, Command; *Band*, Army; *Prowess*, Strength; *I weet*, I know; *I ween*, I think; *whilom*, heretofore; and Two or Three more of that Kind, which I hope the *Ladies* will pardon me, and not judge my MUSE less handsome, though for once she appears in a Farthingal. I have also, in SPENSER's Manner, used *Caesar* for the Emperor, *Boya* for *Bavaria*, *Bavar* for that Prince, *Ister* for *Danube*, *Iberia* for *Spain*, &c.

164. Edward Bysshe

1708

Edward Bysshe (*flor.* 1702) is famous only as the author of *The Art of English Poetry*, which reached its fifth edition in 1714 and reprinted till mid-century. His ignorance of the use of Spenserian stanza is quite remarkable: the admirer of Dryden should not have overlooked Prior. *The British Parnassus* (1714) relies for its examples mainly on poets after Dryden, and seems to contain none from Spenser.

From *The Art of English Poetry* (1708, first edition 1702), p. 40:

Spencer has compos'd his Fairy Queen in Stanzas of 9 Verses, where the 1st rhymes to the 3d, the 2d to the 4th, 5th and 7th; and the 6th to the two last. But this Stanza is very difficult to maintain, and the unlucky choice of it reduc'd him often to the necessity of making use of many exploded Words; nor has he, I think, been followed in it by any of the Moderns . . .

165. William Coward

1709

William Coward (1657?–1725) was a Fellow of Merton College, Oxford. Primarily a physician, he was the author of a religious poem on the lives of the Jewish Patriarchs, now lost.

From *Licentia Poetica discuss'd or the True Test of Poetry* (1709), p. 77:

> SPENCER, in this unfortunately Great,
> New Schemes erected, old ones to defeat.
> But, like *Miltonian Verse*, they pleas'd but few,
> And Those Perhaps, because the Schemes were New.

It was fit I should name some Poem of this Nature, which is *Spencer's Fairy Queen*, wrote in Imitation of the Old Latin Poets, with *Hexameter and Pentameter Verses*, some in this present Age pretend to imitate. But the Grace of that Poem seems to consist more in the *Design*, than *Curiosity of Rhyme* or Expressions; Not but in the Times when he wrote, *viz.* between 1530 to 1596, (at which time he dyed) I have no Reason to doubt that it was an *Approved Poem*, tho' now *unwarrantably* imitable, without Affectation of treading in the Steps of Antiquity.

It is a common Mode of Affectation (as I may call it) when a Man sets up a New Opinion, first by Arguments to endeavour to confute the Old, as absurd, and if he cannot do it, to ridicule and expose it. All poems of Antiquity being seldom valued, as *Horace* says,

> *Si meliora Dies, ut Vina Poemata reddit,*
> *Scire velim pretium chartis quotus arroget Annus.*
> [Ep. II–i. 34–5]

So that we see it is natural enough to carp at our Predecessors. But this is a Grand Mistake, when we see not just Grounds to do it, wherefore take this Rule, *when a Poem has pass'd the Test of several Ages, Antiquity ought to give it a more commendable Character than be a Blemish to it. But if the Language alter, as it may, it then loses its first Grace, and by Time will cease to be Good Poetry, tho' It may still abound with Sound Sense and Solid Reason.*

166. John Dennis

1711, 1722

See headnote to No. 118.

(a) From *Reflections . . . upon An Essay upon Criticism* (1711); repr. E. N. Hooker, *Critical Works* (Baltimore, 1939), I. 410:

Whether the Language of Mr *Dryden* will ever be as obsolete as is at present that of *Chaucer*, is what neither this Author nor any one else can tell. For ev'ry Language hath its particular period of Time to bring it to Perfection, I mean to all the Perfection of which that Language is capable. And they who are alive cannot possibly tell whether that period hath happen'd or not: If that period has not yet happen'd: yet 'tis not the Obsoleteness of Language which makes a Poet fall from the Reputation which he once enjoy'd, provided the Language in which that Poet wrote was at the Time of his Writing come to be capable of Harmony. For *Spencer* is obsolete, yet is still renown'd.

(b) From *Of Prosody* (1722); repr. Hooker, II. 237:

Two of our *Poets*, have writ long *Poems* in *Stanza's*, *Spencer*, and Sir *William Davenant* . . . The *Stanza* of *Spencer* consists of nine Verses, the eight first of *Pentameters*, and the ninth is an *Alexandrine* or an *Hexameter*. But the *Stanza* is certainly very improper for long and noble *Poems*. It seems to belong in a peculiar manner to our *Lyrick* Poetry.

167. Alexander Pope

1713

See headnote to No. 124.

From *The Guardian* No. 40 (27 April 1713); repr. *Literary Criticism of Alexander Pope* ed. B. H. Goldgar (Lincoln, Nebraska, 1965), p. 103:

Lastly, His [Ambrose Philips's] *Elegant Dialect*, which alone might prove him the eldest born of *Spencer*, and our only true *Arcadian*; I should think it proper for the several Writers of Pastoral to confine themselves to their several *Counties*. *Spencer* seems to have been of this Opinion: for he hath laid the Scene of one of his Pastorals in *Wales*, where, with all the Simplicity natural to that Part of our Island, one Shepherd bids the other *Good-morrow* in an unusual and elegant Manner:

> Diggon Davy, *I bid hur God-day;*
> Or Diggon *hur is, or I mis-say.*

Diggon answers,

> *Hur was hur while it was Day-light;*
> *But now hur is a most wretched wight., etc.*

BIOGRAPHICAL NOTICES

See Introduction pp. 25–6.

168. William Camden

1600, 1615

See headnote to No. 43.

(a) From *Reges, Reginae, Nobiles, & Alij in Ecclesia Collegiata B. Petri Westmonasterij Sepulti* (1600), sigs. 12ᵛ–13:

Edward [*sic*] Spencer of London was easily greatest among the English poets of our age, a fact which his poems, written with divine inspiration and with overwhelming genius, confirm. He died prematurely in 1598, and is buried next to Geoffrey Chaucer who was the first great English poet. These lines are written on his tomb:

Here lies Spenser next to Chaucer, next to
him in talent as next to him in death. O Spenser,
here next to Chaucer the poet, as a poet you are
buried; and in your poetry you are more permanent
than in your grave. While you were alive, English
poetry lived and approved you; now you are dead,
it too must die and fears to.[1]

[1] *Edwardus Spencer Londinensis, Anglicorum Poetarum nostri seculi facile princeps, quod eius poemata fauentibus Musis & victuro genio conscripta comprobant. Obijt immatura morte anno salutis 1598. & prope Galfredum Chaucerum conditur que faelicissime poesin Anglicis literis primus illustrauit. In quem haec scripta sunt Epitaphia.*

        Hic prope Chaucerum situs est Spenserius, illi
        Proximus ingenio, proximus vt tumulo.
        Hic prope Chaucerum Spensere Poeta poetam
        Conderis & versu, quam tumulo proprior.
        Anglica te viuo, vixit, plaustique Poesis;
        Nunc moritura timet, te moriente mori.

(b) From *Annales Rerum Anglicarum, et Hibernicarum, Reganante Elizabetha* (1615), II. 171–2; translated by Thomas Browne, *Tomus Alter & Idem: Or the Historie of the Life and Reigne of that Famous Princesse, Elizabeth* (1629), pp. 231–2:

[Three noteworthy men died in the year 1598.] The first was *Thomas Stapleton* Doctour of Diuinity.... The second was *Richard Cosin* a *Cambridge* Man.... The Third was *Edmund Spencer*, a Londoner borne, and a Scholler of *Cambridge*, who was borne to so great a fauour of the Muses, that he surpassed all our Poets, euen *Chawcer* himselfe his fellow Citizen. But labouring with the peculiar destiny of Poets, pouerty; (although hee were Secretary to *Grey* Lord Deputy of *Ireland*) for there hauing scarse time or leisure to write or pen any thing, he was cast forth of doores by the Rebels, and robbed of his goods, and sent ouer very poore into *England*, where presently after hee dyed; and was buried at *Westminster* neere *Chawcer*, at the charges of the Earle of *Essex*, all Poets carrying his body to Church, and casting their dolefull Verses, and Pens too into his graue.[1]

[1] *Primus erat Thomas Stapletonus, Sacrae Theologiae D. ... Alter, Richardus Cosinus Cantabrigiensis. ... Tertius, Edm. Spenserus, patria Londinensis, Cantabrigiensis etiam Academiae alumnus, Musis adeo arridentibus natus vt omnes Anglicos superioris aeui Poetas, ne Chaucero quidem conciue excepto, superaret. Sed peculiari Poetis fato semper cum paupertate conflictatus, etsi Greio Hiberniae proregi fuerit ab epistolis. Vix enim ibi secessum & scribendi otium nactus, cum a rebellibus e laribus eiectus & bonis spoliatus, in Angliam inops reuersus, statim expirauit, & Westmonasterij prope Chaucerum impensis Comitis Essexiae inhumatus, Poetis funus ducentibus, flebilibus carminibus & calamis in tumulum conjectis.*

169. Sir James Ware

1633

Sir James Ware (1594–1666) was educated at Trinity College, Dublin. As an antiquarian and historian of things Irish, his achievement is monumental. Sir James was the editor of Spenser's *View*. Apart from the notice of Spenser's life attached to that edition (which is all that is printed here), a briefer account can be found in *De Scriptoribus Hiberniae* (1639).

The Preface to *A View of the Present State of Ireland* (1633), sigs. ¶³–¶⁴; repr. *Variorum Spenser, The Prose Works*, pp. 531–2:

How far these collections may conduce to the knowledge of the *antiquities* and *state* of this Land, let the fit reader judge: yet something I may not passe by touching Mr *Edmund Spenser* and the worke it selfe, lest I should seeme to offer injury to his worth, by others so much celebrated. Hee was borne in *London* of an ancient and noble family, and brought up in the Vniversitie of *Cambridge*, where (as the fruites of his after labours doe manifest) he mispent not his time. After this he became Secretary to *Arthur* Lord *Grey* of *Wilton*, Lord Deputy of *Ireland*, a valiant and worthy Governour, and shortly after for his services to the Crowne, he had bestowed upon him by Queene *Elizabeth*, 3000. acres of land in the Countie of *Corke*. There he finished the later part of that excellent poem of his *Faery Queene*, which was soone after unfortunately lost by the disorder and abuse of his servant, whom he had sent before him into *England*, being then *a rebellibus* (as *Camdens* words are) *e laribus ejectus at bonis spoliatus*.[1] He deceased at *Westminster* in the yeare 1599. (others have it wrongly 1598.) soone after his returne into *England*, and was buried according to his owne desire, in the collegiat Church there, neere unto *Chaucer*, whom he worthily imitated, (at the costes of *Robert* Earle of *Essex*,) whereupon this Epitaph was framed,

[1] *Annal rer. Anglic. et Hibern. pag.* 729, *edit.* 1625.

[quotes *Hic prope Chaucerum . . .*]

As for his worke now published, although it sufficiently testifieth his learning and deepe judgement, yet we may wish that in some passages it had bin tempered with more moderation.[1] The troubles and miseries of the time when he wrote it, doe partly excuse him, and surely wee may conceive, that if hee had lived to see these times, and the good effects which the last 30. yeares have produced in this land, both for obedience to the lawes, as also in traffique, husbandry, civility, and earning, he would have omitted those passages which may seeme to ay either any particular aspersion upon some families, or generall upon the Nation. For now we may truly say, *jam cuncti gens una sumus*, and that upon just cause those ancient statutes, wherein the natives of *Irish* descent were held to be, and named *Irish* enemies, and wherein those of *English* bloud were forbidden to marry and commerce with them, were repealed by act of Parlament, in the raigne of our late Soveraigne King IAMES of ever blessed memory.[2]

His proofes (although most of them conjecturall) concerning the originall of the language, customes of the Nation, and the first peopling of the severall parts of the Iland, are full of good reading, and doe shew a sound judgment. They may be further confirmed by comparing them with *Richard Creagh's* Booke *de lingua Hibernica*, which is yet extant in the original manuscript, and althogh mixed with matter of story, leaning too much to some fabulous traditions, yet in other respects worthy of light.

Touching the generall scope intended by the author for the reformation of abuses and ill customes, This we may say, that although very many have taken paines in the same subject, during the raigne of Queene *Elizabeth*, and some before, as the author of the booke intituled *Salus populi*,[3] and after him Patrick Finglas,[4] cheife Baron of the Exchequer here, and afterwardes cheife Iustice of the common pleas, yet none came so neere to the best grounds for reformation, a few passages excepted, as *Spenser* hath done in this. Some marginall notes I have added, although not intending any, untill the fourth part of the Booke was printed.

[1] *Ex Bibliotheca Reverendissimi in Christo patris D.* Iacobi Vsserij *Archiep. Armachani.*
[2] *Vid. lib. Statut. Hibern. edit. Dubl. an.* 1621 *pag.* 427.
[3] *Floruit sub initium reg. Edw.* 4.
[4] *Floruit sub Hen.* 8.

170. Robert Johnston

before 1639

Robert Johnston (1567?–1639) was educated at Edinburgh University, but made his fortune in the South.

From *Historia Rerum Britannicarum . . . ab Anno 1572, ad Annum 1628* (Amsterdam, 1655), p. 249 (*Lib.* VIII):

In the year 1598 was taken from the English the greatest ornament of the age, Edmund Spenser, who was born in London of undistinguished parentage. He excelled by a long way all English poets of the century before, and went with the Lord Deputy Gray to Ireland, to forestall poverty, and that he might give his energies to Apollo and the Muses in peace and leisure. There he lost his estate and his goods to predatory brigands, and returned penniless to England. Dying in misery (because it was believed that in *Mother Hubbards Tale* he had savagely maligned the Chancellor Cecil), he was buried in Westminster Abbey next to Chaucer, at the expense of the Earl of Essex.[1]

[1] *Annus & hic abstulit, apud Anglos, Maximum hujus aetatis Ornamentum*, Edmundum Spenserum, Londini in re tenui natum; qui omnes superioris Seculi Poetas Anglicos longe superavit; & ad declinandam Paupertatem, in Hiberniam cum Graio Prorege secessit; ut per Otium ac Requiem, Apollini & Musis operam daret: ubi a Praedonibus Laribus ejectus, & Bonis spoliatus, Inops in Angliam redijt; & Mestitia rebus humanis exemptus, in Vestmonasterij Caenobio sepultus est, apud Chaucerum, impensis Essexiae Comitis; quia ut Creditur, in Cecilium Quaestorem acriter invehitur, in Fabula Hubartae Vetulae. (Mother Huberts tale).

171. Thomas Fuller

1662

Thomas Fuller (1608–61) was educated at Queens' College, Cambridge. As a Fellow-commoner of Sidney Sussex, and later of Lincoln College, Oxford, he enjoyed the leisure which allowed him to pursue his antiquarian researches. The *Worthies* was published posthumously by his son John, a Fellow of Sidney Sussex.

From *The History of the Worthies of England* (1662), pp. 219–20; repr. in edition of P. Austin Nuttall (1840), II. 379–80:

EDMOND SPENCER born in this City,* was brought up in *Pembroke-hall* in Cambridge, where he became an excellent Scholar, but especially most happy in English Poetry, as his works do declare. In which the many *Chaucerisms* used (for I will not say affected by him) are thought by the ignorant to be *blemishes*, known by the learned to be *beauties* to this book; which notwithstanding had been more salable, if more conformed to our modern language.

There passeth a story commonly told and believed, that *Spencer* presenting his Poems to Queen *Elizabeth*: She highly affected therewith, commanded the Lord *Cecil* Her Treasurer, to give him an hundred pound; and when the Treasurer (a good Steward of the Queens money) alledged that sum was too much, then *give him* (quoth the Queen) *what is reason*; to which the Lord consented, but was so busied, belike, about matters of higher concernment, that *Spencer* received no reward; Whereupon he presented this petition in a small piece of paper to the Queen in her Progress,

> *I was promis'd on a time,*
> *To have reason for my rhyme;*
> *From that time unto this season,*
> *I receiv'd nor rhyme nor reason.*

* *Camb. Eliz. in Anno 1598.*

Hereupon the Queen gave strict order (not without some check to her Treasurer) for the present payment of the hundred pounds, the first intended unto him.

He afterwards went over into Ireland, Secretary to the Lord *Gray*, Lord Deputy thereof; and though that his office under his Lord was lucrative, yet he got no estate, but saith my Author,* *Peculiari Poetis fato semper cum paupertate conflictatus est.* . . .

Returning into *England*, he was robb'd by the Rebels of that little he had, and dying for grief in great want, *Anno* 1598. was honorably buried nigh *Chaucer* in Westminster, where this Distick concludeth his Epitaph on his Monument,

> *Anglica te vivo vixit plaustique poesis,*
> *Nunc moritura timet te moriente mori.*

> Whilst thou dids't live, liv'd English poetry,
> Which fears, now thou art dead, that she shall die.

Nor must we forget, that the expense of his funeral and monument, was defrayed at the sole charge of *Robert*, first of that name, Earl of *Essex*.

---

* *Camd. Eliz. in Anno* 1598.

172. John Aubrey

up to 1697

John Aubrey (1626–97) was educated at Trinity College, Oxford, and even from his time as an undergraduate developed his historical interests. The *Brief Lives* were never published in his own time, when his reputation was strictly tied to his achievement as an antiquarian. Outside the *Life*, other mentions of Spenser occur in his accounts of Sidney (repeating first the story about the *Despair* Canto), of the Countess of Pembroke (to the effect that he was not a stranger at Wilton), and of Michael Drayton.

From *Brief Lives*, in the edition of O. L. Dick (1949), pp. 282–3:

Mr Beeston sayes, he was a little man, wore short haire, little band and little cuffs.

Mr Edmund Spencer was of Pembroke-hall in Cambridge; he misst the Fellowship there, which Bishop Andrewes gott. He was an acquaintance and frequenter of Sir Erasmus Dreyden: His Mistris Rosalind was a kinswoman of Sir Erasmus Ladys. The chamber there at Sir Erasmus' is still called Mr Spencers chamber. Lately, at the college takeing-downe the Wainscot of his chamber, they found an abundance of Cards, with stanzas of the *Faerie Queen* written on them.

Mr Samuel Woodford (the Poet who paraphras'd the Psalmes) lives in Hampshire neer Alton, and he told me that Mr Spenser lived some-time in these parts, in this delicate sweet ayre: where he enjoyed his Muse: and writt good part of his Verses. He had lived some time in Ireland, and made a description of it, which is printed.

I have said before that Sir Philip Sidney, and Sir Walter Ralegh were his acquaintance. Sir John Denham told me, that ABp. Usher, Lord Primate of Armagh, was acquainted with him; by this token: when Sir William Davenant's *Gondibert* came forth, Sir John askt the Lord Primate if he had seen it. Said the Primate, Out upon him, with his vaunting Preface, he speakes against my old friend Edmund Spenser.

322

In the South cross-aisle of Westminster abbey, next the Dore, is this Inscription:

Heare lies (expecting the second comeing of our Saviour Christ Jesus) the body of Edmund Spencer, the Prince of Poets of his tyme, whose divine spirit needs no other witnesse, then the workes which he left behind him. He was borne in London, in the yeare 1510, and dyed in the yeare 1596.

173. Edward Phillips

1675

See headnote to No. 97, and also No. 153.

From *Theatrum Poetarum, or a Compleat Collection of the Poets* (1675), pp. 34–6:

Edmund Spencer, the first of our *English* Poets that brought Heroic Poesie to any perfection, his *Faery Queen* being for great Invention and Poetic heighth judg'd little inferiour, if not equal to the chief of the ancient Greeks and Latins or Modern *Italians*, but the first Poem that brought him into Esteem was his *Shepherds* Calendar, which so endear'd him to that Noble Patron of all Vertue and Learning *Sir Philip Sidney*, that he made him known to Queen Elizabeth, and by that means got him preferr'd to be Secretary to his Brother *Sir Henry Sidney*, who was sent deputy into *Ireland*, where he is said to have written his *Faerie Queen*, but upon the return of *Sir Henry*, his Employment ceasing, he also return'd into *England*, and having lost his great Friend *Sir Philip*, fell into poverty, yet made his last Refuge to the Queens Bounty, and had 500 l. order'd him for his Support, which nevertheless was abridg'd to 100 by *Cecil*, who hearing of it, and owing him a grudge for some reflections in Mother *Hubbards* Tale, cry'd out to the Queen, What all this for a Song? This he is said to have taken so much to Heart, that he contracted a deep Melancholy, which soon after brought his life to a Period: So apt is an Ingenious Spirit to resent a slighting, even from the greatest Persons; and thus much I must needs say of the Merit of so great a Poet from so great a Monarch, that as it is incident to the best of Poets sometimes to flatter some Royal or Noble Patron, never did any do it more to the height, or with greater Art and Elegance, if the highest of praises attributed to so Heroic a Princess can justly be term'd Flattery.

174. The *Life* of 1679

The author of this *Life* is not known, but A. C. Judson, 'Seventeenth-Century Lives of Edmund Spenser', *HLQ* (1946–7), 45, records the notion that it might be Brook Bridges. It is also not beyond possibility that Dryden contributed material to it.

A Summary of the Life of Mr Edmond Spenser, in the third Folio *Works* (1679), sigs. A–A2:

Mr *Spenser* was born in *London*, (as his *Epitaph* says) in the Year of our Lord 1510, by his Parent liberally Educated, and sent to the University of *Cambridge*, where he continued a Student in *Pembrook-Hall*; till upon the vacancy of a Fellowship, he stood in competition with Mr *Andrews*, (afterwards *Lord Bishop of Winchester*) in which he miscarried; and thus defeated of his hopes, unable any longer to subsist in the *College*, he repair'd to some Friends of his in the North, where he staid, fell in Love, and at last (prevail'd upon by the perswasions, and importunities of other Friends) came to *London*. His fame in the Art of *Poetry* soon made way to his acquaintance with those that were that way enclin'd, by whose means he quickly inform'd himself who, in likelyhood, might give him Encouragement, and Patronage. Mr *Sidney* (afterward Sir *Philip*) then in full glory at *Court*, was the Person, to whom he design'd the first Discovery of himself; and to that purpose took an occasion to go one morning to *Leicester-House*, furnish't only with a modest confidence, and the Ninth Canto of the First Book of his *Faery Queen*: He waited not long, e're he found the lucky season for an address to the Paper to his hand; who having read the Twenty-eighth *Stanza of Despair*, (with some signs in his Countenance of being much affected, and surpris'd with what he had read) turns suddenly to his Servant, and commands him to give the Party that presented the Verses to him Fifty Pounds; the Steward stood speechless, and unready, till his Master having past over another *Stanza*, bad him give him an Hundred Pound; the Servant something stagger'd at the humour his Master was in, mutter'd to this purpose, That by the semblance of the Man that brought the Paper, Five Pounds would be a proper Reward; but Mr *Sidney* having the following *Stanza*, commands him to give Two Hundred Pounds, and that very speedily, least advancing his Reward, proportionably to the heighth of his Pleasure in reading, he should hold himself oblig'd to give him more than he had: Withal he sent an invitation to the Poet, to see him at those hours, in which he would be most at leasure. After this Mr *Spenser*, by degrees, so far gain'd upon him, that he became not only his Patron, but his Friend too; entred him at *Court*, and obtain'd of the *Queen* the Grant of a Pention to him as *Poet Laureat*: But in this, his Fate was unkind; for it Prov'd only a *Poetical Grant*, the payment, after a very short time, being stopt by a *great Councellour*, who studied more the Queen's Profit than her Diversion, and told Her, 'twas beyond Example to give so great a Pention to a *Ballad-maker*: Of This, the grieved Poet thus complains in his *Tears of the Muses:*

[quotes *R. T.* 449–55]

How much deeper his resentment wrought in *Mother Hubbard's Tale*, may appear to those that list to read it with reflection.

He was in great esteem, and good favour with many of the Nobility whom he Celebrates in his Honorary Verses, and encourag'd by their kindness, he continued in Town, a Poet, a Lover, and a man of Business: A Poet indeed, without a Rival, but not so successful a Lover, for tho' *Hobbinol* as a Gentleman, rather lov'd in Concert with him, than to his grievance, yet *Menalcas* put him to't, whose treachery, together with the Apostacy of his Mistress, gave him occasion bitterly to complain, and having eas'd himself that way, he apply'd himself to Business. Sir *Henry Sidney* had bein three times Deputy of *Ireland*, and after the third being recall'd, *Arthur Lord Grey of Wilton*, was chosen to that Employment, to whom Mr *Spenser* was recommended for *Secretary*. Shortly after, for his Services to the Crown he had bestow'd upon him by *Queen Elizabeth* 3000 Acres of Land in the County of *Cork*: there he finisht the latter part of his *Faery Queen*, which was soon after unfortunately lost by the disorder, and abuse of his Servant, whom he had sent before him into *England*, being then (in the Rebellion of the *Earl of Desmond*) *a rebellibus* (as *Camden's* words are) *e Laribus ejectus, & bonis spoliatus:* His House was in *Kincolman*, the River *Mulla*, so often celebrated by him, running through his Grounds. In this ill posture of his Affairs he return'd into *England*, where he his losses redoubled by the loss of his generous Friend Sir *Philip Sidney*; And thus, yielding to the impressions of a Fortune obstinately adverse to him, he died, without the help of any other Disease save a broken Heart; and was Buried in the Collegiate Church at *Westminster*, near the renowned *Chaucer* (as himself desired) at the Charge of the most Noble *Robert Earl of Essex*, in the year 1596.

His great-Grandchild *Hugolin Spenser* was, after the *King's Return*, restor'd by the *Court of Claims*, to so much of the Lands as could be found to have bin his Ancestors. The remainder of his Works were embezill'd when he was in *Ireland*; for (besides his *Poems* in this Volume, the *View of the State* of Ireland, and some few Letters between himself and his intimate Friend Mr *Harvey* which have bin Printed) many other excellent Pieces of his, highly valued by his learned Friends, are either wholly lost, or unkindly conceal'd from the Publique by private hands: mongst others these his *Nine Comedies*, so much esteemed by Mr *Harvey*. The *Canticles* paraphras'd. The *Ecclesiastes*, and *Hours of our Lord*. His *Seven Psalms*. *The dying Pelican*. *The Sacrifice of a Sinner*. *Stemmata Dudleiana*, and *Purgatory. A Sennight's Slumber. Epithalamium Thamesis. The Hell of Lovers.*

He was a man of extraordinary Accomplishments, excellently skill'd in all parts of Learning: of a profound Wit, copious Invention, and solid Judgment: of a temper strangely tender, and amorous; as appears every where in his Writings, but particularly in his Laments on the Death of Sir *Philip Sidney*, and in his incomparable *Daphnaida*. He excelled all other Ancient and Modern Poets, in Greatness of Sense, Decency of Expression, Height of Imagination, Quickness of Conceit, Grandeur and Majesty of Thought, and all the Glories of Verse. Where he is passionate, he forces commiseration and tears from his Readers; where pleasant and airy a secret satisfaction and smile; and where Bold, and Heroique, he inflames their breasts with Gallantry and Valour. His Descriptions are so easie and natural, that his Pen seems to have a power of conveying *Ideas* to our mind, more just, and to the Life, than the exquisite Pencils of *Titian*, or *Raphael*, to our eyes. He was, in a word, compleatly happy in every thing that might render him Glorious, and Inimitable to future Ages.

175. William Winstanley

1684

William Winstanley (1628?–90?) is best known simply as a compiler. The 1660 edition of *England's Worthies* contains no Life of Spenser (though he is mentioned in the Lives both of Chaucer and Sidney), because Winstanley was unable to find informants who could render a 'full and happy account' of the poet. By 1684 he seems to have overcome his diffidence, without apparently finding any new informants or information.

From *England's Worthies. Select Lives of the most Eminent Persons of the English Nation, From Constantine the Great Down to these Times* (1684), pp. 224–7:

Next to this incomparable Knight Sir *Philip Sidney*, we shall add the Life of his fellow-Poet and contemporary, Mr *Edmond Spenser*, who was born in the City of *London*, and brought up in *Pembroke-hall* in *Cambridge*, where he became a most excellent Scholar, but especially very happy in English Poetry, as his Learned elaborate Works do declare. In which the many *Chaucerisms* used (for I will not say, affected by him) are thought by the ignorant to be blemishes, known by the learned to be beauties to his book: which notwithstanding (saith a learned writer) had been more Saleable, if more conformed to our modern Language.

His first flight in Poetry was that Book of his called *The Shepherds Kalendar*, applying an old name to a new work, being of Eglogues fitted to each moneth in the year: of which work hear what that worthy Knight, Sir *Philip Sidney* writes, in his *Defence of Poesy*: *The Shepherds Kalendar* (saith he) *hath much Poetry in his Eclogues, indeed worthy the reading if I be not deceived. That same framing his Stile to an old rustick Language I dare not allow, since neither* Theocritus *in Greek*, Virgil *in Latine, nor* Sanazara *in Italian did affect it.* Afterwards he translated the *Gnat*, a little fragment of *Virgils* excellency. But his main Book, and which indeed I think Envy its self cannot carp at, was his *Fairy Queen*, a Work of such an ingenious composure, as will last as long whilest times shall be no more.

Now as you have heard what esteem Sir *Philip Sidney* had of his Book, so you shall hear what esteem Mr *Spenser* had of Sir *Philip Sidney*, writing thus in his *Ruines of Time*.

[quotes lines 323–9]

There passeth a story commonly told and believed, that Mr *Spenser* presenting his Poems to Queen *Elizabeth*, she highly affected therewith, commanded the Lord Cecil, her Treasurer to give him an hundred pound; and when the Treasurer (a good Steward of the Queens money) alledged that Sum was too much for such a matter; then give him (quoth the Queen) *what is reason*; to which the Lord consented, but was so busied, belike, about matters of higher concernment, that Mr *Spenser* received no reward: whereupon he presented this Petition in a small piece of Paper to the Queen in her Progress.

> *I was promis'd on a time,*
> *To have reason for my Ryme;*
> *From that time unto this season,*
> *I receiv'd nor Rhyme nor Reason.*

Hereupon the Queen gave strict order (not without some check to her Treasurer) for the present payment of the hundred pounds she first intended unto him.

Now what esteem also this our Poet had amongst learned men may be seen in these verses.

At Delphos *shrine one did a doubt propound* . . .

[quotes epitaph ascribed to Francis Beaumont; see No. 39]

He afterwards went over into *Ireland*, Secretary to the Lord Gray, Lord Deputy thereof; and though that his Office under his Lord was Lucrative, yet got he no estate; *Peculiari Poetis fato semper cum paupertate conflictatus est*, saith the reverend *Cambden*; so that it fared little better with him, than with *William Xilander* the *German*, (a most excellent Linguist, Antiquary, Philosopher, and Mathematician) who was so poor, that (as Thuanus writes) he was thought *Fami non famae scribere*.

Thriving so bad in that Boggy Country, to add to his misery, he was Rob'd by the Rebels of that little he had left; whereupon in great grief he returns into *England*, and falling into want, which to a noble Spirit is most killing, being heart broken, he died *Anno* 1598. and was honourably buried at the sole charge of *Robert*, first of that name Earl of Essex, where this Distick on his Monument.

> *Anglica te vivo, vixit plausitque Poesis;*
> *Nunc moritura, timet te moriente mori.*

> *Whilest thou didst live, liv'd English Poetry,*
> *Which fears, now thou art dead, that she shall die.*

A modern Author writes, that the Lord *Cecil* owed Mr *Spenser* a grudge for some Reflections of his in Mother *Hubbard's Tale*, and therefore when the Queen had ordered him that money, the Lord Treasurer said, What all this for a Song? And this he is said to have taken so much to Heart, that he contracted a deep melancholy, which soon after brought his life to a period: So apt is an ingenious Spirit to resent a slighting even from the greatest persons. And thus much I must needs say of the merit of so great a Poet from so great a Monarch, that it is incident to the best of Poets sometimes to flatter some Royal or Noble Patron, never did any do it more to the height, or with greater art and elegance, if the highest of praises attributed to so Heroick a Princess can justly be termed flattery.

176. George Sandys

1684

From *Anglorum Speculum, or the Worthies of England in Church and State* (1684), pp. 497–8:

Edm. Spencer, bred in *Camb.* A great Poet who imitated *Chaucer*, 'Tis said that he presented Q. Eliz. with a Poem, with which she was so well pleased, that she commanded the Lord Treasurer *Cecil* to give to him 100 l. and when he alledged that Sum was too much, *then give him,* (Quoth the Q.) *what is Reason,* but being delayed he presented these Lines to the Queen:

> *I was promised on a time*
> *To have Reason for my Rhyme;*
> *From that time unto this Season,*
> *I have received nor Rhyme nor Reason.*

Hereupon the Q. gave strict Order for the present payment of the 100 *l.* He was afterwards Secretary to the Lord *Gray,* Deputy of *Ireland.* He was an excellent Linguist, Antiquary, Philosopher, Mathematician, yet so poor (as being a Poet) that he was thought *Fami non Famae scribere.* Returning into *England,* he was robb'd by the Rebels of that little he had, and dying for Grief in great Want 1598, was honourably buried nigh *Chaucer* in *Westminster.* The expence of his Funeral and Monument was defrayed at the sole charge of *Rob.* first of that name, E. of Essex.

177. Thomas Blount

1694

See also No. 158.

From *De Re Poetica: or, Remarks upon Poetry . . . with Characters and Censures of the most Considerable Poets* (1694), II. 213–16:

Edmund Spencer

A Famous *English* Poet, born in the City of *London*, and brought up in *Pembroke-Hall* in *Cambridge*; He flourish'd in the Reign of Queen *Elizabeth*. His great Friend was Sir *Philip Sidney*, by whose mean he was preferr'd to be *Secretary* to his Brother Sir *Henry Sidney*, who was sent Deputy into *Ireland*, where he is said to have written his *Fairy-Queen*; but upon the return of Sir *Henry*, his Employment ceasing, he also return'd into *England*, and having lost his great Friend Sir *Philip*, fell into Poverty; whereupon he addrest himself to Queen *Elizabeth*, presenting her with a Poem, with which she was so well pleas'd, that he had order'd him 500 l. for his support, which nevertheless was abridg'd to One Hundred Pounds by the Lord Treasurer *Cecil*, who hearing of it, and owing him a grudge for some Reflections in *Mother Hubbard's Tale*, cry'd out to the Queen, *What all this for a Song?* This he is said to have taken so much to Heart, that he contracted a deep Melancholy, which soon after brought his life to a Period, *Anno Dom.* 1598.

Edward Phillips, in his *Theatrum Poetarum*, says, That *Spencer* was the first of our *English* Poets that brought *Heroick Poesie* to any perfection; his *Fairy-Queen* being for great Invention and Poetick Heighth, judg'd little Inferiour, if not Equal to the Chief of the Ancient *Greeks* and *Latins*, or Modern *Italians*; But the first Poem that brought him into Esteem, was his *Shepherds Kalendar*. This *Piece* was highly admir'd by Sir *Philip Sidney*.

Cambden, in his *History* of Queen *Elizabeth*, says, That *Edmund Spencer* was a *Londoner* by Birth, and a Scholar also of the University

331

of Cambridge, born under so favourable an Aspect of the *Muses*, that he surpass'd all the *English* Poets of former Times, not excepting *Chaucer* himself, his Fellow-Citizen. But by a *Fate* which still follows *Poets*, he always wrestled with *Poverty*.

Dr *Fuller*, in his *Worthies of England*, affirms, That *Edmund Spencer* was an Excellent Linguist, Antiquary, Philosopher, and Mathematician; yet so poor (as being a *Poet*) that he was thought *Famem* non *Famae scribere*.

Sir *William Temple*, in his *Essay* of *Poetry*, *pag*. 46, 47. remarks, That the *Religion* of the *Gentiles*, had been woven into the *Contexture* of all the *Ancient Poetry*, with a very agreeable Mixture; which made the *Moderns* affect, to give that of *Christianity* a place also in their Poems. But the *true Religion* was not found to become *Fiction* so well, as a *False* had done, and all their Attempts of this Kind, seem'd rather to debase *Religion*, than to heighten *Poetry*. *Spencer*, says *Temple*, endeavour'd to supply *this* with *Morality*, and to make *Instruction*, instead of *Story*, the Subject of an *Epick* Poem. His Execution was Excellent, and his Flights of Fancy very Noble and High, but his Design was poor, and his *Moral* lay so bare, that it lost the Effect; 'tis true, says *Temple*, the Pill was Gilded, but so thin, that the Colour and the Taste were too easily discover'd.

Rimer, in the *Preface* to his Translation of *Rapin's* Reflexions on *Aristotle* of *Poesie*, tells us, That in his Judgment, *Spencer* may be reckon'd the first of our *Heroick Poets*; He had a large Spirit, a sharp Judgment, and a Genius for *Heroick Poesie*, perhaps above any that ever writ since *Virgil*. But our Misfortune is, says *Rimer*, he wanted a true *Idea*; and lost himself, by following an unfaithful Guide. Though besides *Homer* and *Virgil* he had read Tasso, yet he rather suffer'd himself to be misled by *Ariosto*; with whom blindly rambling on *marvellous Adventures*, he makes no Conscience of *Probability*. All is Fanciful and Chimerical, without any Uniformity, or without any foundation in Truth; in a Word, his Poem (says *Rimer*) is perfect *Fairy-Land*.

Dryden, in his *Dedication* to the Earl of *Dorset* before the Translation of *Juvenal*, *pag*. viii. says, That the *English* have only to boast of *Spencer* and *Milton*, in *Heroick Poetry*; who neither of them wanted either *Genius*, or *Learning*, to have been perfect *Poets* and yet both of them are liable to many Censures. For there is no *Uniformity* in the Design of *Spencer*: He aims at the Accomplishment of no one Action: He raises up a *Hero* for every one of his Adventures; and endows each of them with some particular *Moral Vertue*, which renders them all equal, without Subordination or Preference. Every one is most valiant in his own *Legend*; only (says *Dryden*) we must do him that justice, to observe, that *Magnanimity*, which is the Character of Prince *Arthur*, shines throughout the *whole Poem*; and Succours the rest, when they are in distress. The Original of every Knight, was then living in the Court of Queen *Elizabeth*: And he attributed to each of them that Virtue, which he thought was most conspicuous in them: An Ingenious piece of flattery, tho' it turn'd not much to his Account. Had he liv'd to finish his Poem, in the six remaining *Legends*, it had certainly been more of a piece; but cou'd not have been perfect, because the Model was not *true*. But Prince *Arthur*, or his chief Patron, Sir *Philip Sidney*, whom he intended to make happy, by the Marriage of his *Gloriana*, dying before him, depriv'd the Poet, both of Means and Spirit, to accomplish his Design: For the rest, his *Obsolete Language*, and the *ill Choice* of his *Stanza*, are faults but of the Second Magnitude: For notwithstanding the *first* he is still Intelligible, at least, after a little practice; And for the *last*, he is the more to be admir'd; that labouring under such a difficulty, his Verses are so Numerous, so Various, and so Harmonious, that only *Virgil*, whom he has profestly imitated, has surpass'd him, among the *Romans*; And only Mr *Waller* among the *English*, says Dryden.

The Expence of his Funeral and Monument was defray'd at the sole charge of *Robert*, first of that Name, Earl of *Essex*. He lies buried in *Westminster-Abbey*, near *Chaucer*, with this *Epitaph*:

Edmundus Spencer, *Londinensis, Anglicorum Poetarum*
nostri seculi fuit Princeps, quod ejus Poemata,
faventibus Musis, & victuro genio conscripta
comprobant. *Obiit immaturâ morte, Anno Salutis,*
1598. *& prope* Galfredum Chaucerum *conditur, qui*
faelicissimè Poesin *Anglicis literis primus*
illustravit. In quem haec Scripta *sunt* Epitaphia.

> Hic prope Chaucerum *situs est* Spencerius, *illi*
> *Proximus Ingenio, proximus ut Tumulo.*
> Hic prope Chaucerum Spensere *poeta poetam*
> *Conderis, & versu! quam tumulo proprior.*
> *Anglica te vivo vixit, plaustique Poesis;*
> *Nunc moritura timet, te moriente, mori.*

178. John Hughes

1715

See headnote to No. 131. Hughes is the only one of Spenser's biographers in this early period, who has given any thought to the value of his sources. Unfortunately, in the absence of better sources, his scepticism is never materially useful.

The Life of Mr Edmund Spenser, in *Works*, ed. John Hughes (1715), pp. i–xxii:

As the Reign of Queen *Elizabeth* is one of the most shining Parts of our History, and an Age of which *Englishmen* are accustom'd to speak with a particular Pride and Delight; it is remarkable for having been fruitful in Eminent Genius's of very different kinds. Among the *Romans* the Age of *Augustus* is observ'd to have produc'd the finest Wits, but the preceding one the greatest Men. But this was a Period of Time distinguish'd for both; and, by a wonderful Conjunction, we find Learning and Arms, Wisdom and Polite Arts arising to the greatest Heights together.

In this happy Reign flourish'd EDMUND SPENSER, the most Eminent of our Poets till that time, unless we except *Chaucer*, who was in some respects his Master and Original. The Accounts of his Birth and Family are but obscure and imperfect; and it has happen'd to him, as to many other Men of Wit and Learning, to be much better known by his Works than by the History of his Life. He was born in *London*, and had his Education at *Pembroke-Hall* in *Cambridge*. Tho in the Dedications of one or two of his Poems, we find him claiming Affinity with some Persons of Distinction, yet his Fortune and Interest seem at his first setting out to have been very inconsiderable: For after he had continu'd in the College for some time, and laid that Foundation of Learning, which, join'd to his natural Genius, qualify'd him for rising to so great an Excellency afterwards, he stood for a Fellowship, in Competition with Mr *Andrews*, afterwards Bishop of *Winchester*, but without Success. This Disappointment, together with the Narrowness of his Circumstances, forc'd him from the University. And we find him next taking up his Residence with some Friends in the North, where he fell in Love with his *Rosalind*, whom he so finely celebrates in his Pastoral Poems, and of whose Cruelty he has written such pathetical Complaints.

As Poetry is frequently the Offspring of Love and Retirement, it is probable his Genius began first to distinguish it self about this time; for the *Shepherd's Calendar*, which is so full of his unprosperous Passion for *Rosalind*, was the first of his Works of any Note. This he address'd, by a short Dedication in Verse, to Sir *Philip Sidney*; concealing himself under the humble Title of *Immerito*. Sir *Philip* was then in the highest Reputation for his Wit, Gallantry, and Polite Accomplishments; and indeed seems to have been the most universally admir'd and belov'd of any one Gentleman of the Age in which he liv'd. As he was himself a very good Writer, and especially excell'd in the fabulous or inventive part of Poetry, it is no wonder he soon became sensible of our Author's Merit. He was one of the first who discover'd it, and recommended it to the Notice of the best Judges of that time; and so long as this great Man liv'd, *Spenser* never wanted a judicious Friend and a generous Patron.

After he had staid for some time in the *North*, he was prevail'd upon, by the Advice of some Friends, to quit his Obscurity, and come to *London*, that he might be in the way of Promotion. To this he alludes in his Sixth *Eclogue*, where *Hobbinol* (by which Name is meant his intimate Friend Mr *Gabriel Harvey*) persuades *Colin* to leave the hilly Country, as a barren and unthriving Solitude, and remove to a better Soil. The first Step he afterwards made towards Preferment, was, as I have said, his Acquaintance with Sir *Philip Sidney*: but whether that Acquaintance began immediately upon his addressing to him the *Shepherd's Calendar*, as to me seems most probable, or some time after, I will not determine. That which makes it somewhat uncertain, is a Story of him which I shall only set down as I find it related, not knowing how far it may appear worthy of Credit. It is said he was a Stranger to Mr *Sidney* (afterwards Sir *Philip*) when he had begun to write his *Fairy Queen*, and that he took occasion to go to *Leicester*-House, and to introduce himself by sending in to Mr *Sidney* a Copy of the Ninth Canto of the First Book of that Poem. Mr *Sidney* was much surpriz'd with the Description of *Despair* in that Canto, and is said to have shewn an unusual kind of Transport on the Discovery of so new and uncommon a Genius. After he had read some Stanza's, he turn'd to his Steward, and bid him give the Person that brought those Verses Fifty Pounds; but upon reading the next Stanza, he order'd the Sum to be doubled. The Steward was no less surpriz'd than his Master, and thought it his Duty to make some Delay in executing so sudden and lavish a Bounty; but upon reading one Stanza more, Mr *Sidney* rais'd his Gratuity to Two Hundred Pounds, and commanded the Steward to give it immediately, lest as he read further, he might be tempted to give away his whole Estate. From this time he admitted the Author to his Acquaintance and Conversation, and prepar'd the way for his being known and receiv'd at Court.

Tho nothing cou'd have been more happy for him than to be thus introduc'd, yet he did not immediately reap any great Benefit by it. He was indeed created Poet Laureat to Queen *Elizabeth*, but for some time he wore a barren Laurel, and possess'd only the Place without the Pension. The Lord Treasurer *Burleigh* had not, it seems, the same Taste of *Spenser*'s Merit with Sir *Philip Sidney*; and, whether out of Neglect, or any particular Resentment, or from whatever Cause, he is said to have intercepted the Queen's Favour to this unfortunate and ingenious Man. As the most elegant Minds have the quickest Sense of Repulses from the Great and Powerful, who should countenance and protect them, it is no wonder this Misfortune sunk deep into our Author's Spirit, and seems to have dwelt upon him for a great space of his Life. Accordingly we find him in many parts of his Works pouring forth his Heart in Complaints of so hard and undeserv'd a Treatment; which probably would have been less unfortunate to him, if his Noble Patron Sir *Philip Sidney* had not been so much absent from Court, as he was oblig'd to be, by his Employments abroad, and by the share he had in the *Low-Country* Wars.

In the Poem call'd *The Ruins of Time*, which was written some time after *Sidney*'s Death, the Author seems to allude to the Discouragement I have mention'd in the following Stanza.

[quotes ll. 449–56]

And in the Poem call'd *The Tears of the Muses*, in the Speech of *Calliope*, these Lines are apply'd to Persons of Quality and Estates, who are reproach'd for their total Disregard of Learning.

[quotes ll. 469–73]

But it is said that the Lord Treasurer, who perhaps at first only

neglected *Spenser*, conceiv'd afterwards a Hatred of him for some
Reflections, which he apprehended were made on him in his *Mother
Hubberd's Tale*. In this Poem the Author has indeed in the most lively
manner painted out the Misfortune of Dependence on Court-Favour.
The Lines which follow are, among others, very remarkable.

[quotes ll. 895–906]

This, as it was very much the Author's Case, might probably be the
particular Passage in that Poem which gave Offence; for even the Sighs
of a miserable Man are sometimes resented as an Affront by him that is
the occasion of them.

At the end of the Sixth Book of the *Fairy Queen*, the Author plainly
alludes to this Misfortune; where, speaking of *Detraction*, describ'd
as a Monster, he concludes with the following Stanza.

[quotes *Faerie Queene* VI. xii. 41]

I think I ought not here to omit a little Story, which seems founded
on the Grievance I have mention'd, and is related by some, as a Matter
of Fact commonly reported at that time. It is said the Queen, upon his
presenting some Poems to her, order'd him a Gratuity of an Hundred
Pounds; but that the Lord Treasurer *Burleigh* objecting to it, said, with
some Scorn of the Poet, *What! all this for a Song?* The Queen reply'd,
——*Then give him what is Reason. Spenser* waited for some time, but
had the Mortification to find himself disappointed of the Queen's
intended Bounty. Upon this, he took a proper Opportunity to present
a Paper to Queen *Elizabeth* in the manner of a Petition, in which he
reminded her of the Orders she had given, in the following Lines.

> *I was promis'd on a time*
> *To have Reason for my Rhime;*
> *From that time unto this Season,*
> *I receiv'd nor Rhime nor Reason.*

This Paper produc'd the desir'd Effect; and the Queen, not without
some Reproof of the Treasurer, immediately directed the Payment of
the Hundred Pounds she had first order'd.

But tho our Author had no better Interest with the Lord Treasurer,
yet we find him, some time after his Appearance at Court, in considerable Esteem with the most eminent Men of that time. In the Year
1579. he was sent abroad by the Earl of *Leicester*, as appears by a Copy
of *Latin* Verses dated from *Leicester*-House, and address'd to his Friend

Mr *Harvey*: But in what Service he was employ'd, is uncertain. The most considerable Step he afterwards made into Business, was upon the Lord *Grey* of *Wilton*'s being chosen Deputy of *Ireland*, to whom Mr *Spenser* was recommended as Secretary. This drew him over into another Kingdom, and settled him for some time in a Scene of Life very different from what he had known before. There is no doubt but he discharg'd his Employment with very good Skill and Capacity, as may appear by his *Discourse on the State of* Ireland; in which there are many solid and judicious Remarks, that shew him no less qualify'd for Business of the State, than for the Entertainments of the Muses. His Life now seem'd to be free from the Difficulties which had hitherto perplex'd it, and his Services to the Crown were rewarded by a Grant from Queen *Elizabeth* of 3000 Acres of Land in the County of *Cork*. His House was in *Kilcolman*; and the River *Mulla*, which he has more than once so beautifully introduc'd in his Poems, ran thro his Grounds.

It was about this time that he contracted an intimate Friendship with the great and learned Sir *Walter Raleigh*, who was then a Captain under the Lord *Grey*. The Poem call'd, *Colin Clout's come home again*, in which Sir *Walter* is describ'd under the Name of *the Shepherd of the Ocean*, is a beautiful Memorial of this Friendship, which took its Rise from a Likeness of Taste in the Polite Arts, and is agreeably describ'd by our Author, after the Pastoral manner, in the following Lines.

[quotes ll. 56–75]

Sir *Walter* did him some Services afterwards at Court; and by his means Queen *Elizabeth* became more particularly acquainted than before with our Author's Writings.

He was here a more successful Lover than when he courted *Rosalind*. The Collection of his *Sonnets* are a kind of short History of the Progress of a new Amour, which we find ended in Marriage, and gave occasion to an excellent *Epithalamium*, which no one could so well write as himself.

In this pleasant Situation he finish'd his celebrated Poem of the *Fairy Queen*, which was begun and continu'd at different Intervals of Time; and of which he at first publish'd only the Three first Books. To these were added Three more in a following Edition; but the Six last Books (excepting the Two Canto's of *Mutability*) were unfortunately lost by his Servant, whom he had in haste sent before him into *England*. For tho he pass'd his Life for some time very serenely here, yet a Train of Misfortunes still pursu'd him; and in the Rebellion of the

Earl of *Desmond,* he was plunder'd and depriv'd of his Estate. This forc'd him to return to *England,* where his Afflictions were doubled by the want of his best Friend, the brave Sir *Philip Sidney,* who dy'd some Years before of the Wounds he had receiv'd in an Action near *Zutphen* in the *Netherlands.*

SPENSER surviv'd his beloved Patron about twelve Years, but seems to have spent the latter part of that time with much Grief of Heart, under the Disappointment of a broken Fortune. It is remarkable that he dy'd the same Year with his powerful Enemy the Lord *Burleigh,* which was in 1598. He was bury'd in *Westminster* Abbey, near the famous *Geoffry Chaucer,* as he had desir'd. His Obsequies were attended by the Poets of that Time, and others, who pay'd the last Honours to his Memory. Several Copies of Verses were thrown after him into his Grave; and his Monument was erected at the Charge of the famous *Robert Devereux,* the unfortunate Earl of *Essex;* the Stone of which it is made, is much broken and defac'd: the Inscription on it is as follows.

Heare lyes (expecting the second Comminge of our Saviour Christ Jesus) the Body of *Edmond Spencer,* the Prince of Poets in his tyme; whose Divine Spirrit needs noe othir Witness, then the Works which he left behind him. He was borne in *London* in the Yeare 1510. and died in the Yeare 1596.

It is observable that this differs from *Camden*'s Account of his Death, who says it was in 1598. in the Forty First Year of the Queen's Reign. But this Epitaph is, I doubt, yet less to be depended upon for the time of our Author's Birth, in which there must have been a very gross Mistake. It is by no means probable that he was born so early as 1510. if we judg only by so remarkable a Circumstance as that of his standing for a Fellowship in Competition with Mr *Andrews,* who was not born till 1555. Besides, if this Account of his Birth were true, he must have been above sixty Years old when he first publishd his *Shepherd's Calendar,* an Age not the most proper for Love-Poetry; and in his seventieth Year, when he enter'd into Business under the Lord *Grey,* who was created Deputy of *Ireland* in 1580. For those Reasons, I think, we may certainly conclude, either that this Inscription is false, by the Error of the Carver, which may seem the more probable, because the Spelling likewise is very bad even for that time; or that it was put in sometime afterwards, when the Monument perhaps was repair'd, and is wholly different from the Original one; which indeed is mention'd by Dr *Fuller,* and others,* to have been in *Latin.* In a little

---

* *Vid. Kepe's Monumenta Westmonast.*

Latin Treatise, describing the Monuments of *Westminster* in the Year 1600. publish'd, as is suppos'd, by Mr *Cambden,* I find the following Account of it.

[quotes *Reges, Reginae* . . . (1600), sigs. 12ᵛ–13]

The Absurdity of supposing our Author born in 1510. appears yet further by the Expression *immatura morte,* which is here us'd, and cou'd not have been very proper, if apply'd to a Man who had dy'd at eighty eight Years of Age. *Winstanley* and some others have transcrib'd this whole Passage as his Epitaph, not considering that the Prose is only an Eulogy on him, and not a Monumental Inscription. The Reader will likewise observe that the Verses are two distinct Epitaphs; of which, the first and second Couplets are but the same Thought differently express'd. In the last Couplet it is not improbable the Author might have in his eye those celebrated Lines written by Cardinal *Bembo* on *Raphael d'Urbin.*

> *Ille hic est Raphael, timuit quo sospite vinci*
> *Rerum magna Parens, & moriente mori.*

I wish I cou'd give the Publick a more perfect Account of a Man whose Works have so justly recommended him to the Esteem of all the Lovers of *English* Poetry. Besides those Pieces of his which have been preserv'd, we find he had written several others, of which we can now only trace out the Titles. Among these, the most considerable were *Nine Comedies,* in Imitation of the Comedies of his admir'd *Ariosto,* inscrib'd with the Names of the Nine Muses. The rest, which are mention'd in his Letters, and those of his Friends, are his *Dying Pelicane,* his *Pageants, Stemmata Dudleyana, The Canticles Paraphras'd, Ecclesiastes, Seven Psalms, Hours of our Lord, Sacrifice of a Sinner, Purgatory, A Sennight's Slumber, The Court of Cupid,* and *The Hell of Lovers.* It is likewise said he had written a Treatise in Prose, call'd *The English Poet.* As for the *Epithalamion Thamesis,* and his *Dreams,* both mention'd by himself in one of his Letters, I cannot but think they are still preserv'd, tho under different Names. It appears from what is said of the *Dreams* by his Friend Mr *Harvey,* that they were an Imitation of *Petrarch's Visions*; and it is therefore probable, they are the same which were afterwards publish'd under the several Titles of *Visions of the World's Vanity, Bellay's Visions, Petrarch's Visions,* &c. And tho by one of his Letters we find our Author had form'd the Plan of a Poem, call'd *Epithalamion Thamesis,* and design'd, after a Fashion then newly introduc'd, to have written it in *English Hexameters*; yet whoever observes the Account he gives of it there, and compares it with the Eleventh Canto of the Fourth Book of the *Fairy Queen*, will see reason to believe, that he suspended his first Thought, and wrought it after-wards into that beautiful Episode of *the Marriage of the* Thames *and the* Medway, which is so great an Ornament to that Book. And this will appear yet the more probable, if it be consider'd that, with all its Beauty, that Episode is no essential Part of the Poem, but is rather an Excrescence or a Digression from it.

I find no Account of the Family which *Spenser* left behind him, only that, in the few Particulars of his Life prefix'd to the last Folio Edition of his Works, it is said that his Great Grandson *Hugolin Spenser*, after the Return of King *Charles* the Second, was restor'd by the *Court of Claims* to so much of the Lands as cou'd be found to have been his Ancestors: whether this were true or not, I cannot determine; but I think I ought not to omit mentioning another very remarkable Passage, of which I can give the Reader much better Assurance; That a Person came over from *Ireland*, in King *William*'s Reign, to sollicit the same Affair, and brought with him Letters of Recommendation as a Descendent of *Spenser*. His Name procur'd him a favourable Reception; and he apply'd himself particularly to Mr. *Congreve*, by whom he was generously recommended to the Favour of the late Earl of *Halifax*, who was then at the Head of the Treasury; and by that means he obtain'd his Suit. This Man was somewhat advanc'd in Years, and might be the same mention'd before, who had possibly recover'd only some part of the Estate at first, or had been disturb'd in the Possession of it. He could give no Account of the Works of his Ancestor, which are wanting, and which are therefore in all Probability irrecoverably lost.

Addendum

G. W., Senior, and G. W. I.

1595

For identification of the authors of the sonnets below as the two Geoffrey Whitneys, father and son, see Rudolf Gottfried, 'The "G.W. Senior" and "G.W.I." of Spenser's *Amoretti*', *Modern Language Quarterly*, III (1942), 543–6. Geoffrey Whitney Junior, author of *A Choice of Emblemes* (1586), was a personal friend of Sir Robert Needham, to whom Spenser dedicated the *Amoretti*.

(a) From *Amoretti* (1595), sig. ¶3:

> Darke is the day, when *Phoebus* face is shrowded,
> and weaker sights may wander soone astray:
> but when they see his glorious raies vnclowded,
> with steddy steps they keepe the perfect way:
> So while this Muse in forraine landes doth stay,
> inuention weepes, and pens are cast aside,
> the time like night, depriud of chearefull day,
> and few do write, but (ah) too soone may slide.
> The, hie thee home, that art our perfect guide,
> and with thy wit illustrate Englands fame,
> dawnting thereby our neighbors auncient pride,
> that do for poesie, challendge cheefest name.
> So we that liue and ages that succeede,
> With great applause thy learned works shall reede.

(b) *Ibid.*, sig. A:

> Ah Colin, whether on the lowly plaine,
> pyping to shepherds thy sweete roundelaies:
> or whether singing in some lofty vaine,
> heroick deedes, of past, or present daies.
> Or whether in thy louely mistris praise,
> thou list to exercise thy learned quill,
> thy muse hath got such grace, and power to please,
> with rare inuention bewtified by skill.
> As who therein can euer ioy their fill!
> O therefore let that happy muse proceede
> to clime the height of vertues sacred hill,
> where endles honor shall be made thy meede.
> Because no malice of succeeding daies,
> can rase those records of thy lasting praise.

Bibliography

The following is a select list of books and articles containing material, or discussions of material, relevant to the study of Spenser's reputation up to 1715.

ATKINSON, DOROTHY F., *Edmund Spenser: A Bibliographical Supplement*, Baltimore, 1937.

BASKERVILLE, CHARLES R., 'The Early Fame of *The Shepheardes Calender*' *PMLA*, XXVIII (1913), 291–313.

BÖHME, TRAUGOTT, *Spensers literarisches Nachleben bis zu Shelley*, Berlin 1911.

CARPENTER, F. I., *A Reference Guide to Edmund Spenser*, Chicago, 1923.

CORY, H. E., 'The Golden Age of the Spenserian Pastoral', *PMLA*, XXV (1910), 241–67.

The Critics of Edmund Spenser. University of California Publications in Modern Philology, II (1911), 81–182.

Spenser, the School of the Fletchers, and Milton. University of California Publications in Modern Philology, II (1911), 311–73.

ELLIOT, ROBERT, JR., *Prince of Poets*, New York. 1968.

GROSART, A. B., *T..e Works of Edmund Spenser*, Priv. publ., 1882–84.

JUDSON, A. C., 'The Seventeenth-Century Lives of Edmund Spenser', *HLQ*, X (1946), 35–48.

MUELLER, WILLIAM R., *The Critics of Edmund Spenser*, Syracuse, 1959.

MORTON, E. P., 'The Spenserian Stanza before 1700', *MP*, IV (1907), 639–54.

PIERCE, MARJORIE, 'The Allusions to Spenser up to 1650', M.A. Thesis University of Chicago, 1927.

SCHRÖBER, A., 'Zu Spenser im Wandel der Zeiten', *Die Neueren Sprachen*, XIII (1905), 449–60.

This select list is of works listing or describing accounts and imitations of Spenser up to 1715.

ALPERS, PAUL J., *Penguin Critical Anthologies: Edmund Spenser* (1969): an anthology of Spenser criticism from Harvey to the present day: it reprints more early material than any comparable selection and contains the editor's commentary on the selection.

ANONYMOUS, 'MS Notes on Spenser's *Faerie Queene*', *Notes and Queries*, CCII (1957), 504–15: an account of the mainly historical notes in Cambridge University Library Sel. 5.102 (1596 Quarto).

ATKINSON, DOROTHY F., *Edmund Spenser: A Bibliographical Supplement* (Baltimore, 1937): contains lists of early Spenser criticism supplementary to those in Carpenter, and draws on the unpublished *Spenser Allusion Book*.

CARPENTER, FREDERIC IVES, *A Reference Guide to Edmund Spenser* (Chicago, 1923): the chief source for information about Spenser's early reputation.

CORY, H. E., *The Critics of Edmund Spenser, University of California Publications in Modern Philology*, II (1911), 81–182: a slightly dated but unfairly neglected account of Spenser's earlier critics.

——, *Spenser, the School of the Fletchers and Milton, University of California Publications in Modern Philology*, II (1911), 311–73: the fullest account before Miss Grundy's of Spenser's influence on seventeenth-century poetry.

ELLIOT, JOHN R., JR., *The Prince of Poets: Essays on Edmund Spenser* (New York, 1968): an anthology of Spenser criticism from Harvey to the present day, but the earlier period is only casually represented.

FOWLER, A. D. S., 'Oxford and London Marginalia to *The Faerie Queene*', *Notes and Queries*, CCVI (1961), 416–19: demonstrates early interest in historical and iconological topics.

GODSHALK, W. L., 'Prior's Copy of Spenser's *Works*, 1679', *Papers of the Bibliographical Society of America*, LXI (1967), 52–5: an account of Prior's marginalia on Spenser, showing his interest in pageant sequences, iconographies, and historical identifications.

GRUNDY, JOAN, *The Spenserian Poets* (1969): the fullest critical account of Spenser's imitators.

HOUGH, GRAHAM, ed., *The First Commentary on the 'Faerie Queene'* (privately published, 1964): an edition of the marginalia of John Dixon in Lord Bessborough's copy of the *Faerie Queene*.

MUELLER, WILLIAM, *The Critics of Edmund Spenser* (Syracuse, 1959): an anthology of Spenser criticism from Hughes to the present day with a historical introduction.

WURTSBAUGH, JEWEL, *Two Centuries of Spenser Scholarship* (Baltimore, 1936): a full account of the fortunes of Spenser's text from 1609 to Todd's edition of 1805.

Select Index

Index references are grouped as follows: I. authors of material collected; II. allusions to Spenser's works, to passages from them, or to characters in them; III. proper names referred to in the material collected; IV. topics to which Spenser's work is related. Neither III nor IV attempt completeness.

I

Addison, Joseph, 224–5
Alabaster, William, 101
Anonymous criticism, 63 ('Ignoto'),
  116–17 (author of *Returne from
  Parnassus*), 136–7 (author of *Apollo
  Christian*), 213 (*A Pastoral*), 215
  (following Rymer), 216–20
  (Preface to *Spenserus Redivivus*),
  223 (*Athenian Mercury*), 233 (on
  Spenser's influence), 289 (on
  'trew Hexameters'), 324–7 (*Life*,
  1679)
Atterbury, Francis, 302–3
Aubrey, John, 322–3
Austin, William, 172–3
Aylett, Robert, 140

B., H., 64
Barnfield, Richard, 94
Basse, William, 111, 190
Beaumont, Francis, 108; the elder, 286
Beaumont, Joseph, 183
Bentley, Richard, 309
Blackmore, Sir Richard, 226–7
Blount, Sir Thomas Pope, 304–5,
  331–3
Bodenham, John, 290
Bolton, Edmund, 292
Breton, Nicholas, 102
Browne, William, 133

Bryskett, Lodowick, 119–21
Burton, Robert, 141
Butler, Charles, 287
Bysshe, Edward, 311

C., E., 84, 165
C., R., 189
Camden, William, 114, 315–316
Carew, Richard, 95, 291
Chalkhill, John, 104
Chatwin, John, 209–11
Chetwood, Knightly, 214
Churchyard, Thomas, 76–7
Cobb, Samuel, 231–2
Cockayne, Sir Aston, 194–5
Collins, Thomas, 132
Covell, William, 85
Coward, William, 312–13
Cowley, Abraham, 185
Culpepper, Sir Thomas, 298

Daniel, George, 178
Daniel, Samuel, 74–6
D'Avenant, Sir William, 187
Davies, John, 296
Decker, Thomas, 122
Denham, Sir John, 198
Dennis, John, 229–30, 313
Digby, Sir Kenelm, 147–59
Dorrell, Hadrian, 283
Drayton, Michael, 78–81
Drummond, William, 139–40

II

K., E., 44, 56, 57, 196, 197

L., W., 197
Langland, William, 292
Longinus, 245, 265
Lucan, 95, 96
Lucian, 51, 204
Lucilius, 205
Lucretius, 96, 205, 270, 294
Lydgate, John, 35, 50, 135, 138, 193, 286, 292
Lyly, John, 83

Machiavelli, Niccolò, 52
Macrobius, 41
Mantuan, Baptista, 39, 98, 235
Marlowe, Christopher, 96, 189, 195
Marot, Clément, 39
Marston, John, 114
Martial, 95, 171
Mary, Countess of Pembroke, 197, 275
Mary, Queen of Scots, 136
Massinger, Philip, 193
Menander, 52
Michelangelo, 44
Milton, John, 203, 205, 223, 225, 227, 228, 229, 230, 243, 246, 247, 249, 254, 263, 266, 273
More, Sir Thomas, 49, 55
Museus, 195

Nashe, Thomas, 54, 83

Ovid, 77, 88, 95, 96, 118, 189, 245, 264, 269, 271, 287
Owen, John, 193

Palingenius, 49
Pasquil, 51
Paul, St, 47
Petrarch, Francesco, 39, 50, 51, 55, 66, 72, 75, 77, 79, 149, 170, 222, 276, 340

Phaer, Thomas, 50, 289
Philips, Ambrose, 274
Philo, 175
Pindar, 62, 96, 183
Plato, 46, 150, 157, 171
Plautus, 52
Plutarch, 251
Prodicus, 258
Pythagoras, 89

Rabelais, François, 79
Ralegh, Sir Walter, 50, 98, 135, 136, 189, 197, 229, 231, 249, 275, 322, 338
Raphael, 327, 340
Rich, Lady Penelope, 275
Ronsard, Pierre, 189, 222
Rosalind, 52, 168, 322, 335
Rubens, Peter Paul, 250
Rymer, Thomas, 215, 263, 332

S., R., 197
Sackville, Thomas, Lord Buckhurst, 68
Sannazzaro, Jacopo, 39, 98, 204, 280, 328
Sappho, 137
Scaliger, J.C., 150, 217
Scaliger, J.J., 215
Scotus, Duns, 164
Shakespeare, William, 50, 95, 96, 97, 98, 114, 193, 197, 214, 223, 246, 262
Sidney, Sir Philip, 40, 43, 49, 50, 54, 55, 57, 62, 65, 66, 75, 85, 87, 88, 89, 92, 95, 96, 97, 98, 114, 129, 130, 132, 137, 140, 142, 178, 179, 184, 189, 195, 197, 203, 261, 265, 274, 275, 276, 277, 278, 283, 322, 323, 324, 326, 327, 328, 331, 333, 335, 336, 339
Silius Italicus, 96
Skelton, John, 53, 193, 292
Sophocles, 96

IV

heroic poetry—*contd.*
238, 253, 254, 257, 270, 293, 297,
299, 323, 331, 332; epic, 81, 225,
226, 227, 229, 246, 299; romance,
163, 172, 184, 261
history, 47, 79–80, 138, 139, 151,
201, 223; legend, 81, 92, 141, 202,
209

love, 36, 59, 97, 105, 141, 142, 189,
209, 239–41, 272, 276, 325, 339

morality, 36, 45–6, 58, 77, 81, 88,
91, 119, 120, 121, 127, 131, 150,
162, 164, 170, 171, 175, 184, 199,
203, 218, 222, 223, 231, 237, 252,
255, 258, 263, 265, 271, 275, 331;
philosophy, 45, 119, 150, 157,
171, 172

obsolete words, 36, 74, 130, 148,
182, 188, 201, 203, 216, 235, 243,
248, 274, 275, 278, 282, 285, 286,
288, 294, 298, 299, 300, 320, 327;
dialect, 36, 204, 216, 235, 291

painting, 37, 188, 204, 226, 230, 233,
250, 259, 264, 270–1, 327.
panegyric, 61, 72, 75, 83, 84, 85,
124, 133, 203, 204
pastoral, 36, 40, 60, 81, 97, 98, 132,
235, 238, 246, 270, 272–5;
Spenser as Colin Clout, 35, 52,
78, 79, 82, 84, 87, 92, 100, 104,
111, 112, 133, 134, 166, 167, 168,
178, 179, 180, 183, 190, 194,
209–10, 213, 270

verse, 37, 43, 44, 54, 57, 92, 120,
124, 148, 180, 186, 188, 191, 199,
203, 204, 205, 208, 216, 220, 232,
233, 237, 244, 277, 284, 285, 287,
289, 293, 297, 299, 326, 333;
quantitative verse, 43, 278–9
virtue, 46, 132, 159, 160, 163, 176,
244; chastity, 46, 67, 141, 209,
244; courtesy, 209, 244, 270;
friendship, 142, 209, 244; holiness,
46, 125, 146, 209, 244; justice, 160,
164, 209, 244, 270; temperance,
46, 67, 125, 160, 209, 211, 244,
266